Greening the Children of God

Princeton Theological Monograph Series
K. C. Hanson, Charles M. Collier, D. Christopher Spinks,
and Robin A. Parry, Series Editors

Recent volumes in the series:

Riyako Cecilia Hikota
*And Still We Wait:
Hans Urs von Balthasar's Theology of Holy Saturday
and Christian Discipleship*

Guillaume Bignon
*Excusing Sinners and Blaming God:
A Calvinist Assessment of Determinism, Moral Responsibility,
and Divine Involvement in Evil*

Jeff McDonald
*John Gerstner and the Renewal of Presbyterian and
Reformed Evangelicalism in Modern America*

James P. Haley
*The Humanity of Christ:
The Significance of the Anhypostasis and Enhypostasis in
Karl Barth's Christology*

Karlo V. Bordjadze
Darkness Visible: A Study of Isaiah 14:3–23 as Christian Scripture

Graham H. Twelftree
The Nature Miracles of Jesus: Problems, Perspectives, and Prospects

William M. Marsh
*Martin Luther on Reading the Bible as Christian Scripture:
The Messiah in Luther's Biblical Hermeneutic and Theology*

Benjamin J. Burkholder
*Bloodless Atonement?
A Theological and Exegetical Study of the Last Supper Sayings*

Greening the Children of God
Thomas Traherne and Nature's Role in the Ecological Formation of Children

CHAD MICHAEL RIMMER

☙PICKWICK *Publications* • Eugene, Oregon

GREENING THE CHILDREN OF GOD
Thomas Traherne and Nature's Role in the Ecological Formation of Children

Princteon Theological Monograph Series 241

Copyright © 2019 Chad Michael Rimmer. All rights reserved. Except for brief quotations in critical publications or reviews, no part of this book may be reproduced in any manner without prior written permission from the publisher. Write: Permissions, Wipf and Stock Publishers, 199 W. 8th Ave., Suite 3, Eugene, OR 97401.

Pickwick Publications
An Imprint of Wipf and Stock Publishers
199 W. 8th Ave., Suite 3
Eugene, OR 97401

www.wipfandstock.com

PAPERBACK ISBN: 978-1-5326-5330-8
HARDCOVER ISBN: 978-1-5326-5331-5
EBOOK ISBN: 978-1-5326-5332-2

Cataloguing-in-Publication data:

Names: Rimmer, Chad Michael, author.

Title: Greening the children of God : Thomas Traherne and Nature's Role in the Moral Formation of Children / by Chad Michael Rimmer.

Description: Eugene, OR : Pickwick Publications, 2019 | Princteon Theological Monograph Series 241 | Includes bibliographical references and index.

Identifiers: ISBN 978-1-5326-5330-8 (paperback) | ISBN 978-1-5326-5331-5 (hardcover) | ISBN 978-1-5326-5332-2 (ebook)

Subjects: LCSH: Traherne Thomas— -1674—Criticism and interpretation. | Christian poetry, English—History and criticism.

Classification: PR3736.T7 R56 2019 (paperback) | PR3736.T7 R56 (ebook)

Manufactured in the U.S.A.   09/16/19

To Paul Michael and Luke

May you always follow the whispering instinct of nature to become
as a little child,
renewing your infant eye so that you will never become a stranger to
the shining skies.

May you always play among the creatures who minister to you,
wonder at the Creator who teaches you that you are cared for in all
creation,
and, being sensible of the Creator's mercy, feel the joy of being a
friend of God.

Contents

Acknowledgments | ix

Introduction | 1

1. Platonist, Poet, or Paracelsian? Locating Thomas Traherne among the Science of the New Philosophy | 17

2. "Between Ants and Angels": Outlining the Empirical Basis of Traherne's Moral Theory in *The Kingdom of God* | 55

3. Retirednes: Understanding the Principles of the Perceiving Child | 110

4. Retirednes: The Role That Created Objects Play in the Formation of a Child's Inter-Subjective Moral Identity | 167

5. Retirednes: Interest as the Motivation for Moral Formation | 191

6. Cultivating the Careful Child: The Pro-formative Role That Ecology Plays in Educating Caring Children | 217

7. Conclusion | 252

Bibliography | 257

Acknowledgments

I WANT TO ACKNOWLEDGE those people who have accompanied me during the completion of this book. Thomas Traherne is first among them. In a time of war and shifting paradigms, he saw the beatific vision of the Creator's peace that is woven into creation. I thank him for sharing that vision with us in prose and poetry, and for being an inspiring witness among the communion of saints. I am also thankful to those Traherne scholars who have gone before me. Specifically I want to thank the late Dr. Denise Inge and Dr. James Balakier for graciously sharing thoughts, emails, electronic copies of various resources, and the general encouragement to join this small but inspired group of Traherne devotees. I thank Dr. Robbie Nicol of the Moray House Institute, School of Education for his time and willingness to talk about things related to phenomenology and the pedagogical implications for environmental education. I thank my friend and colleague Jeremy Kidwell for hours of mutual reflection, critique, and encouragement over coffee at St. Giles. I thank Jennifer for being willing to patiently edit her little brother's thoughts with eagle eyes. I thank Professor Jolyon Mitchell and Dr. Rowan Williams for dedicating their time to engage my research and discuss my contribution to our field, especially during Lord Williams's Giffords Lectures. For the depth of your expertise and faithful encouragement I will forever be grateful.

I want to particularly thank Professor Michael Northcott. I came to Scotland believing that our relationship to creation is an important part of our pursuit of peace. He helped me cultivate that passion into research by inviting me to work in this field that he has faithfully and masterfully tended for decades. When I would produce a paper or chapter that was not well ripened, he would insist that I start over with better questions so that I could bear the fruit of theological ethics. I am incredibly grateful to my supervisor for his patient teaching. But I am also thankful to him as a fellow priest and friend who shared his home, his faith, his time and his garden for these years, and those that followed.

Finally, I wish to thank my wife, Natalie, and our two sons, Paul Michael and Luke. They were willing to sacrifice so much for this project. I thank them for their patience while I spent so much time huddled in the corner at my desk in Edinburgh. I pray that they are blessed with all the felicity, love, joy and peace that I receive from our life together. I thank them for tending the garden as a family, and for helping to turn the natural wonder of Arthur's Seat, the Sahara, the Blue Ridge Mountains and the Swiss Alps into our playground. In so doing, they constantly remind me what this thesis is all about.

Introduction

GREENING THE CHILDREN OF God uncovers theological roots of the growing ethical imperative to reconnect children with their natural environment. The crisis in our moral responsibility to care for the earth has caused a rapid loss of habitats, biodiversity, and the degradation of ecosystems that have accelerated the effects of climate change. In her book *Gaia and God: An Ecofeminist Theology of Earth Healing*, Rosemary Radford Ruether writes, "We do not have thousands of years to unlearn the wrong patterns that were established over thousands of years. The exponential speed-up of these cumulative patterns of destruction means we have to both learn new patterns and put them into practice on a global scale within the next generation."[1] Human beings have to quickly learn to make ecologically sound decisions regarding every aspect of our lives. But as we consider our choices for transportation, the food we consume, the homes that we live in, the goods that we buy, or the investments we make, what motivates people to make decisions to care for non-human members of the earth community? People may be convinced by climate data and various economic or pragmatic rationales. But thoughtful, empathetic and altruistic decisions for the common good are also motivated by relationships. Being able to identify with "the other" who is impacted by any given decision generates degrees of empathy that shape our moral discernment.

The connection between experience and ethical discernment is natural, given that humans are not merely rational beings. We are relational creatures. Embodied relationships are theologically, psychologically and ethically significant, because we do not only derive knowledge from what we think. We make meaning out of what we experience. This is true for Christian moral discernment as well. While the apostolic seed of Christianity is rooted in a text, that text refers to acts of divine revelation—the giving of the Law, the incarnation, acts inspired by the Holy Spirit—which are phenomena, experiences, and encounters with the Divine. Religious and sacred texts are derived from lived experiences of those phenomena and

1. Ruether, *Gaia and God*.

refer us back to the relationship which gave them meaning. Jesus teaches that the summary of the entire Mosaic Law is love—to love God and our co-creatures. But the letter of 1 John (4:7–21) is clear that the motivation to love comes not from a legal prescription, but from the experience of being loved. Because we are loved, therefore we are motivated to love. Perhaps love can be commanded or explained rationally. *(Parents tend to exhaust themselves commanding siblings to love one another!)* But there is surely no more effective way to communicate love to someone than to love them. A relationship creates the potential for love to be fully known. In this way, relationships are grounds for moral knowledge.

In terms of environmental ethics, this means that rational scientific or economic information is not the only way to motivate people to extend the common good to non-human creation. The phenomenal encounter with another creature creates the possibility of a morally significant relationship. This interdisciplinary study explores how a child's relationship with non-human creatures forms their moral identity and why that relationship is a significant part of making meaning in our ecological age.

Knowing as a Child

This study addresses the ways in which a child comes to know who they are as a human creature, and how they cultivate moral significance from that knowledge. In his letter to the Corinthians, St. Paul recognizes that we use different ways or modes to make meaning at different stages of our life. He wrote,

> We know only in part, and we prophesy only in part; but when the complete comes, the partial will come to an end. When I was a child, I spoke like a child, I thought like a child, I reasoned like a child; when I became an adult, I put an end to childish ways. For now we see in a mirror dimly, but then we will see face to face. Now I know only in part; then I will know fully, even as I have been fully known. (1 Cor 13:8–13)

If this passage is read in a cognitivist fashion, "childish" seems to suggest a deficient rational state that will be perfected as the child transitions to adult modes of knowing. But the subject of Paul's letter is the ultimate knowledge of God that comes from the experience of standing in the unmasked presence of Divine Love. In that eschatological moment of perfect union with the Divine, we will know the full truth about the essence of God and ourselves as we are "fully known" by God. Relative to that unmediated encounter, Paul acknowledges that all forms of knowing are limited or at least mediated, as if looking in a mirror dimly. Read in this light, Paul's statement on the childlike mode of knowing is not necessarily negative—it is simply a different way of perceiving. Human knowledge is always mediated by our perceptual capacities, which naturally change as we develop.

In the second Hebrew creation narrative, the animals were brought before the earthling, *Adam*, so that he could name them (Gen 2:18–20). In Hebrew scripture, the power to name or rename implies a deep knowledge of the nature of the creature or place that is named. What was the relationship between the earthling and other creatures, and what modes of perception did the earthling use to "know" these creatures deeply enough to name them? Anthropologists help us hypothesize about early humans' capacity to reason and make meaning. But in the earliest days of our species, knowledge was certainly not derived linguistically. Language is a part of culture that evolves over time. The first earthlings were preverbal, as are all children when they first engage the world with wonder and playfulness in their morally formative years. In this way, the Genesis narrative affirms that knowing is not a mere cognitive, intellectual exercise. Knowing is the result of being deeply embedded in a web of right relationships. Any effort to reify knowledge outside of that holistic mode of meaning making results in a willful isolation of the individual. Genesis figures this disintegration from the created whole as sin.

Throughout the Bible, a variety of human capacities are used to derive knowledge about the Truth that is woven into the fabric of creation. The Magi used inductive physical science to triangulate the position of a newly revealed star. Pontius Pilate's wife derived meaning about Jesus from dreams. Paul used Athenian philosophy and poetry to communicate the nature of revealed truth. The psalmist and prophets were able to interpret the significance of a changing landscape and fluctuating crop yields. The Torah ritualizes a legal system of health, hygienic, dietary, social, agricultural, and economic practices as a way to communicate moral knowledge of God's will for life. Elizabeth's pre-natal baby leapt *in utero* when it sensed the resonance of Mary's voice. Jesus urged his followers to contemplate creation, notice the change of seasons, respect natural cycles of vegetation, consider animal behavior, and adopt the epistemological mode of a child in their midst. The Biblical narrative brims with a diverse range of ways to perceive God's self-revelation, and to derive meaning from that divine self-communication.

So to return to Paul's text, we should not interpret this text as denigrating a child's mode of knowing, for he affirms many times that all human ways of knowing Truth are incomplete. His letter acknowledges that a child's ways of knowing are particularly suited to their stage in life. So without contradiction we are free to ask, what are childlike ways of knowing? How do children perceive their world? How do children create meaning and what motivates them to find moral significance? And perhaps most significantly, what are the ethical consequences when adults put aside childlike modes of engaging the natural world in which we live and move and have our being? This book will show how this sort of epistemological departure—disintegrating our rational selves from our ecological place in the web of life—has played a tremendous role in the ecological crisis of our age, and why it is important that we cultivate a childlike knowledge of creation in every age.

Age-Appropriate Ways of Knowing

Between birth and death, life can be divided into ages. In each age an organism will express different qualities, engage the environment with different capacities and respond from a different social location. Insects develop from egg to larva to pupa to adult. Humans develop from embryo to infancy to childhood to adolescence to adulthood. Woodland ecosystems develop from prairies to pine stands to old growth deciduous forests.

Since its formation, our planet has developed as well. During the Hadean age, the moon was formed and the surface of the young earth was bombarded by celestial bodies. During the Archean age, life formed from the dust of the earth, and plants began to synthesize solar energy into oxygen. During the Proterozoic age, the oxygen rich atmosphere gathered above the waters of the earth, early animals thrived in earth's energetic richness. During the Paleozoic age, the lands shifted among the seas that teemed with life, while vertebrates and arthropods roamed coniferous forests. The great reptiles ruled the Mesozoic age until the earth cooled into the Cenozoic age when mammals began to thrive. Through the Paleogene, Neogene and Pleistocene periods, a diversity of small and large mammals evolved alongside birds, amphibians, reptiles, marine and plant life. Then humans emerged from the dust and the earth entered its Holocene period.

The whole course of human history—our agrarian and artisanal cultures, our languages, our making, our systems of familial, economic and legal society, our commerce and conflicts, our built environments and technological advances, everything that we know—has developed in this briefest of all ages. From the human activity that dominates this short period we derive the name, Anthropocene.

Since the Industrial Revolution, the Anthropocene devolved into a geologically and ecologically destructive period. The impact of human activity began to physically alter the face of the earth, like wrinkles in the skin of a body entering its middle age. Delicate habitats, like organs, are failing, and earth's body is slowly becoming septic. Wetlands are the earth's liver that cleans toxins from its streams. But they are undergoing cirrhosis from coastal development. Mountaintops are the earth's kidneys that purify the circulatory system of contaminants. But they are being surgically removed or occluded by mining. The vast forests are earth's lungs that filter pollutants from the air. But they are being cleared, leaving vast deserts of scar tissue that cannot exchange CO_2 for Oxygen. The oceans are the earth's endocrine system that maintains a proper chemical balance. But abnormal temperature shifts have rendered the oceans too acidic to support the great reefs and vital supplies of probiotic micro-fauna that maintain the digestive health of the body. When biological systems are compromised, tissues begin to breakdown. The rapid disintegration of delicately balanced habitats is causing an unsustainable loss of biodiversity.

We extract nutrients from the earth's energy cycles at levels that overrun the earth's capacity to heal itself. By draining its nutrient reserves, we are compromising the earth's immune system. The steady rise in average temperatures, like a fever, is a sign that the earth is struggling to conserve the energy it needs to restore equilibrium. This planetary breakdown is the result of our violent lifestyles; I say violent, because our demands violate reasonable limits of sustainable consumption. The Ecumenical Patriarch Bartholomew I of Constantinople observed that violating biological and planetary limits which sustain the created order constitutes a sin:

> We have traditionally regarded sin as being merely what people do to other people. Yet, for human beings to destroy the biological diversity in God's creation; for human beings to degrade the integrity of the earth by contributing to climate change, by stripping the earth of its natural forests or destroying its wetlands; for human beings to contaminate the earth's waters, land and air—all of these are sins.[2]

In Romans 8, Paul related the travails of creation to our sinfulness. Paul knew that creation groaned as a result of our sinfulness. He also believed that the redemption of creation was integrally tied to ours. When the children of God are harmoniously restored to right relationships, creation will also be liberated from its struggle. Patriarch Bartholomew I had such an age in mind when he co-wrote the following statement with Pope John Paul II for their Common Declaration on the Fourth Ecological Symposium in June 2002:

---

2. Bartholomew, *Cosmic Grace, Humble Prayer*, 190.

It is not too late. God's world has incredible healing powers. Within a single generation, we could steer the earth toward our children's future. Let that generation start now.³

Bartholomew I and John Paul II were calling us to put aside the old ways of the Anthropocene that led to the gross injustices against the earth and her creatures, and renew our knowledge of what it means to be a human creature today. Catholic priest and eco-theologian Thomas Berry also wrote about the inauguration of a new ecological age. In his 1991 E. F. Schumacher Society Lecture, Berry observed that "we have already terminated the Cenozoic period of the geo-biological systems of the planet. . . . A renewal of life in some creative context requires that a new biological period come into being; a period when humans would dwell upon the Earth in a mutually enhancing manner." He dubbed this new period of redemptive mutuality, the Ecozoic Age.⁴

Knowledge in the Ecozoic Age

What are the epistemological hallmarks of our "new mode of being"⁵ in the Ecozoic Age? In *Laudato Si*, Pope Francis affirms that the task of understanding our peculiar role as humans and establishing the conditions for justice and peace for the whole inhabited earth necessarily demands ecumenical and interdisciplinary conversation. He appeals for a new multilateral dialogue between the arts, science and religion.⁶ Pope Francis recognizes that while "specialization leads to a certain isolation and the absolutization of its own field of knowledge,"⁷ we should expand the epistemological conversation and seek solidarity among scientific, theological, cultural and aesthetic modes of knowing. Only an interdependent approach can overcome the disintegrating forces of economic and materialist theories that have colonized our human self-understanding for centuries.

While we research new ways to green our technological and economic sectors, we must also help one another rediscover what it means to be a human creature in the Ecozoic age. The Pope highlights the role that awe, wonder and loving relationships play in discovering our ecological selves.⁸ He points to his namesake, St. Francis of Assisi, as one who knew that "an

---

3. Bartholomew, *Cosmic Grace, Humble Prayer*, 281.
4. Berry, "Ecozoic Era," 196.
5. Berry, "Ecozoic Era," 196.
6. Francis, *Laudato Si*, 14, 62.
7. Francis, *Laudato Si*, 201.
8. Francis, *Laudato Si*, 11.

integral ecology calls for openness to categories which transcend the language of mathematics and biology, and take us to the heart of what it is to be human."[9] We are beings, made from the dust of the earth, whose spiritual and material well-being is ecologically embedded. As Lutheran theologian Dietrich Bonhoeffer put it, we must remember that "we do not have a body, we are a body."[10] To this end, chapter 6 of *Laudato Si* is devoted to the wisdom of reconciling Ecological Education and Spirituality. The Pope's instinct is affirmed by the growing consensus between environmental educators, eco-philosophers, theological ethicists, naturalists, poets and scientists who agree that a paramount ethical goal of our time is to reconnect children to their natural ecology as a means to know what it means to be human, and form an ecological notion of the self.

This interdisciplinary convergence is a consistent hallmark of our emerging Ecozoic Age. However, above I used the word "reconciling" to describe this convergence because scientific and moral knowledge have not always been estranged as they were during the Anthropocene. There was a time when every discipline was understood as being part of an epistemological whole. There was a time when truth was equally pursued in the laboratory, in religious devotion, in our social interactions, in the humanities and in the daily perception of our relationship to the natural world around us. In *Laudato Si*, Pope Francis quotes Ali al-Khawas, the ninth-century Sufi mystic, who wrote, "Prejudice should not have us criticize those who seek ecstasy in music or poetry. There is a subtle mystery in each of the movements and sounds of this world. The initiate will capture what is being said when the wind blows, the trees sway, water flows, flies buzz, doors creak, birds sing, or in the sound of strings or flutes, the sighs of the sick, the groans of the afflicted."[11] At the time of Ali al-Khawas, natural and moral knowledge were still two parts of one science, both contributing to a full understanding of what it meant to be human.

Returning to the Source of the Epistemological Schism

In Europe, relationship between scientific and ecclesial authority became contentious during the late Renaissance. But the bond between scientific and moral epistemology began to disintegrate in the sixteenth and seventeenth centuries. The Scientific Revolution was ushered along by the intellectual pursuits of Francis Bacon, Renée Descartes and Isaac Newton among

9. Francis, *Laudato Si*, 11.
10. Bonhoeffer, *Creation and Fall*, 77.
11. Francis, *Laudato Si*, 153n159.

others. Most heralded the liberation of natural science from the confines of metaphysical deduction as a necessary step for humanity to pass from the dark childhood of religious superstition into the enlightened knowledge of inductive truth. However, there were those who had a firm understanding of the morally pro-formative quality of our relationship to the natural world and warned against the consequences of alienating scientific and moral reasoning. One such clairvoyant was the seventeenth-century Anglican priest and poet Thomas Traherne. He was a poet, a priest, a theologian and a naturalist trained at Oxford in the sciences of his day. He embraced the epistemological nexus of theology, aesthetics, science and a childlike engagement with the natural world. From what we would now call an interdisciplinary perspective Thomas Traherne developed a moral theory that promoted the "sweetest and most delightful methods"[12] of forming an ecologically rooted moral identity. He developed an ethic of care that could overcome the disintegrating violence of his age, that is remarkably suited for our Ecozoic age.

Thomas Traherne was five years old when the violence of the English Civil War reached the walled city of Hereford in the autumn of 1642 and again in 1645.[13] The son of a Herfordshire shoemaker[14] and a family of committed royalists, Thomas lost his parents while still an infant, was adopted by his uncle Philip, and witnessed the violence of at least two sieges of his home city by the time he was 12.[15] Traherne was not only a witness to violent conflict, but was educated amongst the philosophical, social, theological and scientific upheaval that defined seventeenth-century England. We might assume that the vision of political and ecclesiastical roots of such violence would cause an orphaned child to join the growing ranks of those skeptical of faith in a loving, just God. The writings of Traherne's early contemporary, Thomas Hobbes, reveal such noticeable scars of war. Basil Willey suggests that the violence and bloodshed led Hobbes to surmise that humanity was locked in a "war of all against all" according to its natural tendencies towards competition, diffidence and glory.[16] In the words of Willey, Hobbes concluded that "through the disgust of chaos" humankind would be willing "to swallow the medicine of despotism" and come to rely on the social covenant of government as the source, or force, of peace.[17] Thomas Traherne,

---

12. Traherne, *Centuries, Poems, and Thanksgivings*, 1:17.

13. Traherne, *Centuries, Poems, and Thanksgivings*, 1:xxxii.

14. Anthony Wood records this vital biographical information in his entry on Thomas Traherne in his *Athenae Oxonienses*, which is reprinted in its entirety in Traherne, *Centuries, Poems, and Thanksgivings*, 1:xxiii.

15. Traherne, *Centuries, Poems, and Thanksgivings*, 1:xxxvii.

16. Willey, *English Moralists*, 158.

17. Willey, *English Moralists*, 158. I will explore this theme in chapter 1.

however, is a radical exception to Hobbes's rule. In an unsigned preface to the posthumously published edition of Traherne's *A Serious and Pathetical Contemplation*, the editor acknowledged that Traherne lived during "disordered Times when the Foundations were cast down and this excellent Church laid in the dust, and dissolved into *Confusion* and *Enthusiasme*."[18] Yet his "Soul was of a more refin'd allay, and his Judgment in discerning for things more solid, and considerate then to be infected with that Leaven."[19] In the midst of conflict, Thomas Traherne found a focal point of consideration that helped him perceive the peaceableness of the Kingdom.

Rather than being distracted by the image of humanity's ability to do violence, young Thomas kept his gaze set upon Creation. In communion with creation he felt the manifestation of God's beauty and peaceableness. In the opening of his *Centuries*, he writes:

> Beauty being a thing consisting of variety, that body could be not one simple being, but must be sweetly tempered of a manifold and delightful mixture of fixtures and colours . . . how do we know, but the world is that body, which the Deity hath assumed to manifest His Beauty and by which He maketh Himself as visible, as it is possible He should? Since therefore this visible World is the body of God, not His natural body, but which He hath assumed; let us see how glorious His wisdom is in manifesting Himself thereby. It hath not only represented His infinity and eternity which we thought impossible to be represented by a body, but His beauty also, His wisdom, goodness, power, life and glory, His righteousness, love and blessedness: all which as out of a plentiful treasury, may be taken and collected out of this world.[20]

Traherne claims that the plenitude of virtues such as beauty, goodness, and wisdom are manifest in creation in ways that can be apprehended by the senses. Therefore, these virtues can be "collected out of this world." In the opening pages of his *Centuries*, he suggests it is his intention to teach others the methods to "know" these virtues through communion with creation.

> The fellowship of the Mystery which from the beginning of the World hath been hid in God lies concealed! The thing hath been from the Creation of the World, but hath not so been explained as that the interior Beauty should be understood. It is my design therefore in such a plain manner to unfold it that my friendship

18. Traherne, *Centuries, Poems, and Thanksgivings*, 1:xxxii.
19. Traherne, *Centuries, Poems, and Thanksgivings*, 1:xxxii.
20. Traherne, *Centuries, Poems, and Thanksgivings*, 1:65–66.

> may appear in making you possessor of the whole world. I will not by the noise of bloody wars and the dethroning of kings advance you to glory: but by the gentle ways of peace and love. As a deep friendship meditates and intends the deepest designs for the advancement of its objects, so doth it shew itself in choosing the sweetest and most delightful methods.[21]

He desires to share those "methods" by which a child is able to sense the goodness, blessedness, and love of God that is revealed in the "plentiful treasury" of Creation. His writings suggest the deep connection between a child's direct interaction with creation and the formation of a moral identity that is rooted in the virtues of goodness, peaceableness and care. For those who sought a "method" to nurture the virtues in their lives, he counselled:

> Above all, pray to be sensible of the Excellency of the Creation, for upon the due sense of its Excellencey the life of Felicity wholly dependeth. Pray to be sensible of the Excellencey of Divine Laws, and of all the Goodness which your Soul comprehendeth. Covet a lively sense of all you know, of the Excellency of God, and of Eternal Love; of your own Excellencey, and of the worth and value of all Objects whatsoever. For to feel is as necessary, as to see their Glory.[22]

Traherne's claim about the role of the senses in moral formation invites questions regarding his moral theology and epistemological questions about the relationship between scientific knowledge and revealed knowledge. Traherne offers a particularly interesting subject for this enquiry because he lived during the age when empiricism and rationalism, science and faith, moral philosophy and social theory were all beginning to part ways. This book will explore his moral theory and demonstrate why he believed retiring into creation was one "method" of knowing the loving, peaceable goodness of the Creator, and therefore forming our moral identity as peaceable creatures. It will demonstrate the theological and scientific reasons why he believed a relationship with creation is a significant component of the moral formation of a child. It will also demonstrate how his "methods" are helpful to our contemporary pursuit of moral theology, epistemology, and the moral formation of children in our Ecozoic Age.

---

21. Traherne, *Centuries, Poems, and Thanksgivings*, 1:17.
22. Traherne, *Christian Ethicks*, 6.

Traherne's Moral Theory: A New Look at Old Questions

Traherne scholars have long noted the central role that childhood and nature play within his poetry and prosaic meditations. However, explaining the rationale for his understanding of nature and childhood has proven enigmatic. According to personal accounts of his life, his knowledge of the peace that was woven into the fabric of creation could be understood as a simple extension of his naturally felicitous and perhaps optimistic personality. The editor of Traherne's first published writings remembers Traherne as a "Divine of the Church of England," who was "so wonderfully transported with the Love of God to Mankind" that he would discourse with anyone he met "whether they had any sense of Religion or not." But "his company was very acceptable to all such as had any inclinations to Vertue." He was

> a man of a cheerful and sprightly Temper, free from any thing of the sourness or formality, by which some great pretenders of Piety rather disparage and misrepresent true Religion, than recommend it and therefore was very affable and pleasant in his Conversation, ready to do all good Offices to his Friends, and Charitable to the Poor almost beyond his ability.[23]

At the time of Traherne's death at the age of 36, in October 1674, Thomas Good wrote to the Dean of Worcester, "I believe it is not news to you that Tom Traherne is dead, one of the most pious ingenious men that ever I was acquainted with."[24] While accounts of his personal peaceableness seem unanimous, his mix of piety and ingenuity has been difficult to articulate. His writings are notoriously eclectic and his influences diverse. Many scholars have sought to explain his use of childhood and nature according to contemporary literary[25] and theological[26] influences, while others attribute his ability to discern the Divine virtues in nature to a mystical charism.[27] However, Traherne research in the twentieth century was based on the two

---

23. The following quotes come from the unsigned preface to the first edition, which can be read in Traherne, *Centuries, Poems, and Thanksgivings*, 1:xxxi–xxxii.

24. Traherne, *Centuries, Poems, and Thanksgivings*, 1:xxviii.

25. Such theses include Ellrodt, *L'Inspiration personnelle*; Martz, *Paradise Within*; Ponsford, "Poetry of Thomas Traherne."

26. Grant, *Transformation of Sin*; "Original Sin," 40–61; Marks, "Thomas Traherne and Cambridge Platonism," 521–34; Cefalu, "Thomistic Metaphysics and Ethics," 248.

27. Wöhrer, *Thomas Traherne*; Salter, *Thomas Traherne*; Clements, *Mystical Poetry of Thomas Traherne*; Sherrington, *Mystical Symbolism*; Matar, "Thomas Traherne's Solar Mysticism."

collections of Traherne's poetry and meditations known as the Dobell and Margoliouth sequences. While his poetry and meditations are extensive, the poetic style that continues to inspire[28] also has a masking effect that evades systematic analysis or reflection.

However, in 1997 a new corpus of Traherne manuscripts was discovered in the Lambeth Palace and Folger Libraries. These new manuscripts more than double the size of Traherne's previously known writings.[29] Most of these writings are explicitly theological in nature and clearly reflect the theological, scientific and social milieu of his day. Denise Inge commented that after centuries of relative obscurity at worst and literary interest at best, Thomas Traherne is ready to "come home" to his Anglican roots and be considered not only as one of Britain's metaphysical poets, but as a priest and theologian.[30]

This discovery has opened up new fronts in the field of Traherne research. The new documents make possible a more rigorous study of Traherne's moral theory as well as the scientific and social influences that contributed to his "ingenious" contribution to moral theology. I will demonstrate that Traherne's moral theory was far more sophisticated than previously thought. He did not merely derive his notion of childhood and nature from the Platonist theologians and poets of his day. Traherne was studying the rationale for a Trinitarian moral theology at the nexus of his own scientific education, personal observations of the mutuality that exists within creation and the peculiar way that children perceive the benefits of being in relationship to nature. His moral theory is well suited to provide guidance and insight to the moral and scientific vocation of our Ecozoic Age.

The Shape of This Study

Chapter 1 will locate Traherne among his philosophical and theological predecessors. It will demonstrate the limitations of previous attempts to suggest Traherne is merely derivative of Platonism and metaphysical poetry. This chapter will outline his relationship to the new modes of scientific thought that were developing in his day, and compare him to the Paracelsian and

---

28. D. Elton Trueblood writes, "Traherne's many modern admirers include Thomas Merton, as well as C. S. Lewis, who extolled the Meditations as 'almost the most beautiful book in English'" (Kurian and Smith, *Encyclopedia of Christian Literature*, 607).

29. Denise Inge recounts the stories of Dobell's discovery of Traherne's poetry and *Centuries of Meditations*, as well as the recent discovery of the new Traherne text (Inge, *Wanting Like a God*, 267). Prior to this discovery, Traherne's works amounted to two volumes plus *Select Meditations*.

30. Inge, "Poet Comes Home," 335–48.

mechanical scientists. Finally it will locate Traherne among the Paracelsian school of science, and propose the impact that this new system of inductive reasoning had on his education and moral theory.

Chapter 2 will outline the empirical basis of Traherne's moral theory, with particular attention on his manuscript *The Kingdom of God*. This chapter outlines the theological and empirical means by which creation communicates goodness. Optical theories and knowledge of the atom play a significant role in the way creatures communicate their virtues to one another. This empirical aspect of his theory provides the basis of his critique of atheistic skepticism, particularly the theory of Thomas Hobbes. This chapter concludes by suggesting the role that the senses play in the perception of moral epistemology.

Chapter 3 begins a three-part study of *Inducements to Retirednes*. This chapter explores Traherne's understanding of the principles of human perception, particularly that of children. Among the "rules" of perception, wonder plays a significant role in a child's interaction with nature. By engaging their naturally social sense of wonder, Traherne suggests that a child can perceive the moral communication of creatures and the environment. This chapter engages the work of Maurice Merleau-Ponty, and various contemporary psychologists to understand the moral significance of the environment and the nature of the ecological self.

Chapter 4 continues the study of *Inducements*, and considers the role that nature plays in creating a theatre for forming an inter-subjective moral identity. Utilizing current themes in developmental child psychology, it demonstrates that Traherne understands how a significant relationship to the environment and other creatures helps a child form a moral identity as a creature in relationship to the Creator.

Chapter 5 continues the study of *Inducements*, and explores how discerning our mutual "interest" in being in relationship with other creatures provides the moral motivation to care. This chapter contrasts Traherne's notion of interest with that of Immanuel Kant in order to demonstrate the theologically positive effect that can be derived from realizing the way in which local environments care for the child. The chapter ends by suggesting knowledge of mutual care can motivate moral responses and nurture the basis for a caring moral identity.

Finally, chapter 6 considers the pedagogical implications of Traherne's moral theory. Within the current field of moral education, Traherne's moral theory represents what may be called an ethic of care. Relationships of care have a pro-formative impact on the child's development of a relational, caring moral identity. The chapter shows how Traherne's concept of our relationship with creation resembles a pro-formative ethic of care that is not very different from contemporary forms of environmental and place-based education. It explores current trends in the field of environmental and moral education. Then it suggests Thomas Traherne provides a model for deploying environmental or place-based education as a part of the Christian moral formation of children that resonates with the work of current moral theologians. Finally, the book concludes by showing how Traherne's writing on the festival of Rogation outlines a liturgically embedded, place-based moral relationship with creation.

The Significance of This Study

At its core, the current book is a study of the moral theory of Thomas Traherne. This endeavor has merit in its own right. However, Traherne makes it clear that questions of moral theology cannot be removed from questions regarding social theory, philosophical and scientific understandings of human nature, and the moral significance of our relationship to other creatures. Traherne warned of the consequences of disassociating these disciplines.

Through an ecological reading of recently discovered manuscripts, *Greening the Children of God* shows how Traherne anticipated the pedagogical and ethical consequences of divorcing scientific and moral reasoning, and the promise of recovering his theological voice for our age. Traherne affirmed that in order to fully form virtues such as goodness, peaceableness and care, humans needed to be embedded in God's creation. Being among the diversity of creatures in their natural place creates a relational theatre, or "communion," in which we can perceive how the thread of mutual "interest" among creatures is woven into the fabric of nature. This morally significant place-based knowledge becomes a motivation to care for creation. For Traherne a phenomenological engagement with nature is especially suited to the moral formation of children, who apprehend nature with their senses. Their innate wonder equips them to form an ecological identity in relationship to the earth, and become human beings that are morally and intellectually equipped for the dynamic synergies of our Ecozoic Age.

Traherne's moral theory offers significant theological and pedagogical insight for our age when environmental educators and care ethicists promote the morally pro-formative benefits of a child's relationship with other creatures in their natural environment. In conversation with child psychologists such as Darcia Narvaéz and Colwyn Trevarthen, Christian ethicists such as Rowan Williams, Michael Northcott and John Inge, and educational philosophers such as David Carr and Carol Gilligan, *Greening the Children of God* articulates a constructive theological perspective on how a child's experience in the local ecology of their parish can play a pro-formative role in developing a moral identity in relationship to a caring Creator.

These moral educators, theologians, psychologists and environmentalists are responding to the call to restore the relational nexus that exists between social, scientific and moral knowledge. This study shows that Traherne's counsel to retire into creation makes a significant pedagogical impact on the formation of a child's moral identity as a creature who knows they are cared for, and are motivated to care. It represents a significant recovery of theological roots of the ethical imperative to reconnect children to their local ecology, and to attend to the childlike ways of knowing that are regaining significance in our Ecozoic age.

This recovery is an ethical imperative, because it is a question of motivation. We know the climate science and the data regarding the harsh realities of climate change. But if we are going to respond to the mandate to rectify the economic, social, political, anthropological and biological injustices that are caused by the commodification and misuse of creation, where will we derive the motivation to act in ethical ways?

At the time of publishing this book, the United Nations Framework Convention on Climate Change (UNFCCC) has entered into the phase of implementing the Paris Agreement. This agreement proposed economic and political mechanisms for addressing climate change. However the next step is perhaps the most important. Countries must introduce their own Nationally Determined Contributions (NDCs) in order to make the Paris agreement operational. This stage comes at a period of time when many climate scientists, advocates and observers to the various COP and national processes are detecting a decline in the political and social will to push their governments to enact policies that will affect real change in the energy, economic, environmental, agriculture and trade sectors. We are witnessing an "Ambition Gap," or a gap between knowing what we need to do, and mustering the moral will to do it. Perhaps there is no more significant time to consider the reasons that people are motivated to take morally significant action.

As this study will demonstrate, there have always existed many theories about ethical motivation. We can be motivated ba a sense of duty to what we think is right or just. We can be motivated to act out of sheer pragmatism, or emotion, or according to an evaluation of likely consequences, or perhaps out of self-less altruism. Each of us will appeal to every one of these theories at some point in our moral deliberation, and for different reasons. However, this study will demonstrate that our fundamental concept of what it means to be human orient us towards certain ethical decisions. In other words, we tend to care for, act on behalf of, or advocate for those with whom we closely identify. Our moral identity motivates us.

We may be motivated by rational decisions, but we go a long way to bridge the ambition gap if we help one another understand that creation is a part of us, and we are a part of creation. Our motivation to care for creation comes not only from altruism, pragmatism, duty or justice, but the knowledge that creation cares for us, because we are part of creation. And from where does that moral knowledge come? That is the fundamental question at the heart of this book, and the ethical significance of its contribution to our age.

Platonist, Poet, or Paracelsian?

Locating Thomas Traherne among the Science of the New Philosophy

Introduction

IN ORDER TO UNDERSTAND the contribution that Thomas Traherne can make to our contemporary attempt to recover the relationship between environmental and theological ethics, it is important to understand Traherne within his own historical, philosophical, theological and scientific context. This requires a bit of historical, theological and philosophical "brush clearing." This first chapter will take us deep into the rough weeds of the philosophical and scientific controversies of the seventeenth century that led to the disintegration of scientific and theological epistemology. But this critical exercise in the history of knowledge is important. In order to understand a theologian or philosopher, one must understand the context and controversies that informed their thinking and shaped their response. For example, to really understand the explanatory power Darwin's theory in *Origin of Species*, we need to grasp the framework of natural theology and natural philosophers that he was critiquing. In order to see the scope and limits of Luther's doctrine of justification that triggered the Reformation, we need to grasp the medieval scholastic theology from which he sought liberation. And, understanding something about Newtonian physics magnifies the paradigm shifting genius of Einstein's theory of relativity. In the same way, going deep into detail about the Traherne's own philosophical, scientific and educational context will help us emerge with a better understanding of the problem that he was addressing, and the repair that he was proposing. That critical perspective will help us to interpret the current state of our own epistemological paradigm, and consider the way that Traherne's moral theology can equip us to speak to our own moment in the history of knowledge.

In the years following the nineteenth-century discovery of Thomas Traherne's manuscripts, a scholarly consensus quickly emerged that associated him with the seventeenth-century Cambridge Platonists and metaphysical poets.[1] This consensus went largely unchallenged for the next century. However, Margoliouth's 1958 textual analysis of Traherne's *Centuries* and poetry suggested that Traherne utilized many Aristotelian concepts in addition to Platonism. Marks and Guffey's form critical textual analysis of Traherne's *Ethicks* demonstrated Traherne's dependence upon the scholasticism of Eustache de St. Paul for both the form and content of his ethics.[2] Paul Cefalu leads a group of literary scholars who recognize the influence of Aristotelian scholasticism and Thomism on the writings of Thomas Traherne.[3] There are good reasons to pursue these textual critiques of Traherne's writings. Traherne's *Commonplace Book* and his *Ficinio Notebook* from his days at Oxford provide students of Traherne with a great variety of source-critical paths to pursue. However, debating the relative influence of Platonism versus scholasticism on the form and logic of Traherne's ethics only really serves to confirm what we know about the complexity of seventeenth-century England. The political and intellectual conflict that took place within that century led to an abundance of new political, moral and scientific theories. But for all the complexity and eclecticism of Traherne's sources, many scholars have concluded that he actually achieves very little in the field of ethics.

As editors of Traherne's *Ethicks*, Marks and Guffey paint a picture of an aspiring student and young priest writing during an age of ethics.[4] During the seventeenth century, John Scott, Richard Allestree, Thomas Bayly, and the Puritans Jeremy Taylor and Richard Baxter[5] all produced popular devotional works that flooded the print market. In comparison to Traherne's contemporaries Grotius and Pufendorf, Marks and Guffey claim that Traherne and many other contemporary Platonists were merely summarizing

---

1. This thesis was solidified by the Robert Ellrodt, who conducted a landmark study of seven English metaphysical poets, and included Traherne among them. Ellrodt's study is a literary analysis of the social and psychological influences on the poets. See Ellrodt, *L'Inspiration personnelle*.

2. Marks and Guffey were the editors of Cornell's 1968 edition of Thomas Traherne's *Ethicks*. The original manuscript of *Ethicks* was sent to the publisher for editing at the time of Traherne's death. The work was published posthumously, by Thomas's brother Philip. See Traherne, *Christian Ethicks*.

3. Cefalu, "Thomistic Metaphysics and Ethics," 248.

4. Marks and Guffey explore the works of contemporary moralists in the section titled "Ethical Thought and its Students at Mid-Century" in Traherne, *Christian Ethicks*, xv.

5. Traherne, *Christian Ethicks*, xxiii.

the past.⁶ They suggest that the better known moralists of the seventeenth century were rebooting centuries-old deductive systems, and that Traherne achieves little more than an epitome of contemporary Platonic notions through Aristotelian logic.⁷ In form and logic, Traherne's *Ethicks* is little more than a précis of Eustache de St. Paul's *Ethica*.⁸ They suggest Traherne's lack of ethical originality resulted from the "stultifying traditional academic training to which Englishmen were still being subjected in 1650."⁹ Marks and Guffey suggest that Traherne "only partly escaped" from his age and ultimately "failed to set forth a new ethical theory."¹⁰ They base their conclusion on a limited body of Traherne's writings, which is now nearly doubled in size, and a very limited consideration of Thomas Traherne's actual education. They fully recognize that more work should be done on the realities of Traherne's actual education.¹¹ In their section on "Ethics as an Academic Subject" in the seventeenth century, they acknowledge that a portion of this section "must be construed as suggestions rather than as conclusions, for few scholars have dealt in any thorough way with the subject."¹² In this chapter, we will deal with the subject. The results open up a new path out of the established scholarly consensus regarding Traherne's relationship to the Cambridge Platonists and the metaphysical poets. I will join another emerging conversation interprets Traherne through his interaction with another school of thought that emerged during his lifetime—the new science of natural philosophy.

This chapter begins by complicating the scholarly consensus that attempts to define Traherne's work in terms of Cambridge Platonism, and secondly metaphysical poetry. Thirdly, I will expand the view of Thomas Traherne's own education, specifically as it relates to the "new" science. I will highlight the methods of the Paracelsian scientists who were shaping scientific thought during Traherne's undergraduate days, and suggest the impact of this New Philosophy on Traherne's own education and moral theory. Finally, based on a reading of Traherne's *Kingdom of God*, I will demonstrate the extent to which Traherne embraced and critiqued the ethical implications of this new "science." I will show that Traherne was not a conservative, albeit gifted, practitioner of a dying method of deductive moral

6. Traherne, *Christian Ethicks*, xxiv.
7. Traherne, *Christian Ethicks*, xvi.
8. Traherne, *Christian Ethicks*, xv.
9. Traherne, *Christian Ethicks*, xxii.
10. Traherne, *Christian Ethicks*, xxii.
11. Traherne, *Christian Ethicks*, xv.
12. Traherne, *Christian Ethicks*, xv.

philosophy. He embraced the scientific realities of his age, and yet firmly critiqued the logical ethical consequences of this new age of empiricism. This chapter provides a critical piece of interpreting the ethical contribution of Thomas Traherne in his own age, and in ours.

More Than a "Platonist"

Seventeenth-century England was full of political, social, and intellectual conflict.[13] In its worst manifestations, this conflict took the form of a bloody and protracted Civil War between the Parliamentarians and the Royalists. But there were other disputes that, while perhaps less violent, were no less divisive. Ecclesial and liturgical divisions had been escalating within the Anglican Church. The "Prelatists" ascribed to the high liturgical establishment of Bishop Laud, and the Puritans' pietistic movement was more Calvinist in nature.[14] The differences between Calvinist and high church Anglicans were not confined to pamphlets and pulpits. As a result of the theological differences in the area of political theology, the Puritans often found themselves allied with the so called "Roundhead" Parliamentarians against the Royalists who maintained the Divine right of Kings as part of the created and natural political order. This theological position often put them at odds with the more conservative Anglican Divines, which injected an element of sectarian conflict into the political struggle of the day.[15] In the midst of this conflict, a group of Platonist Professors and tutors in Cambridge University emerge as a peace-seeking group of theologians that appealed to the rational middle ground that lay between the Puritan/Laudian, Roundhead/Royalist divisions. Graham Parry concludes that the Cambridge Platonists "tried during the 1640s and 1650s to elabourate a system of belief that transcended the acrimonious doctrinal squabbles that divided English Christians so profitlessly."[16]

But the goal of the Cambridge Platonists' project was not merely to proclaim peace to the political division between Parliamentarians and Royalists. Their goal was to overcome a much more fundamental philosophical and theological divide between faith and reason. Basil Willey suggests that the political conflict between the Parliamentarians and the Royalists was

---

13. For an outstanding primer into the political, cultural, and intellectual climate of the seventeenth century, I recommend Parry, *Seventeenth Century*.

14. Willey, *Seventeenth-Century Background*, 113.

15. Traherne's place in this seventeenth century milieu has been explored through a close reading of the political ramifications of his Select Meditations in Blevins, *Re-Reading Thomas Traherne*, 65.

16. Parry, *Seventeenth-Century Poetry*, 121.

related in large part to the great skepticism that had taken hold of the religious, political and scientific imagination by the end of the sixteenth century.[17] Skepticism of the religious foundations of political theories such as the divine right of kings was part of the general skepticism of ecclesiastical authority. For instance, the same skepticism that led the Parliamentarians to question the Divine right of a monarch was present in Thomas Hobbes's skepticism of a created moral order and his subsequent theory that the social contract was the only basis for sustainable peace. In the same way emerging social and epistemological theories were skeptical of scholasticism's deductive method of reasoning, whereby knowledge of the natural world was deduced from previously held theological principles about the hierarchical order of creation. Skepticism of this deductive logic led to Francis Bacon's paradigm shift towards an early scientific method of inductive, experimental enquiry about natural phenomena. Bacon writes:

> Our method, though difficult to practise, is easy to formulate. It is to establish degrees of certainty, to preserve sensation by putting a kind of restraint on it, but to reject in general the work of the mind that follows sensation; and rather to open and construct a new and certain road for the mind from the actual perceptions of the senses.[18]

Bacon's method was to create knowledge according to what we could observe through our senses. This method began with what we observe, and then suggest theories based on that experience of the world. Baconian empiricism was decidedly atheistic in the sense that knowledge (moral and otherwise) was not deduced from prior knowledge of a divinely instituted natural order. In some form, this would be the fundamental epistemological cadre of natural theologians and deistic scientists, including Charles Darwin, during subsequent centuries of the scientific revolution.[19] Natural phenomena did not have to be deduced from Divine causes. Rather, through inductive experimentation natural phenomena could be explained in terms of their material or mechanical causes. It was simply no longer necessary to invoke God's will to understand natural phenomenon or construct the social order. In the same way, Hobbes proposed that the moral order of the political sphere could be constructed in terms of any socially agreed ends,

---

17. Willey specifically explores this reality in his chapter on Thomas Hobbes and the Cambridge Platonists in Willey, *English Moralists*, 148–89.

18. Bacon, *New Organon*, 28.

19. For an exceptional and nuanced understanding of Darwin's struggle between the theism, deism, and natural theology of his day, see Johnson, *Ask the Beasts*.

not only those deduced from God's will or commands for human society.[20] In this new social and scientific age, the basis for reason no longer had to be deduced from the traditional Christian theological, doctrinal or canonical sources.

This new science appeared to dismiss the role of faith in ethical discernment. One reaction to this perceived atheism was a revival of evangelical fideism, which sought to root conceptualizations of the social and natural order in Scriptural revelation.[21] But the perception that this new science was thoroughly atheistic was misdirected. There is no room to engage in a close reading here, but it is sufficient to say that scientists like Bacon and Hobbes were not necessarily atheists in the sense that they did not believe in God. Bacon and Hobbes simply believed that natural phenomena were "causeless."[22] In other words, observable natural phenomena are not necessarily the result of or proof of God's will, as revealed in the sources of the Christian tradition. Therefore, knowledge about the natural and social sciences could be induced from sources that were different from the sources of religious knowledge, which were deduced from grace and revelation. By the late sixteenth and early seventeenth centuries, systems of moral philosophy could be inductively reasoned from political, social, natural or economic science just as well as it could be deduced from Divine revelation.[23]

This new epistemological method set up a fundamental conflict between "causes." Will we deduce moral, social, and scientific knowledge from Divine causes, or will we create knowledge through inductive observations

---

20. Hobbes's concept is explored more fully in chapter 2 of the current study.

21. Pascal's Wager is an excellent example of the fideistic reaction against this kind of inductive reasoning. Blaise Pascal did not try to suggest that inductive reasoning was invalid, he simply suggested that it was unneccessary, thereby sidestepping the very question that Bacon and Hobbes were introducing. See Willey, *English Moralists*, 153. An excellent critique of Pascal's fideistic wager is found in Jordan, *Pascal's Wager*.

22. Basil Willey supports this view that is suggested in Professor Michael Oakshott's introduction to Hobbes, *Leviathan*, 9–20.

23. Robert Watson puts it thus: "In a world habitually struggling—in Christian modes from contemptus mundi to Neoplatonism and Protestantism—to look past the material object to its meaning for the human soul, Shakespeare and his fellow artists (no less than Bacon and his fellow scientists) begin to ask whether it isn't at least as hard to look truly at any object without that distorting imposition of human meaning. The battle between words and things for ontological, epistemological, and teleological superiority was thus partly a surrogate for the emerging war between the needs of Reformed Christianity and the needs of reformed science, which usually seemed good neighbors. The idea that things were ultimately more real than words—the dominant idea in schools, derived from a standard Aristotelian position—threatened to carry a corollary valuation of temporal history as ultimately more real than religious intuitions (debates about the historical Jesus still reflect this tention)" (Watson, *Back to Nature*, 43).

of the natural world? While epistemological differences between faith and reason were already well articulated in ancient philosophy, the Late Renaissance was a time in which we begin to see the perception of independence, or even a conflict between faith and reason.[24] A real methodological gap was developing between moral theology and the natural and political "sciences."

The Cambridge Platonists attempted to bridge this growing distance between faith and reason. Benjamin Whichcote summarized their perspective when he said in a public debate, "I oppose not rational and spiritual, for spiritual is most rational."[25] By 1636, Whichcote had become a Tutor in Emmanuel College where he began a lecture series which K. W. Salter suggests was an attempt "to preserve a spirit of sober piety and rational religion in the University and Town of Cambridge, in opposition to the fanatic enthusiasm of senseless canting then in vogue."[26] Soon after Whichcote, John Smith, Ralph Cudworth, and Nathanael Culverwell followed at Emmanuel College, and Henry More came to Christ College, Cambridge. The rational skepticism of Thomas Hobbes was a favorite target of most of these Platonists. John Smith's *Discourse Concerning the Immortality of the Soul*, Ralph Cudworth's *The True Intellectual System of the Universe*, and Nathanael Culverwell's *The Light of Nature*, were all written against Hobbes's determinist notion that the human mind was subject to the effects of material motion on the body (*i.e., emotions are caused by physical forces on the body*).[27] As a means of tamping down the emotionally conflicted "ranting" between Divine command fideists and atheistic materialists, these Puritan Cambridge Platonists attempted to create a theological system that appealed to reason based on what Henry More called "Divine Sagacity."[28] Their belief was that faithful reason should be able to overcome the duality of body and spirit that was held by atheistic materialists and fideistic Calvinists (who maintained an extreme interpretation of Augustine's doctrine of original sin). The Cambridge Platonists appealed to Augustine's Neo-Platonism, Plotinus, and Plato himself for an understanding of the relationship between the Divine form of Truth, Goodness and Beauty, and the truth, goodness and beauty that can be discerned through the inductive study of creation.[29]

24. Robert Watson outlines several of these paradigm shifts as they apply to urbanization, capitalism, skepticism, empirical sciences, and optical technology. Some of these theories will be explored in the current study, especially in chapter 2.

25. Whichcote quoted in Willey, *English Moralists*, 305.

26. Willey, *English Moralists*, 173.

27. Willey, *English Moralists*, 174.

28. Dowell, *Enjoying the World*, 48.

29. Dowell summarizes this perspective nicely in his section on the "Platonist Tendency" in Dowell, *Enjoying the World*, 45–50.

But for all of their striving towards peaceableness, Graham Parry concludes that the irenic nature of their broad system of belief came at a cost. The Cambridge Platonists were called "latitudinarians" because they took great theological latitude in their appeals to Plato, Plotinus,[30] the Hermetic tradition and the Bible.[31] Parry critically summarizes that "the Cambridge Platonists, active from the 1650s to the 1670s, have an air of sweet if at times bland reasonableness about them."[32] Because of that perceived blandness, he concludes that "it may be imagined such abstract and rarefied debate had little popular impact."[33] Parry is offering no praise of Cambridge Platonism. His perspective provides a bit of support for Marks's critique of Traherne. It is true that, Traherne's *Ethicks* bears the marks of this "rarefied debate," and its posthumous publication does not seem to have had much of an impact on moral theories in his day.

I do not quarrel with Parry's interpretation of the methods or impact of the Cambridge Platonists. But I do challenge the assumption that Traherne should be categorized as a mere Platonist on the basis of his theological latitude. The term "Platonist" cannot simply be deployed to describe a seventeenth-century theologian who uses latitude in constructing their theological system. A seventeenth-century "Platonist" will utilize theological latitude, but not all latitudinarians are "Platonists." Parry himself recognizes the "complexities of religious belief in this period are such that generalizations do not readily stick; in the end each individual evolved his own combination of beliefs and prejudices, and in the 1640s the choice became much wider and the combinations more confusing than ever before."[34] However, when it comes to Thomas Traherne, he uncritically reports:

> Some recent critics question how much [Traherne's *Centuries*] owes to personal inspiration, and how much to ancient meditative traditions derived from St Augustine or St. Buonaventura. Others represent it as primarily a case of Christian Platonism in an English setting.[35]

---

30. Willey demonstrates the way in which Smith, Coleridge, and Cudworth each appeal to Plato and Plotinus to refute Hobbes's materialist view of the mind as mechanical, affective responses to the motion of bodies in Willey, *English Moralists*, 177–81.

31. Dowell, *Enjoying the World*, 47; Parry, *Seventeenth Century*, esp. 181–201. For a fine exposition on the nature of their latitudinarian tendencies, see Willey, *English Moralists*, 172.

32. Parry, *Seventeenth Century*, 201.

33. Parry, *Seventeenth Century*, 202.

34. Parry, *Seventeenth Century*, 192.

35. Parry, *Seventeenth Century*, 116.

Rather than address the critical question, Parry too easily joins the "others" and suggests that Traherne demonstrates an "affinity to that loose group of thinkers known as the Cambridge Platonists."[36] I admit that the word "affinity" does not bind Parry to a thoroughgoing diagnosis of Traherne as a Platonist. But most scholarly interpretations of Traherne's writings default to this theory that Traherne's moral theology simply restated those of the seventeenth-century Platonists. This theory has its problems, and fails to appreciate the significance of Traherne's contribution. He was more than one among the Cambridge Platonists.

Parry suggests that the only "long-term significance of the Cambridge movement would be found in the changed temper of religious belief in the next century." He is right that Christian theistic moral theories would move "towards a deistic view of the Creation that would prevail widely among the more pensive classes of the eighteenth century."[37] Basil Willey agrees that the Cambridge Platonists' appeal to right reason "points towards the Deisms and the "Moral Sense" philosophies of the eighteenth century,"[38] including natural theologians like William Paley. In other words, the Platonic atmosphere of "bland reasonableness" in the face of Descartes and Hobbes created the space for Kantian rationalism and Humean empiricism to emerge, which ultimately disassociated moral reason and human sensibility. This played a role in the disassociation of religion and natural science. The following paragraph offers a rough outline of that shift.

On the one hand, the Reformed view of human depravity claimed that knowledge of the Divine could only be known through revelation, not reason. On the other hand, Bacon and Hobbes asserted an atheistic, empirical philosophy in which reason was the basis for moral knowledge. As a response to this binary, the Platonists generally asserted that moral theology could claim reason as its basis as much as philosophy. Ralph Cudworth believed that moral knowledge is based on eternal, unchanging Divine forms or ideas that existed prior to and independent of the individual. He wrote that knowledge "is a thing independent upon singular bodies [i.e., empirical details or sense-data], or proleptical to them, and in order of nature before them."[39] In other words, our ability to grasp moral knowledge has less to do with our perception of the world, and more to do with our ability to

---

36. Parry, *Seventeenth Century*, 121.

37. He goes on to claim that the foundation of Cambridge Platonism allowed later moral theorists to move "away from the concept of special truths enshrined in Christianity alone towards a broad justification of man's spirituality in nature" (Parry, *Seventeenth Century*, 202).

38. Willey, *English Moralists*, 186.

39. Willey, *English Moralists*, 176.

understand eternal ideas or forms. Based on the Christian Neo-Platonic idea that the soul is eternal, the Platonists believed that our soul is capable of intelligibly reasoning the immutable nature of morality.[40] Reason was our "organ of spiritual vision." Whichcote called reason the "candle of the Lord" that led humans to seek God within themselves through a kind of spiritually enlightened "supersensuousness" that could recognize the eternal and universal form of God's goodness.[41] But while the Cambridge Platonists meant to affirm human reason as a locus for God's grace to override our sensual passions and inspire moral knowledge, their efforts led to the kind of cognitive rationalism that would be postulated in the seventeenth century by Renée Descartes,[42] expressed in the eighteenth century through the deistic "Ideas" of John Locke[43] and find its full ethical application in Immanuel Kant's rationalist moral epistemology in which "Reason exerts a dominion over sensibility in order to extend it in conformity with its own realm (the practical)."[44] By the nineteenth century, moral philosophers generally adopted the position that religious knowledge was discontinuous with our sensible nature, and the two needed to be liberated from one another. And in the end, the divorce between moral and religious knowledge was successful.

C. S. Lewis recognized that by separating reason and sensibility, moral theorists of the late renaissance began "discarding the image" of the created order that embodied the very moral order that they were seeking.[45] The disembodiment of ethics went hand in hand with the separation of moral knowledge from our sensory knowledge of the natural world. In the seventeenth century, the Platonists did not challenge the dualistic binary of

40. Willey, *English Moralists*, 183.

41. Willey, *English Moralists*, 207.

42. Descartes famously constructs his meditations and methods based on the notion that his senses deceive him. He can only "know" something to be true that he conceives rationally. These references can be found throughout his methods and meditations. See Descartes, *Discourse*. Willey explores the consequences as I have stated them here in Willey, *Seventeenth-Century Background*, 76.

43. Locke writes that "perception is that which we call the understanding," which is to say, the "perception of ideas in our minds" or the "connexion or repugnancy, agreement or disagreement, that there is between any of our ideas" (Locke, *Essay Concerning Human Understanding*, 151). He goes on to say that "knowledge is the perception of the agreement or disagreement of two ideas." In other words, understanding of moral knowledge is not related to sensory perception, only cognitive ideas. The theory is footnoted with the comment that "the placing of certainty, as Mr. Locke does in the perception of the agreement or disagreement of our ideas, the Bishops of Worcester suspects may be of dangerous consequence" (Locke, *Essay Concerning Human Understanding*, 385).

44. Kant, *Critique of Judgment*, 78.

45. Lewis, *Discarded Image*, 11.

body and mind, or sensuality and reason, and therefore abetted the disembodiment of ethics which came to fruition in Kant's rationalism. The last chapters of this study will explore recent developments in the philosophy of moral education which, according to Thomas Wren, are struggling to climb out of the shadow of Kant's rationalism by reaffirming that direct, sensory contact with ecology has something to do with the moral formation of children.[46]

Given that genealogy, it may seem obvious why I wish to read Traherne apart from the group of moral theologians who are part of a philosophical trajectory between Platonism and Kantian rationalism. However, associating Traherne too closely with the Platonists is not merely inconvenient for this thesis. Such an uncritical assumption overlooks a significant difference between Traherne's moral theory and that of the Platonists. In an effort to deny the sufficiency of Hobbes's atheistic moral theory, the Platonists' subjugated the bodily senses and elevated the role of reason to the "supersensual." Basil Willey suggests that the Cambridge Platonists' suspicions of the moral import of the senses fit very naturally with their Puritan skepticism of Laudian ecclesiastical ritual with its appeal to smells, images, and metaphorical liturgy. In contrast, sensuality is an entire *leit motif* that runs throughout Traherne's work. Rather than discarding the body or subjugating sensuality, Traherne writes a whole poem in praise of the human senses.[47] The human being's ability to derive knowledge of the Divine moral order is related to the human being's physical, sensual interaction with the earth.

> Therefore hath God created living ones, that by lively motions, and sensible desires, we might be sensible of a Deity. They breathe, they see, they feel, they grow, they flourish, they know, they love. O what a world of evidences! We are lost in abysses, we now are absorpt in wonders, and swallowed up of demonstrations. Beasts, fowls, and fishes teaching and evidencing the glory of their creator. But these by an endless generation might succeed each other from everlasting. Let us therefore survey their order, and see by that whether we cannot discern their governor.[48]

46. Thomas Wren writes that "cognitive and developmental psychologists who focus on children's moral reasoning have also worked in the long shadow of Kant ever since Jean Piaget wrote *The Moral Judgment of the Child*, referring to Kant's understanding that moral reasoning is based on his version of the "fully functional" adult living in a basically decent environment" (Nucci and Narvaéz, *Handbook*, 25).

47. "Thanksgivings for the Body" gives thanks for all things "Visible, Material [and] Sensible" (Traherne, *Centuries, Poems, and Thanksgivings*, 2:220). This "Thanksgiving for the Body" and other poems will be explored in later chapters.

48. Traherne, *Centuries, Poems, and Thanksgivings*, 1:70.

Given that a major motif of his moral epistemology is related to the senses in a way that runs contrary to the "supersensual" trajectory of Cambridge Platonism, it seems Traherne is trying to make a unique contribution to the moral and scientific landscape of his day and ours. A close study of his newly discovered manuscripts will demonstrate that Traherne's moral theory is based on a synthesis of sensory experience, inductive science and theology.

More Than a "Poet"

While Thomas Traherne has yet to be fully recognized for his theological and ethical import as an Anglican priest of the high liturgical Laudian church of the restoration, he has definitely achieved celebratory status as a superlative poet. However, just as many historians are too quick to corral Traherne among the Cambridge Platonists, many interpret Thomas Traherne according to the cadre of seventeenth-century metaphysical poetry. Highlighting the subtle differences between Traherne's poetry and that of the metaphysical poets will help us fully appreciate Traherne's unique contribution to ethics.

The roster of metaphysical poets includes George Herbert, John Donne, Andrew Marvell, Henry Vaughan and Henry More. Samuel Johnson first created the category of "metaphysical poet" in his 1781 seminal work, *Lives of the Most Eminent English Poets*.[49] From Johnson's work we can derive three basic characteristics that define the metaphysical poet. The first characteristic is the time period, which runs from Shakespeare through the seventeenth century. The second characteristic is that the poet's metaphorical concepts, known as "conceits," give the poets their eternal, "metaphysical" quality. The conceits of the metaphysical poets are generally Platonic because the goal is not to describe the emotional or sensual experience of life as it is. The goal is the intellectual knowledge of the eternal that lies behind the sense of the object. Thirdly, Johnson suggests the metaphysical poets generally focus on the occult, or hidden, nature of that knowledge.

---

49. Samuel Johnson wrote: "About the beginning of the seventeenth century, appeared a race of writers that may be termed the metaphysical poets. . . . The metaphysical poets were men of learning, and to show their learning was their whole endeavor. . . . Their thoughts are often new, but seldom natural; they are not obvious, but neither are they just; and the reader, far from wondering that he missed them, wonders more frequently by what perverseness of industry they were ever found. . . . But [their] wit, abstracted from its effects upon the hearer, may be more rigorously and philosophically considered as a kind of discordia concors; a combination of dissimilar images, or discovery of occult resemblances in things apparently unlike. . . . From this account of their compositions it will be readily inferred, that they were not successful in representing or moving the affections" (Johnson, *Lives*, 8–9).

Knowledge is hidden under or behind the thing itself. When these poets engage the natural world as a metaphor to explain the human or divine, they tend to dabble in magicalism. The metaphysical poets regularly appeal to the Heremetic tradition and specifically the *Divine Pymander* for their occult references.[50]

Based on Johnson's summary, it is easy to understand why Traherne has been included in the roster of metaphysical poets. On the first quality, Thomas Traherne did write his poetry within the seventeenth century. However, Traherne was late born among the poets, and entering university in 1652, was the latest of those poets that are generally considered among this group. I will demonstrate below that, when mapped onto the nature of Paracelsian science being taught at Oxford at the time of his matriculation, we can see how Traherne's scientific education illuminates a unique perspective on moral theology in the shadow of Milton, Donne and Vaughan.

On the third quality, Traherne does reference Hermes Trismegistus's *Divine Pymander*. But clarifying Traherne's nuanced use of the *Divine Pymander* will help us understand the epistemological goals of his poetry and other writings.[51] Traherne uses the Heremetic texts to harness an historical case against the materialist philosophy that began to dissociate the Creator from creation. I base this claim on the difference between what Traherne recorded from the Hermetic corpus in his personal notebooks, and what he actually used in his *Ethicks*. We could expect Traherne to quote large sections of Trismegistus in his notebook out of intellectual curiosity towards the major Hermetic revival that was begun by Ficino.[52] But while Traherne does record large quotations of the *Divine Pymander* in his *Commonplace Book*, he refers to Trismegistus very sparingly in his own writing.[53] Traherne consistently references Trismegistus for two specific philosophical purposes. First, Traherne cites the *Divine Pymander* as a witness to the way in which God's goodness is present in creation, which follows the orthodox

---

50. Examples of this hermetically induced magicalism is recorded in Diane McColley's treatment of seventeenth-century poetry. See McColley, *Poetry and Ecology*, 59.

51. Wade demonstrates how metaphysical poets—such as Cudworth and Vaughan—couple Hermetic texts with the methods of alchemy and theurgy to convey knowledge of God which would otherwise be hidden. See Wade and Parker, *Thomas Traherne*.

52. The relationship between Ficino and Hermes Trismegistus are well documented in the chapter on Marsilio Ficino in Hedley and Hutton, *Platonism at the Origins*. Denise Inge often cites Traherne's indebtedness to Ficino and Hermes. For references to the Common Place Notebook, see Inge, *Happiness and Holiness*, 16. For references to the Ficino Notebook, see Inge, *Happiness and Holiness*, 47.

53. Traherne's use of quotes from the *Divine Pymander* are in Traherne, *Christian Ethicks*, 228–30.

notion of Divine plenitude found in the Church fathers such as Tertullian, Gregory of Nyssa and St. Augustine to whom he also constantly refers. He also cites the *Pymander* in reference to God's love as the formal power by which God infinitely communicates through each creature.[54] In this regard, the *Pymander* is not referred to for its occult magicalism but its affirmation of basic Thomism in which God's being is both formal creative power and efficient communicative act.[55]

Traherne's use of *Pymander* is a philosophical reaction against the nominalist tradition that was present in the sixteenth-century reformation theologies.[56] Nominalists suggest that creation is not the overflowing plenitude of God's goodness, but rather the logical and linguistic result of God's free will to create. Since God can speak that will into reality from afar, the nominalists affirm that God's goodness remains linguistically and spatially separate from creation, and do not participate in one another. Put another way, nominalists profess that a perfectly free God is not bound to creation in any way. That spatial separation ultimately allows Hobbes's to posit his atheistic materialist theory about natural phenomena. In the face of nominalism and atheism, Traherne is keen to assert the value of every creature because God communicates goodness in the fact of its being. Traherne frequently rejoices in the knowledge that God is manifestly known in his works. In the following quote the italics are quotations from *Pymander*.

> His Close is most divine; *And yet thou sayest, God is Invisible; but be advised: for who is more manifest than he? For therefore he made all things, that thou by all things mightst see him. This is the Good of God, his Vertue is this, to appear and be seen in all Things.* This is the bottom of all other Greatnesses whatsoever: God is infinitely communicative, infinitely prone to reveal himself, infinitely Wise and able to do it. He hath made the Soul on purpose that it might see him.[57]

As opposed to using Hermes to poetically reinforce occult, preternatural ideas, Traherne sparingly uses Hermes Trismegistus to reinforce the way that God is present and "infinitely communicative" in all things. This quote

54. Traherne, *Christian Ethics*, 227.

55. Paul Cefalu makes this point as evidence that Traherne is fundamentally a Thomist rather than a Platonist. See Cefalu, "Thomistic Metaphysics and Ethics."

56. Norman Wirzba recognizes nominalism as a cause of the separation between God and the nature of creation in Wirzba, *Paradise of God*, which borrows its title from Traherne's *Centuries*.

57. Traherne, *Christian Ethics*, 227. This quote of Traherne's is taken from Hermes's chapter entitled, "That God is not manifest, and yet most manifest." See Hermes Trismegistus, *Divine Pymander*.

also points to the second reason that Traherne refers to Trismegistus. Traherne cites Trismegistus in order to underline his belief that human beings have the capacity to intuit the communication of God's goodness in creation. His references to Trismegistus only occur in his chapter on the virtue of "Magnanimity."[58] In this chapter, Traherne equates the Soul with man's capacity to perceive the presence of the Divine in creation. He affirms that God "hath made the Soul on purpose that it might see him." The Magnanimous Soul has the "Capacity" to

> become ETERNITY, as *Trismegistus* speaketh, or ONE SPIRIT with God, as the Apostle. And then it must needs be present with all things *in Heaven, and in the Earth, and in the Sea*, as GOD is: for all things will be in it, as it were by Thoughts and Intellections.[59]

We can see here the way in which Traherne associates the rational, cognitive function of the human being with the spiritual. While this formula may be theosophical, it is not an allusion to occult magic or vitalist theurgy. Rather, it is an epistemological defence of the human senses. Traherne refers to the Hermes who writes in his chapters "Of Sense and Understanding" that "God is the workman of all things, and when he worketh, he useth Nature," and "It is, therefore, a thing proper to man, to communicate and conjoin Sense and Understanding."[60]

In an effort to avoid any trace of occult magic in his references to Trismegistus, Traherne recognizes and willingly points to the limits of referring to "the Philosophy of the ancient Heathen." He writes "wherein though there be some Errors, yet was he guided to it by a mighty sence of the interiour Excellencey of the Soul of Man, and the boldness he assumes is not so profane, but that it is countenanced here and there in the Holy Scripture."[61] Traherne's usage of Trismegistus is only for the reason of affirming the human being's ability to perceive Eternity in nature, and he only refers to Trismegistus in situations where the *Pymander* agrees with Scripture's witness to this "capacity" for human beings to be of one Spirit with God. He is certainly not looking to the *Pymander* in order to repair a perceived gap in Christian orthodoxy. On the contrary, he sees the limitations of the Pymander's occult goals. He writes:

---

58. "Of Magnanimity" is chapter 28 in Traherne, *Christian Ethicks*, 224.
59. Traherne, *Christian Ethicks*, 228.
60. Traherne, *Christian Ethicks*, 94–98.
61. Traherne, *Christian Ethicks*, 226.

Trismegistus (or whoever else was the Author of that Book) saw the deep Capacity of his own Soul, but if a Conjecture may be made by the residue of the discourse, did not understand the end (at least not clearly) for which it was implanted. Some knowledge he had, that all the things in Eternity were Objects of the Power, by reason of which he calls them *Fair and Good*: but that they were to be the *Treasures and Enjoyments* of the Soul I do not find him affirming.[62]

Traherne explicitly states that the *Pymander* affirms there are different ways of seeing and knowing, and that human beings have the capacity to "see" and therefore know God. But the ethical question remains, how does a person "see"? Thomas Traherne, even in his most latitudinal poetic mode, is no occult magician. Gladys Wade suggests that Traherne is "perfectly free from any taint" of the Hermetic, or Cabalistic occult magic that Samuel Johnson detects in the other poets of this century.[63] Wade's observation urges us to clarify the contribution that Traherne was trying to make to the moral theory of his day. He never made an appeal to the occult aspects of the Hermetic tradition because he was making his peace with another way of knowing. The new "science" of Bacon's natural philosophy employed the senses for inductive reasoning, and I will show that this epistemological method shaped Traherne's contribution to ethical theory.

In the time of the metaphysical poets, scientists such as Bacon and Galileo were plumbing the depths of the earth and pushing the boundaries of the heavens and humanity. The new Paracelsian chemistry, toxicology, and medicine were atomizing the body, and Gilbert was exploring geology while quantifying the physical forces of magnetism and gravity. All of these new inductive means of "knowing" creation were based in Bacon's inductive method. Marjorie Hope Nicolson suggests that the poets understood these concepts, and were concerned over the "death of a world."[64] She writes that while the Copernican revolution expanded the bounds of the physical universe into infinity, Kepler's planetary calculations revealed the elliptical orbits which broke the circle of perfection. The Elizabethan concept of the

---

62. Traherne, *Christian Ethicks*, 230.

63. Gladys Wade hints at this when she summarizes that while Vaughan displays a great tendency towards the magicalism and Cabalism utilized by Donne and More before him, Traherne is nearly devoid of this "taint" of magicalism. While she does not explain the reasons for this summary, it resembles Parry's "hunch" about the quality of Traherne's work. See Wade and Parker, *Thomas Traherne*, 219, 233.

64. Nicolson, *Breaking of the Circle*, 65. While unrelated to the metaphysical poets as such, Carolyn Merchant uses the term "death of nature" to describe the espistemological consequences of this particular age of scientific thought. See Merchant, *Death of Nature*.

concentric model of the universe, in which the macrocosm contained the geocosm and the geocosm contained the human microcosm, provided the poets with their metaphor of man as the geometric centre of a meaningful world. When this circle was "broken" by the new science, the earth was revealed as a wandering collection of chemical and mechanical forces. Human beings were no longer the epitome of God, but individuals competing for space who acted according to the motions and influences of other bodies. In the face of this new Baconian, Hobbesian, and eventually Newtonian reality, the old Elizabethan metaphors of the living earth and our sensibility of it no longer had meaning, or were relegated to the occult world of magic.[65]

Based upon this inductive, scientific revolution, T. S. Eliot claimed that the metaphysical poets were attempting to maintain the connection between our empirical senses and our moral sensibility. He wrote, "In the seventeenth century, a dissociation of sensibility set in, from which we have never recovered."[66] In the face of this "dissociation of sensibility," the metaphysical poets seemed to seek the shadows of transcendent forms and the magic of Hermetic vitalism to regain a lost sense of mystery. Samuel Johnson claims that the metaphysical poets yoked together concepts such as Platonism and Rosicrucian alchemy.[67] For Johnson the *discordia concors* of this poetic method was intended to maintain the role of emotion and the senses as epistemologically significant in the face of the emerging mechanistic world view.[68] Like Nicolson, Eliot believes that the poets were not yoking concepts that they did not understand, and they were not merely resorting to occultism to defend against the new science. Eliot suggests that the metaphysical poets maintained a commitment to the integration of thoughts and feelings, reason and sensuality. He writes, "A thought, to Donne, was a feeling; it modified his sensibility." However, the directionality of Eliot's observation is significant. For the metaphysical poets, contemplating the transcendent realm generated feelings of spiritual ecstasy. This tends to be the same methodology of mystics and theosophists. Contemplating eternity and infinity causes intense feelings of joy. Thinking modifies our perception. It is interesting to note that for Traherne, however, the writ also ran the other way.

For Traherne, felicity did not begin with the cerebral contemplation of a rational or eternal concept. Traherne's method of reasoning began with

---

65. Carolyn Merchant traces the Baconian roots of the mechanization of the earth in Merchant, *Death of Nature*.

66. From Eliot's "Metaphysical Poets," in Eliot, *Selected Essays*, 247.

67. Johnson, *Lives*, 9. For the complete quotation, see footnote 49 in this chapter.

68. Johnson, *Lives*, 8.

sensual engagement with the finite in his presence. "For to *feel* is as important as to *see* their *Glory*," writes Traherne in the introduction to his *Ethicks*.[69] Nicolson agrees that Traherne is familiar with the new "science" of natural philosophy. But she overlooks the significance of the fact that when the macro-, geo-, micro-cosmic pattern was broken by the new science, Traherne did not retreat to the safe and infinite recesses of the eternal and rational. When that circle was broken, Traherne actually advanced towards a deeper contemplation of the finite geocosm with the new Baconian method in mind. Rather than reapply the ancient methods of deductive reasoning, Traherne believed that through sensual, empirical engagement of the natural world, the human can derive moral knowledge.

In his summary of the seventeenth-century poets, Graham Parry remarks that there seems to be a qualitative difference between Traherne and the other poets. He writes that "Traherne seems to have had no poetic model, and no successor."[70] However, he attributes the difference to a belief that Traherne was happily ensconced in his peaceful, Platonic spirituality. He writes that Traherne's "religious life is so private and apart that it seems scarcely to touch the boundaries of his age."[71] Parry assumes that Traherne stands full square with the seventeenth-century Platonists and poets, and does not attempt to understand the "seemingly" unique quality of his writings. In an age when Baconian empiricism threatened to water the seeds of skeptical atheism, many Neo-Platonists and metaphysical poets turned towards infinity to affirm deductive reasoning as the beginning of moral knowledge. I will show that in light of this trend, Traherne's focus on the geocosm sets him apart from the rationalist genealogy that runs from seventeenth-century Platonism to Kant. That geocosmic focus, I will argue, is the source of Traherne's distinct ethical voice.

A closer reading of Traherne will help us realize that Traherne is not only interested in poetically representing the relationship between the One Creator and the many of creation. He is interested in the ethical implications of that unity, and the means by which we can discern the goodness of the One in the naturally, ecologically cooperative goodness of the many. I will demonstrate that his Oxford education led Traherne toward the geocosm with a fairly sophisticated degree of scientific acumen.

---

69. Traherne, *Christian Ethicks*, 6.
70. Parry, *Seventeenth-Century Poetry*, 122.
71. Parry, *Seventeenth-Century Poetry*, 118.

Summary

In the first two sections, I have attempted to complicate the two prevailing methods of categorizing Thomas Traherne. There are limitations to interpreting Traherne according to seventeenth-century Platonism and metaphysical poetry. Having been born and educated in seventeenth-century England, we should expect that Traherne would employ the literary techniques of Platonists and poets. But these categorical assumptions have tempted many scholars to look past Traherne's real contribution to moral philosophy. When we associate Thomas Traherne too closely with either Cambridge Platonism or the metaphysical poets, it is possible that the details of his life become overlooked. Parry begins his survey of Traherne by stating that "The mundane career of Traherne is neither well-documented nor very remarkable."[72] He concludes that the "wonder" of Traherne's own spiritual discovery "renders the details of his ordinary life insignificant."[73] He is ready to set aside the realities of Traherne's journey. But like most of us, the engagement with ordinary life left discernible impressions on Traherne's poetry, theological prose, and moral theory.

It is admittedly difficult to piece together the biographical history of a man who was so rarely documented. However, I will demonstrate that the details of his education are significant factors in the way that Traherne grappled with the tumult of his age. I believe the reason that Traherne had no model and no successor was because he was writing at the boundaries of an age. In a time of military, political violence and theological conflict, Traherne did not retreat into a Platonic solace with heterogeneous allusions to new scientific concepts that he did not understand. He attempted to advance a Christian moral theology into a new empirical age. His education in the "new philosophy" helped him harness the epistemological and ethical significance of our inductive senses.[74] Therefore, contrary to Parry's conclusion, I will argue that Traherne's spiritual sense of "wonder" did not render the details of his ordinary life insignificant. Rather, the profound moral significance of the ordinary details of the geocosmic Creation that surrounded him was revealed through the sensory engagement of his natural sense of wonder.

---

72. Parry, *Seventeenth-Century Poetry*, 116.
73. Parry, *Seventeenth-Century Poetry*, 117.
74. Several scholars have begun to explore this thesis, most notably, Nicolson, *Breaking of the Circle*; Akers, *From the Hexaemeral*; Dowell, *Enjoying the World*; Balakier, "Pre-Newtonian Gravitational Trope," 32–41.

Teaching Thomas: Reconciling a Deductive and Inductive Education

Thomas Traherne's autobiographical reflections reveal the profound joy he took in studying the inductive methods of the New Philosophy at the age of 15 during his undergraduate days in Oxford. In order to appreciate the revolution that resulted from his engagement with this new, Baconian, inductive method of science, we must first understand that Thomas received a deductive, scholastic, catechetical grammar school education as a child. There is a lingering debate regarding whether young Thomas was a student at the Hereford Cathedral School, or if he received private tutelage funded by his uncle, Philip Traherne. The Hereford Cathedral School claims Thomas Traherne as one of their alumni.[75] Conversely the records of Brasenose College suggest that Traherne was admitted as a "commoner," as opposed to being admitted among the cadre of Cathedral School graduates.[76] Based on this registration, Gladys Wade assumes that Traherne received a private education.[77] This would explain his high level of achievement, as well as the peculiarities of Traherne's reception into Brasenose.[78] While the lack of documentation does not allow us to settle the question regarding the means by which he received it, the point remains that he received a deductive, scholastic, seventeenth-century grammar school education. And Traherne remembers that, as a child who needed a sense of peace in troubled times, this standard deductive education did not provide comfort or contentment.

Young Thomas was orphaned sometime after the age of four.[79] He and his brother were moved to the care of his uncle Philip who enjoyed Royal privilege as a wealthy leader in Hereford. Thomas seemed overwhelmed by the qualitative difference between his "Fathers poor House"[80] and the rich urban interior of his uncle's city life. In his new life of wealth, Thomas was quickly taught that "the Tinsild Ware upon a Hobby hors was a fine

---

75. This claim was confirmed to me by the resident historian at the Hereford Cathedral School. They proudly record Thomas Traherne as one of their distinguished "graduates," even though this is not confirmed by any extant record.

76. This information is recorded in the Brasenose College Register, 1509–1901, found in Traherne, *Centuries, Poems, and Thanksgivings*, 1:xxiv. See also Wade and Parker, *Thomas Traherne*, 38.

77. Margoliouth comes to the same conclusion in Traherne, *Centuries, Poems, and Thanksgivings*, 1:xxxvii.

78. Wade and Parker, *Thomas Traherne*, 39.

79. Traherne, *Centuries, Poems, and Thanksgivings*, 1:xxxvii.

80. A memory is recorded from his father's "poor house" in the sixteenth meditation of his third century (Traherne, *Centuries, Poems, and Thanksgivings*, 1:119).

thing," that a "Purs of Gold was of any valu," "a fine Coat, a Peny, a Gilded Book &c," "Beads and Glass Buttons Jewels" had value and meaning.[81] In this new environment, Thomas felt he was being "Swallowed up therefore in the Miserable Gulph of idle talk and worthless vanities," and "thenceforth I lived among Shadows like a Prodigal Son feeding upon Husks with Swine." The urban life of his later childhood was "A Comfortless Wilderness full of Thorns and Troubles the World was, or wors: a Waste Place covered with Idleness and Play, and Shops and Markets and Taverns."[82] Reflecting on his education, he laments that:

> As for Churches, they were things I did not understand. And Scholes were a Burden: so that there was nothing in the World worth the having, or Enjoying, but my Game and Sport which also was a Dream and being passed wholy forgotten. So that I had utterly forgotten all Goodness Bounty Comfort and Glory: which things are the very Brightness of the Glory of God: for lack of which therfore [God] was unknown.[83]

Here Traherne inverts common understanding of what makes "civil society." The things of human civilization were the wild thorns that choked out the beauty and glory of God as revealed in Creation. This group of meditations reveals a child who was struggling to reconcile the confines of his deductive, scholastic education with the "Liquid Clear Satisfactions"[84] that he intuited from his native experience of nature. In contrast to the seemingly Edenic tutelage that the book of nature provided Traherne in his early childhood, he was struggling to reconcile his new urban environs with the education that he was receiving in Church and school. His meditations record his desire to receive a "Book of Heaven" that would confirm the "Causes of Peace" that he discerned as a child, when he gazed upon "the Beauties of the Earth" and "was made to hold a Communion with the Secrets of Divine Providence in all the World."[85]

> Among other things, there befel me a most infinit Desire of a Book from Heaven. For observing al things to be rude and superfluous here upon Earth I thought the Ways of felicity to

---

81. Traherne, *Centuries, Poems, and Thanksgivings*, 1:116.
82. Traherne, *Centuries, Poems, and Thanksgivings*, 1:118.
83. These quotes are all found from the ninth to the fourteenth meditation of the third century (Traherne, *Centuries, Poems, and Thanksgivings*, 1:118).
84. Traherne, *Centuries, Poems, and Thanksgivings*, 1:123.
85. Traherne, *Centuries, Poems, and Thanksgivings*, 1:124.

> be known only among the Holy Angels: and that unless I could receiv information from them, I could never be Happy.[86]

Eventually he came to realize that God "had sent the Book I wanted before I was Born: and prepared it for me, and also commended, and sent it unto me, in a far better manner then I was able to imagine."[87] But in all of his grammar school education, he never "received" the Bible as a young child. After leaving school, he realized:

> there are thousands in the World, of whom I being a Poor Child was Ignorant, that in Temples, Universities and Secret Closets enjoy felicity. Whom I saw not in Shops, or Scholes or Trades; Whom I found not in Streets, or feasts, or Taverns and therefore not to be in the World: Who Enjoy Communion with God, and hav fellowship with the Angels evry Day. And these I discerned to be a Great Help unto me.[88]

He came to discover that there were great temples, universities and "Secret Closets" in which "thousands" of people enjoyed the felicity of discerning truth in communion with God and fellowship with the Angels every day through their Baconian inductive methods of observing the Book of Creation. Traherne began to rediscover that childhood satisfaction of interacting with the Creator in creation not through his deductive, grammar school education of his youth, but through his undergraduate education in the "secret closets" of his University. This explains the joy that he felt upon entering Oxford in 1652 as a fifteen year old.[89]

> Having been at the University, and received there the Taste and Tincture of another Education, I saw that there were Things in the World of which I never Dreamed, Glorious Secrets, and Glorious Persons past Imagination. There I saw that Logick, Ethicks, Physicks, Metaphysicks, Geomtery, Astronomy, Poesie, Medicine, Grammer, Musick, Rhetorick, all kind of Arts Trades and Mechanicismes that Adorned the World pertained to felicity At least there I saw those Things, which afterwards I knew to pertain unto it: And was Delighted in it. There I saw into the Nature of the Sea, the Heavens, the Sun, the Moon and Stars, the Elements, Minerals and Vegetables All which appeared like the Kings Daughter, All Glorious within, and those Things which

---

86. Traherne, *Centuries, Poems, and Thanksgivings*, 1:127.
87. Traherne, *Centuries, Poems, and Thanksgivings*, 1:127.
88. Traherne, *Centuries, Poems, and Thanksgivings*, 1:128.
89. The record of his matriculation can be found in the Brasenose College Register, 1509–1901 (Traherne, *Centuries, Poems, and Thanksgivings*, 1:xxiv).

my Nurses and Parents should hav talkt of, there were taught unto Me.[90]

At university he received "the Taste and Tincture of another Education" which he feels like he should have been taught as a child. This new education ranges from logic and ethics to grammar, poetry, astronomy, medicine and "Mechanismes" which is likely a reference to the budding field of physics. His joy is oriented towards the study of the elements and mechanisms "within" minerals, vegetables, the sea, the heavens, and the body. These words reflect the goals of inductive science, and the turning of his attention towards the geocosm which we will explore in later chapters. Traherne was experiencing the wonder of an inductive curriculum which he missed in the deductive "scholes" of his childhood. Through this new scientific eye, he saw the things that he longed to confirm about the glory and wonder of creation that he had viewed as a young child in the Book of Nature.

Traherne Embraced a New Science, but Which Science?

After the deductive nature of his primary education, Traherne was inspired by his undergraduate exposure to the new inductive science. There is, however, one distinction to be made. There was a major educational shift from the Galenist, deductive philosophy towards a Baconian, inductive science. But the debate between John Webster and Seth Ward demonstrates that the seventeenth century cannot simply be divided between "ancient" deductive philosophers and "modern" inductive empiricists.[91] The New Philosophy of inductive science was far from monolithic. Within the scientific revolution itself, there were many avenues of inductive sciences being pursued. So while Traherne was inspired by "modern" science, the question remains, in what form? The answer to this question will give a bit more precision about the way in which inductive science shaped Traherne's moral theory.

Debus classifies one group of scientists as mechanical philosophers. These scientists studied on the laws of physics, as well as biological and physiological mechanics. These mechanical philosophers relied on the precision of mathematics as a means to measure and predict movements and

---

90. Traherne, *Centuries, Poems, and Thanksgivings*, 1:132.

91. Debus, *Science and Education*, explores the controversy that existed at Oxford during the early 1650s. In doing so, Debus's research highlights the impact that this Baconian paradigm shift had upon education at Oxford during Traherne's undergraduate education, as well as the significant nuance that exists between the Paracelsian, chemical, and mechanical scientists. For more on the Paracelsian aspects of this "new philosophy," see Yates, *Rosicrucian Enlightenment*.

motions. Mathematicians such as Pythagoras, astronomers such as Galileo and Kepler, and physicists such as Isaac Newton would be associated with this classification. This genealogy of mechanical philosophers eventually gave rise to empiricists, such as David Hume, whose moral sense theories relate to the motion of objects. Within this group of scientists, you find many astronomers who focused on the precision of optical theories related to the telescope, compass and clock. The Oxfordian astonomer Seth Ward was a champion of this mathematical and mechanical method of inductive reasoning.[92] Ward actually believed that "it was a misfortune to the world, that my Lord Bacon was not skilled in Mathematicks, which made him jealous of their Assistance in Naturall Enquiries."[93] Here is one inductive scientist of the philosophical revolution critiquing the method of another. So there were at least two ways to apply inductive reasoning, and the mechanical philosophers were not the only practitioners of the Baconian method.

The chemical philosophers were a group of inductive scientists who were not specifically interested in the mechanics of motion. They were interested in the microscopic and chemical properties of the biosphere. Chemical philosophers were trying to discern truths about the mystical wisdom of the Creator's universe by prying into the microscopic, chemical relationships that occur within the creaturely microcosm. Rather than turning their mathematical gaze towards the heavens, this group of scientists generally focused on the inner workings of the geo- and bio-chemical world.

It may be helpful to illustrate the subtle philosophical difference between these two approaches to inductive science. The seventeenth century saw great breakthroughs in the area of anatomy and physiology, including ground-breaking work on the body's circulation of blood. Robert Fludd and William Harvey were two pioneers in the study of circulation. Robert Fludd was a chemical philosopher, who based his study of circulation on a microcosmic/macrocosmic analogy. He suggested that the circulation of blood in the body respected the circulation of the universe. The sun is the centre of circulatory motion in the heavens. It is the origin of light and continuously radiates that life giving energy to other celestial bodies. In the same way the heart circulates blood and the brain circulates perception throughout the body. Fludd was deeply concerned with the relationship between the

---

92. Debus, *Science and Education*, demonstrates that Ward took particular offence to Webster's charge that Ptolemy's theories were still being taught at Oxford. He opposed Ptolemy's theories on account of contemporary precision of astronomical observations. More on Ward's mathematical and mechanical approach to the Baconian method can be found in Vickers, *Occult Scientific Mentalities*; Roux and Garber, *Mechanization of Natural Philosophy*; Lindberg and Numbers, *God and Nature*.

93. Debus, *Science and Education*, 59.

physical and metaphysical truths of this circulatory revelation. The title of his most famous works, *Ultriusque Cosmi, Maioris scilicet et Minoris, metaphysica, physica, atque technica historia* (*The metaphysical, physical and technical history of the two worlds, namely the greater and the lesser*) suggests his ultimate goal.[94] However, William Harvey, a Padua trained medical doctor, was less concerned about metaphysical truths, and was more concerned about the mechanics of circulatory motion. The title of his book *On the motion of the heart and blood in animals*[95] demonstrates that he is mostly concerned with anatomical mechanics.

The mechanical astronomer Seth Ward was impressed by the sufficiency of Harvey's mechanical approach. But John Webster insisted that a mechanical knowledge of life was not sufficient. While praising the brilliant inductive skills of observation by which "Dr. Harvey discovered that wonderful secret of the Bloods circulary motion," Webster laments that his mechanical application of Bacon's methods are:

> defective as to that vive and *Mystical Anatomy* that discovers the true *Schematism* of that invisible *Archeus* or *spiritus mechanicus*, that is the true opifex, and dispositor of all the salutary, and morbifick lineaments, both in the seminal *guttula*, the tender *Embrio*, and the formed Creature, of which *Paracelsus*, *Helmont*, and our learned Countryman Dr. *Fludd*, have written most excellently.[96]

Webster represents a group of inductive, Baconian scientists who distrust those scientists who observe mechanics without keeping their eye on the proper goal of knowledge, "the true opifex," which is knowledge of the Creator. Webster praises Fludd's study of the blood because it respects a Christian application of inductive reasoning that is best demonstrated by the work of "Paracelsus."

By highlighting the Paracelsian nature of inductive science that prevailed in Traherne's day, we can be precise about the goals and methods of contemporary scientific theory that Traherne was referencing. On that basis, this study can be more specific about the moral consequences of his use of the new science. In the next section, I will explore the philosophy of the Paracelsian chemical scientists and its relationship to the Hermetic tradition. From this location, we can better understand the impact that this group of metaphysical chemists had upon the empirical aspects of

---

94. This writing is included as chapter 2 in Huffman's anthology of Fludd's writings, Huffman, *Robert Fludd*, 58–81.
95. Harvey, *Motion of the Heart*.
96. Webster quoted in Debus, *Science and Education*, 59.

Traherne's moral theory. Referring to the Paracelsian emphasis on the moral nature of the geocosm, rather than mere empirical mechanics, I will show that Traherne found a way to associate the "liquid clear satisfactions" of his childhood experience of nature with his moral theory.

Paracelsian Chemistry and the Inductive Method

In order to interpret the significance of his education in the New Philosophy's method of inductive reasoning, I will take an excursion into the methods of the Paracelsian branch of science. The name of this early and influential school of inductive science is derived from the sixteenth-century Swiss physician, botanist and chemist known as Paracelsus. As a late Renaissance scientist, Paracelsus was reacting against the deductive scholasticism of the Aristotelian and Galenist tradition. He wrote, "I do not here write out of speculation, and theorie, but practically out of the light of Nature, and experience, lest I should burden you and make you weary with many words."[97] More than merely valuing the idea of inductive reasoning, he provided a practical method to attend the theory. His method was to burn everything.

Paracelsus is commonly known as the father of modern chemistry because of his belief that everything could be reduced to its constituent elements by subjecting it to heat. There is no space to discuss the merits of his science *per se*, except to note that his pyrotechnical methods of oxidizing elements led him to isolate and name Zinc as a constituent element of nature. His impact on chemistry has endured the test of time, as oxidation is a fundamental aspect of modern day chemistry. Debus summarizes that "The Paracelsian chemical physician is a man who is not afraid to work with his own hands. He is a pious man who praises God in this work and who lays aside all those vanities of his Galenist competitor and instead finds his delight in a knowledge of the fire while he learns the degrees of the science of alchemy."[98] John Bostocke, who was instrumental in the scientific reform of the English university wrote in 1585 that the new chemists and physicians in the English universities should turn away from Aristotelian and Galenian curricula, and "learn of those Bookes which Paracelsus hath most Godly and learnedly expressed in this Labyrinth. In comparison of which all other Authorities in thos matters are small or none."[99] Bostocke's scientific curricula followed Paracelsus's method of trying "all things by fire whereby the vertue, nature, and propertie of each thing appeareth to the palpable

---

97. Paracelsus quoted in Debus, *Science and Education*, 15.
98. Debus, *Science and Education*, 15.
99. Debus, *Science and Education*, 16.

and visible experience."¹⁰⁰ By doing so, the chemical physician would be following Paracelsus in his faithful attempt to "seek out God through nature." Bostocke suggested:

> We must turn to the book of the heavens, the book of the elements, the book of man, the book of alchemy and the book of medicine. In effect, published books [of deductive reasoning] are nothing for science and knowledge must be based on experience and observation.[101]

Paracelsian chemistry challenged the deductive education of Aristotle and Galen because they did not necessarily lead to any direct knowledge of the Creator. The inductive, Paracelsian method was not proposed as a new school of "science" which was separate from revealed or inspired knowledge. Inductive reasoning was being proposed as a "scientific" method towards knowledge of the Divine. Bostocke's quote confirms Debus's suggestion that the Paracelsian chemists of the sixteenth and early seventeenth century all refer "to the two-book theory of knowledge. Man may obtain truth both through the Holy Scriptures or some mystical religious experience and also through his diligent study of nature, God's book of Creation."[102]

For most of the Paracelsian chemists, the study of Scripture and nature overlapped. Debus refers to chapter 38 of Ecclesiasticus in which "the priestly office of the physician is described, and where medicine is referred to as a divine rather than a mundane science."[103] Rooted in this Biblical understanding of the divine significance of their pursuit, chemists in this age generally interpreted Genesis as describing creation "as a divine *chemical* separation in which special emphasis was placed on the elements from which all other substances derive."[104] Debus notes that whether chemists relied on the four elements of Aristotle or the modern table of chemical elements that was developing, the interpretation was still the same. Creation was a chemical process. Debus confirms that "the significance placed on this Biblical account goes far to explain why there exists such a voluminous literature relating to element theory in the Renaissance."[105] This also goes far to explain the reason that these early scientists would rely on Hermes's ancient occult texts.

---

100. Debus, *Science and Education*, 16.
101. Debus, *Science and Education*, 16.
102. Debus, *Science and Education*, 18.
103. Debus, *Science and Education*, 17.
104. Debus, *Science and Education*, 18.
105. Debus, *Science and Education*, 18.

The Hermetic texts emphasize the mystery revealed in the process of elemental creation. Paracelsians understood that the Hermetic tradition was not in conflict with the revelation in Christ Jesus or Scripture. Knowledge of the elemental nature of the microcosm was embraced as a compliment to knowledge about the macrocosm's creation and redemption that is revealed in Scripture. In his 1609 *Basilica Chymica*, Oswald Croll wrote:

> Heaven and Earth are Mans parents, out of which Man last of all was created; he that knowes the parents, and can Anatomize them, hath attained the true knowledge of their child man, the most perfect creature in all his properties; because all things of the whole Universe meet in him as in the Centre, and the Anatomy of him in his Nature is the Anatomy of the whole world.[106]

The mystical pursuit to uncover the macrocosmic truth that is hidden (occult) in the microcosm of nature was well recognized by the leading Paracelsian (alternatively called Rosicrucian[107]) scientists of the sixteenth century. The Paracelsian scientists were associated with occultism, because they referred to the Hermetic tradition. However, Paracelsian scientists on the order of Pierre Gassendi, Robert Fludd, Johnnes Kepler and Galileo Galilei should hardly be considered occultist. These researchers and teachers of Bacon's new philosophy were not simply alchemists who maintained an ancient devotion to magicalism. They were scientists who believed that all knowledge about the nature of creation would confirm truth about the Creator. In his major scientific work, Fludd writes a passage that should be considered in its fullness:

> Infinite nature, which is boundless Spirit, unutterable, not intelligible, outside of all imagination, beyond all essence, unnameable, known only to the heart, most wise, most merciful, FATHER, WORD, HOLY SPIRIT, the highest and only good, incomprehensible in height, the unity of all creatures, which

---

106. Croll quoted in Debus, *Science and Education*, 19.

107. The name "Rosicrucian" is derived from the legend of a fourteenth century named Christian Rosenkreuz. The legend states that Rosenkreuz gathered their chemical, elemental, and atomic knowledge of nature in relationship to various Sufist, Zoroastrian, and Christian wisdom traditions. Those scientists who participated in this epistemological movement were known as "Rosicrucians," and scientists such as Pierre Gassendi, Robert Fludd, Johnnes Kepler and Galileo were found among their ranks. In 1614, an anonymous book titled *Fama Fraternitis* was published. The *Fama* recorded the goals of the Rosicrucians as well as the knowledge that informed their pursuit. Included among these writings were vast references to Hermes. A history and exposition of the Rosicrucian movement can be found in Heindel, *Rosicrucian Mysteries*; Yates, *Rosicrucian Enlightenment*.

is stronger than all power, greater than all distinction, more worthy than all praise, indivisible TRINITY, most splendid and indescribable light, in short, the divine mind, free and separate from mortal matter, glory of all, necessity, extremity and renewal: Here, I say, GOD, the highest and greatest of all, whose name was made blessed in eternity, skilfully formed the admirable machine of the entire Macrocosm, and beautifully adorned his structure. Even all the Philosophers, both ancient and more recent, except the Peripatetics who maintain that that world exists from eternity, had generally preserved, with unanimous consent, this most divine founder of the Universe with many appellations, giving fitting surnames to any quality of his action. Among these Hermes calls him eternal. . . . However impossible it may be correctly to describe the true essence of this triple Creator, nevertheless, following certain learned men's ideas, he is depicted thus, namely, in human form. "Man, made in the image of God is his representative, for he contains Mind, Word and Spirit." . . . "The Father of all, existing as Mind, Life, and Light, created man like himself, just as he made his Son, with whom he was pleased because he was beautiful, in the image of the Father." . . . "Man is made of Life and Light; God is made of Life and Light" (Trismegistus, *Pymander*). "God made man in his own image (Gen 1)."[108]

Fludd offers a Trinitarian rationale for utilizing a Baconian scientific method of inductive reasoning to study creation. The essence of God is light and life, and the nature of matter is life and light. In the opening paragraph of this seminal work, we can see that Fludd invokes Genesis, and Hermes's *Pymander* to demonstrate the relationship between revealed truth and scientific knowledge. This Paracelsian/Rosicrucian chemical scientist was not only well respected; he was admitted as a fellow to the Royal College of Physicians in 1609. In 1660, Fludd and several of his fellow Rosicrucian scientists became founding members of the Royal Society.[109]

The purpose of exploring this Paracelsian genealogy is to demonstrate that by the seventeenth century, the goal of the Paracelsian enlightenment was to provide an inductive path away from scholasticism, towards a "more perfect knowledge of the 'Son of Jesus Christ and Nature.'"[110] This Christian epistemology was part of the rationale for significant advances in the new

108. Huffman, *Robert Fludd*, 59–60.

109. This is the subject of Purver, *Royal Society*, in which Purver approaches the differences between Webster and Ward (Purver, *Royal Society* 110). It is also highlighted in Debus, *Science and Education*, 22.

110. Debus, *Science and Education*, 21.

philosophy that occurred in the budding scientific faculties of seventeenth-century British universities. Reference to the Hermetic texts is a hallmark of a theistic, scientific movement. This means that Traherne's references to Hermes are not necessarily tendencies of a metaphysical poet attempting to defend an Elizabethan or Platonic view in the face of the onslaught of empirical science. On the contrary, references to Hermes can be a sign of a young theologian who has embraced the faithful pursuit of Paracelsian, inductive science as a path between knowledge of the elemental realities of the microcosmic creation and knowledge of the Creator. In the next section, I will demonstrate the hallmarks of this new science in the new Traherne manuscripts.

Signs of Paracelsian Science in the Kingdom of God

Traherne's poetry and Meditations contain myriad references and allusions to the most contemporary scientific contexts of his day. Traherne's poem "Circulation"[111] is based on Fludd's theory of circulation. A decade before Newton published his *Principia*, Traherne relates the force of planetary gravity to the forces exerted by a magnetic "loadstone," which is a reference to Gilbert's seminal work on magnetism.[112]

> I have found that things unknown have a secret influence on the soul, and like the centre of the earth unseen violently attract it. We love we know not what, and therefore everything allures us. As iron at a distance is drawn by the loadstone, there being some invisible communications between them, so is there in us a world of Love to somewhat, though we know not what in the world that should be.[113]

While there are many references and metaphors in those previously known works, the recent discovery of Traherne's most mature and theologically systematic manuscripts provides a whole new set of texts which reveal the direct impact of Paracelsian science on his moral theory. In *The Kingdom of God*, Traherne includes a specific catalogue of "Modern Divines and Philosophers":

> Among Modern Divines and Philosophers there are many that follow the Ancients, Copernicus, Vossius, Grotius, Ametius, Descartes, Gassendus, Hevelius, Serranus, Stobaeus, Dr.

---

111. Traherne, *Centuries, Poems, and Thanksgivings*, 2:152.
112. James Balakier explores this topic in Balakier, *English Language Notes*, 32–41.
113. Traherne, *Centuries, Poems, and Thanksgivings*, 2:3.

Charleton, Dr. Willis, the learned Gale, and Mr Richardson our countrey Man. Thomas ab Angelis, my Lord Bacon, Sr Kenelm Digby and the Incomparable Mr Robert Boyl are not far from the opinion: Whose Names I mention as a Topic of Authoritie in so doubtfull a Matter, to countenance the Truth, and Encourage weak Apprehensions in the Belief of that, which they cannot by Reason discerne.[114]

Traherne is obviously aware of the theories of "my Lord" Francis Bacon, Renee Descartes, Robert Boyle, who pioneered a theory of pneumatics and combustion, the astronomy of Nikolai Copernicus, the pansophistic physics of the educational reformer Comenius, and the atomic theory of Peter Gassendi. We can couple this list with similar earlier references in his poetry and centuries of meditations.

It must be said that Traherne strings together that roster of scientists and philosophers in a rather haphazard manner. It may be difficult to discern the exact connection that Traherne would draw between the likes of Copernicus, Grotius, Gassendi, Theophilus Gale, Kelnem Digby, Robert Boyle, Francis Bacon, and Comenius. However, we can derive a clue from its textual location. This catalogue is included in chapter 23, "Of the Nature of Influences in Particular; and first of the Suns." In this chapter, Traherne considers the significance of the Sun. This catalogue comes in the midst of a larger quote from Theophilus Gale's *Court of the Gentiles*. Specifically, Traherne is quoting a very tightly argued portion of Gale's work that claims various ancient philosophers such as Plato, Theophrastus, Democritus, Pythagoras and the Phoenicians derived their knowledge of the sun from Hebrew sources. Gale's work was part of a well-known debate among the Platonists as to whether Plato and the ancients derived their knowledge of natural phenomenon from the Hebrews or vice versa. Gale, Cudworth, More, and Shaftesbury openly disagreed about the direction in which this knowledge was transmitted.[115] While Traherne was clearly aware of this debate about the origins of deductive philosophy, he is not particularly concerned with Gale's claim about the genealogy between the ancient and the modern philosophers. He perceived it to be a distraction. He wishes, "not to spend Time in questions, that may better be Employed in Material and Important discoveries Delightfull and Happy; it may Easily be Granted, that that Light which was Scatterd over the Hemisphere, and Expanded the three first Days of the Creation, was contracted into the Body of the Sun, the

---

114. This catalogue of "Modern Divines and Philosophers" comes from Traherne, *Kingdom*, 377.

115. This debate is taken up in Hedley and Hutton, *Platonism at the Origins*, 105.

fourth."[116] He is more interested in demonstrating the scientific consensus that exists about the value of inductive reasoning, namely the "Material and Important discoveries" about the nature of the sun.[117] Traherne's reference to the sun's role as the origin of stellar circulation is an adaptation of Fludd's Paracelsian notion of the microcosmic/macrocosmic model of inductive reasoning, which was explored above.

Traherne's references to fire and heat are classic hallmarks of the Paracelsian scientist who desires to put everything to the fire in order to understand the chemical workings of creation. Debus claims that the Paracelsian educational reform required students "to spend the bulk of their time learning the true facts of nature through observation and chemical operations with the fire."[118] The chemical and pyrotechnic nature of Traherne's references closely associates him with the Paracelsian/Hermetic branch of the new scientists, as opposed to the mechanical philosophers of the new science.

Traherne's Critique of the Mechanical Sciences

I have just spent several sections of this study demonstrating Traherne's embrace of the Paracelsian methods of Bacon's inductive science that was being taught by the time of Traherne's matriculation at Oxford in 1652.[119] However, we should also attend to Traherne's critique of the new science. For this reason, defining Traherne's embrace of the Paracelsian branch of the new science helps us understand the exact nature of the critique that he levies against the New Philosophy. Just after reflecting on his elation at receiving the tincture of this new, inductive education at Oxford he writes:

> Nevertheless some things were defective too. There was never a tutor that did professly teach Felicity, though that be the mistress of all other sciences. Nor did any of us study these things but as *aliena*, which we ought to have studied as our own enjoyments. We studied to inform our knowledge, but knew not for what end we so studied. And for lack of aiming at a certain end we erred in the manner. Howbeit there that we received all those seeds of knowledge that were afterwards improved; and our souls were

---

116. Traherne, *Kingdom*, 377.

117. This subject will be the focus of the next chapter, as I explore the way empirical science shapes Traherne's moral theory in Traherne, *Kingdom*, 377.

118. Debus, *Science and Education*, 28.

119. The record of his matriculation can be found in the Brasenose College Register, 1509–1901 (Traherne, *Centuries, Poems, and Thanksgivings*, 1:xxiv).

awakened to a discerning of their faculties, and exercise of their power.[120]

While he was fully inspired by the way in which the new science was taught at Oxford, there were deficiencies. The major deficiency is that the new science was taught as *aliena*, or separated from the full *telos* of our knowledge, which for Traherne is communion with God. In this case he describes that communion as happiness or "Felicity." It seems he assumes that knowledge gained through the inductive study of creation will naturally play a part in communion. However, the way in which he was taught this new science tended to be disembodied from that goal. Traherne felt a mechanical scientific curriculum missed the mark when it came to the *telos* of observing creation. He goes on to explain that inductive reasoning has two purposes that must be pursued together in their fullness:

> It is the Glory of god to give all things to us in the best of all possible manners. To study things therefore under the double notion of interest and treasure, is to study all things in the best of all possible manners. Because in studying so, we enquire after God's Glory and our own happiness. And indeed enter into the way that leadeth to all contentments, joys and satisfactions, to all prises, triumphs and thanksgivings, to all virtues, beauties, adorations and graces, to all dominion exaltation, wisdom, and glory, to all Holiness, Union and Communion with God, to all patience and courage and blessedness, which it is impossible to meet any other way. So that to study objects for ostentation, vain knowledge or curiosity is fruitless impertinence, tho God Himself and Angels be the object. But to study that which will oblige us to love Him, and feed us with nobility and goodness toward men, that is blessed. And so is it to study that which will lead us to the temple of Wisdom, and seat us in the Throne of Glory.[121]

Communion with God, formation in the virtues and contentments of peace are a goal of knowledge. If inductive knowledge of creation is pursued as *aliena*, in isolation from this metaphysical goal, it is "vain," "fruitless," "ostentation." In the next meditation, he lists other "sciences" which are fruitless if alienated from this unified theory of knowledge.

> He that studies polity, men and manners, merely that he may know how to behave himself, and get honor in this world, has not that delight in his studies as he that contemplates these things that he might see the ways of God among them, and

120. Traherne, *Centuries, Poems, and Thanksgivings*, 1:132.
121. Traherne, *Centuries, Poems, and Thanksgivings*, 1:133.

> walk in communion with Him. . . . He that knows the secrets of nature with Albertus Magnus, or the motions of the heavens with Galileo, or the cosmography of the moon with Hevelius, or the body of man with Galen, or the nature of diseases with Hippocrates, or the harmonies in melody with Orpheus, or of poesy with Homer, or of Grammar with Lilly, or of whatever else with the greatest artist, he is nothing if he knows them merely for talk or idle speculation, or transient and external use. But he that knows him for value, and knows them his own shall profit infinitely. And therefore of all kinds of learnings, humanity and divinity are the most excellent.[122]

In one fell swoop he links the goals of scientists as diverse as Galen and Galileo. The former misses the mark for his deductive reasoning, the latter for his mechanical scientific study of motion. It seems that regardless of how one pursues knowledge of creation, both miss the mark if they do not keep the ultimate goal of communion with God in focus. The mechanical pursuit of inductive reasoning missed the mark for Traherne. Traherne goes on to suggest:

> Natural philosophy teaches us the causes and effects of all bodies simply and in themselves. But if you extend it a little further, to that indeed which its name imports, signifying the love of nature, it leads us into a diligent inquisition into all natures, qualities, affections, relations, causes and ends, so far forth as by nature and reason they may be known. And this noble sciences as such, is most sublime and perfect: it includes all Humanity and Divinity together. God, Angels, Men, Affections, Habits, Actions, Virtues, everything as it is a solid, entire object singly proposed being a subject of it, as well as material and visible things. But taking in as it is usually bounded it its terms, it treateth only of corporeal things, as Heaven, Earth, Air, Water, fire, the Sun and Stars, Trees, herbs, Flowers, Influences, Winds, Fowls, Beasts, Fishes, Minerals, and Precious Stones, with all other beings of that kind.[123]

Having rejoiced in the wonders of creation that were opened up to him through the "tincture" of his Oxford education, he was ready to criticise the short-sighted manner of teaching the natural sciences according to simple mechanics. However, keeping in mind the above discussion of the Paracelsian chemical methods, we can now understand that Traherne's critique is

---

122. Traherne, *Centuries, Poems, and Thanksgivings*, 1:134.
123. Traherne, *Centuries, Poems, and Thanksgivings*, 1:136.

not of the new science *per se*. Rather he is critiquing the mechanical, atheistic version of the New Philosophy. What good would it be to turn away from the "irreligious" nature of an Aristotelian/Galenist deductive philosophy if we were to simply embrace an atheistic, mechanical New Philosophy?

It has been the opinion of Traherne scholars such as Helen Wade that Traherne's critique of the new science naturally signalled a turn towards the conceits of Cambridge Platonism. Because of scant biographical information and a textual corpus which was less than half of what we have today, Wade necessarily had to form a *post-hoc* hypothesis. Wade implies that upon his dissatisfaction with his undergraduate education, he retreated towards the safety of Cambridge Platonism. She assumes that Traherne would have come into contact with these Cambridge Platonists at a later stage, specifically during his time of service as Chaplain to Orlando Bridgeman in London.[124] And so she makes the further estimation that Platonism would have provided the resting place for Traherne's mature theological perspective.

However, there are two problems with that thesis. First, we now have Traherne's latest, and therefore most mature theological manuscripts. These manuscripts are so late that they were in the process of editing upon Traherne's death. *The Kingdom of God* reveals his theological embrace of Paracelsian science as a mature position, which explains his references to Ficino and Hermes far better than a nebulous association with the Cambridge Platonists. Therefore, his Hermetic references and critique of the new science are not the mark of one retreating from the new science into a conservative revival of Platonism. Secondly, I have demonstrated that Traherne's reaction to the New Philosophy was much more nuanced than Wade could have known based on the texts that were available to her. We can see now that Traherne did not retreat from the New Philosophy at all. He criticised those natural philosophers who used their inductive skills of observation to promote a simple mechanistic knowledge of creation. But *The Kingdom of God* shows us that his theological defence took the form of embracing a Paracelsian form of inductive science that maintained an integral link between the study of nature and communion with the divine.

In an age when astronomy and physics threatened to break the divine circle and the metaphysical relationship between the microcosm and the macrocosm, as Marjorie Hope Nicolson so aptly puts it, Traherne did not simply embrace the notion of astronomical infinity as a defence against the mechanical study of creation. Rather, he followed Paracelsus and Fludd into the nature of the human microcosm, and our geocosmic place. Traherne embraced a radically new, inductive means of knowing creation in pursuit

124. Wade and Parker, *Thomas Traherne*, 224.

of communion with God. I believe this Paracelsian, geocosmic turn made a profound impact on Traherne's moral theory.

Proposing the Impact of Paracelsian Science on Traherne's Moral Theory

Immediately following the meditation on the sciences and the fact that God and all virtue can be discerned through knowledge of God's creatures, he writes a meditation on ethics:

> Ethics teach us the mysteries of morality, and the nature of affections, virtues and manners, as by them we may be guided to our highest happiness. The former for speculation, this for practice. The former furnisheth us with riches, this with honors and delights, the former feasteth us, and this instructeth us. For by this we are taught to live honourably among men, and to make ourselves noble and useful among them. It teacheth us how to manage our passions, to exercise virtues, and to form our manners so as to live happily in this world. And all these put together discover the materials of religion to be so great, that it plainly manifesteth the Revelation of God to be deep and infinite. For it is impossible for language, miracles, or apparitions to teach us the infallibility of God's word, or to shew us the certainty of true religion, without a clear sight into truth itself, that is into the truth of things. Which will themselves when truly seen, by the very beauty and glory of them, best discover, and prove religion.[125]

For Traherne, Ethics exist in a matrix that includes "language, miracles, or apparitions" which are all part of true religion. Traherne's vast quotations of the Bible and the role of the "Book of Heaven" demonstrate that scripture and Christian tradition do ultimately perform significant heavy lifting in his moral epistemology. However, "the Revelation of God" is also plainly manifested through "a clear sight into truth itself, that is into the truth of things." In the previous meditation quoted above, he outlined the creatures within God's Kingdom that help us to see the truth in their beauty. Just following his meditation on ethics, he remembers with great fondness the time:

> When I came into the country, and being seated among silent trees and meads and hills, had all my time in mine own hands, I resolved to spend it all, whatever it cost me, in search of

125. Traherne, *Centuries, Poems, and Thanksgivings*, 1:137.

happiness, and to satiate that burning thirst which Nature had enkindled in me from my youth.[126]

Here Traherne is referring to his first charge in the rural Herefordshire parish of Credenhill. Traherne took up the Credenhill parish following his first ordination in 1557.[127] This first charge immediately followed his graduation from undergraduate studies and preceded his master's level theological studies. This time period is also a full decade prior to his association with Orlando Bridgeman and the Cambridge Platonists that he would have encountered in Teddington and London in 1667.[128] His parish in "the country" gave him time to reconnect and explore the forests of his childhood, and turn his gaze from the infinite realms to his local geocosm. In the beauty of that creation which surrounded him, he tried out his newly budding moral theory. After his undergraduate exposure to the new sciences, this parish would have provided the location to prove the Baconian methods of inductive reasoning and the Paracelsian commitment to discerning the Trinitarian wisdom that gave form to creation. Wade suggested that these years in the rural countryside of Credenhill "are clearly the ten years of 'mending' the ten in which, by deliberate effort of will and sheer tenacity of purpose, he actually remade himself into another person."[129]

I believe it is clear that the seeds of his Paracelsian education were reinvigorating his awareness of the role that creation played in his moral formation at a rather early stage. And in the next chapter we will see that his experience and education will develop into a mature moral theory that incorporates Paracelsian science with a thoroughgoing Trinitarian moral epistemology.

Conclusion

The main goal of this chapter was to challenge the conclusion of Marks and Guffey that Traherne did not contribute anything new to the ethical theories of his age. They base their claim on a reading of Traherne's *Ethicks*, and suggest that he could not break out of the stultifying education of his age. Based on the scientific and educational reforms that took place within his lifetime, I claim that Traherne did not suffer at all from the stultifying parameters

---

126. Traherne, *Centuries, Poems, and Thanksgivings*, 1:137.

127. As reprinted in Traherne, *Centuries, Poems, and Thanksgivings*, 1:xxiv.

128. Gladys Wade constructs a remarkably complete biographical sketch of Traherne's life in her groundbreaking work on the subject. See Wade and Parker, *Thomas Traherne*, 69.

129. Wade and Parker, *Thomas Traherne*, 69.

of his deductive education. He was educated in an age of inductive reasoning, and emerged with a fairly nuanced theory of moral epistemology that shows a close affinity with the Paracelsian scientists. Graham Parry felt there is some nebulous quality about Traherne's writing which shows he is not simply derivative of the past, or reproduced in the future. This study will confirm Parry's hunch. Traherne is a metaphysical poet and a Christian Neo-Platonist in as much as Christian theologians of his age were deeply influenced by those forms of thought. However, as a Paracelsian he is so much more.

A close reading of *The Kingdom of God* will demonstrate that he was able to augment the deductive conceits of his age with a Paracelsian empiricism that maintained an association between the embodied senses and metaphysical reality. His moral theory was based on a unified science between revealed, deductive reasoning, and inductive experience. His theory does not fit neatly within the rationalist genealogy that Basil Willey draws between the Cambridge Platonists and Immanuel Kant because it relies too heavily on the value and role that empirical, inductive reasoning plays within moral formation. By virtue of his Trinitarian commitments, he also does not align with the mechanical or atheistic empiricists whose theories lead to the moral sense theories of David Hume and Adam Smith. In these ways, Traherne's moral theory seems to have stood between several extremes that began to part ways within Traherne's lifetime. Over the next few centuries, moral sense, rationalist and existentialist moral theories would try to fill the void that was created by that disassociation. In the time when, as T.S. Eliot recognized, there was a disassociation of the senses from moral theory, Traherne saw the inherent dangers of pursuing epistemological, theological and ethical theories in isolation from either creation or the Creator. He was trying to maintain a unified moral theory between our inductive sensibility and metaphysical truths.

In doing so, Traherne made a significant contribution to the moral theories of his age, or would have had his work not been interrupted by his untimely death at the age of 36. The discovery of a new body of manuscripts helps us complicate the historical picture and better understand his moral theory. With that claim in mind the next chapter will engage in a close reading of *The Kingdom of God*. I will explore the way Traherne develops his mature moral theory into a significant contribution to his age and ours that demonstrates a great affinity to Christian moral theologians who stand on our side of the moral *aporia* trying to reconnect an embodied theory of inductive sensibility and metaphysical truth.

2

"Between Ants and Angels"

Outlining the Empirical Basis of Traherne's Moral Theory in The Kingdom of God

Introduction

IN THE PREVIOUS CHAPTER, I demonstrated that Traherne was educated according to the seventeenth-century science of the "New Philosophy," and familiar with its latest concepts. While many of the divines and metaphysical poets turned to Neo-Platonism as a defence against the atheistic tendencies of the mechanical scientists, I suggested that Traherne did something different. He began to synthesize an empirical Baconian method into a system of moral formation. The purpose of this chapter is to demonstrate that claim through a close reading of his mature work, *The Kingdom of God*.

Following the lead of Marjorie Hope Nicolson, a few Traherne scholars have begun to reassess Traherne's relationship to the emergence of modern science. Most of these attempts have been rooted in a reassessment of Traherne's literary form,[1] or his relationship to emerging theories of rational consciousness.[2] According to the inertia of the perspective regarding Tra-

---

1. In Matthew Akers's unpublished dissertation, "From the Hexaemeral," Akers explores the *Kingdom of God* in an attempt to re-evaluate Traherne's relationship to science. However, Akers is largely concerned with demonstrating a literary point about the way in which Traherne represents a physico-theological form of writing as opposed to the popular hexameral tradition that was the model of reflection on creation coming into the seventeenth century. Likewise, Akers follows Nicolson's thesis by focusing on Traherne's focus on cosmology. My thesis differs in the fact that, while I agree that Traherne is fascinated by the new cosmology, his real ethical contribution can be detected through his focus on the microscopic terrestrial sciences.

2. This line of critique has been most recently pursued in Blevins, *Re-Reading Thomas Traherne*. Specifically, Kuchar's article, "Traherne's Specters"; Balakier, "Traherne, Husserl." While Balakier's research does venture into the realm of phenomenology, as the title suggests, his main concern is to understand Traherne's notion of consciousness, and therefore ends up primarily comparing Traherne to fourth level Vedic meditation. These two streams of Traherne studies have been largely influenced

herne's indebtedness to Neo-Platonism and the metaphysical poets, these studies stay well within the bounds of reading Traherne as a proto-Rationalist. Most follow Nicolson's original thesis about Traherne's gaze towards the new cosmological infinity as a "mirror" of internal modes of rational consciousness.[3] However, they rarely consider Traherne's contemplation of his place among the finite geocosm, and the epistemological significance of his external relationship to creation.[4] Additionally, all of these studies were conducted prior to the discovery of the new corpus of Traherne's writings which, I claim, give us more insight into the depth of his empirical knowledge of creation, and the significant effect that his wondrous relationship with other creatures had on his moral theory.[5]

This chapter will explore one of Traherne's latest and most systematic writings, *The Kingdom of God*.[6] Through a close reading of *Kingdom*, I will demonstrate the way in which he uses a Baconian/Paracelsian empirical method within his system of moral theology. I will focus specifically on his theory of light as a vehicle for communicating the natural goodness of creatures. I will conclude by suggesting the ethical implications of that communication. Because knowledge of goodness is communicated through those physical means, or exhalations, Traherne acknowledges the role that empirical senses play within Christian moral formation. He suggests that a relational nexus between the human and non-human creation is a critical component of our capacity to become human beings whose moral nature lies somewhere between ants and angels.

---

by DeNeef's expanded study of Traherne (DeNeef, *Traherne in Dialogue*). Of the three comparisons, DeNeef's study of Lacan's psychology of "mirroring" comes the closest to a consideration of Traherne's empirical interaction with creation. Because Traherne does speak of creation as a "mirror" of the Divine, and of nature, Lacan makes a fine interlocutor for comparing Traherne's contemplation of creation with modern psychology. See DeNeef, *Traherne in Dialogue*.

3. For instance, see DeNeef, *Traherne in Dialogue*; Balakier, *Thomas Traherne*.

4. One significant exception to this is Allchin et al., *Profitable Wonders*. Allchin's work, however, is much more aligned to a consideration of the role that concept of participation plays in Anglican theology of his day, rather than the ethical implications of his relationship to creation, nor did Allchin have the new corpus of manuscripts.

5. One exception to this timeline is Ellrodt, *Seven Metaphysical Poets*. In this work, however, Ellrodt only goes so far as to call Traherne's relationship to creation a "sensual idealism" (Ellrodt, *Seven Metaphysical Poets*, 281).

6. Traherne's *Kingdom of God* forms the largest part of the first volume of Traherne's newly discovered and published works.

A Brief Word regarding the Textual Apparatus

Before I begin to interpret *Kingdom*, I will briefly comment on the textual apparatus. Traherne's writing bears his distinct idiosyncrasies in spelling, grammar and form. *Kingdom* is part of that bound folio which was written by hand, and it bears many edits and marginal references. When this folio of manuscripts was discovered in the Lambeth Palace Library, these idiosyncrasies helped identify them as belonging to Traherne. For that reason, a few comments on the systematic structure of the text and the physical manuscript may be helpful in interpreting Traherne's writing.

Unlike most of Traherne's most well known works, *Kingdom* is neither poetry nor a prosaic meditation. It is a work of systematic moral theology, and as such, it has a clear internal system. *Kingdom* is divided into forty two chapters. Within each chapter, Traherne makes no subdivisions. However, he uses marginal glosses throughout the manuscript that suggest headings may have been intended for a final published document. Having never been published, these marginal glosses remain as such. I may refer to a marginal gloss if it provides a helpful reference, or if it emphasizes a point that assists in my interpretation of the text. As an example of a helpful reference, marginal glosses often refer to a passage of scripture that was not directly referred to in the text. As an interpretive tool, consider the title of chapter 5:

> A Philosophical Account of God's
> > Kingdom drawn from the Inclinations
> and powers of the Soul, and from the Nature
> > of Infinitie. All which Shew his Kingdom
> to be Compleat and Perfect.

In this case, the title is a very descriptive outline of the content to follow. However, within the chapter, line 243 contains the marginal gloss, "The Benefit of the natural power whereby we are able impartialy to Examine the Works of God." In this case the marginal gloss clearly highlights Traherne's intention to focus on the natural power by which human beings can examine creation. In the course of interpreting a passage that has descriptive marginalia such as this one, I may refer to the gloss in order to accent Traherne's intentions.

Finally, I will offer a brief comment on the systematic structure of *Kingdom*. While Traherne does not group the 42 chapters into sections, chapter titles suggest seven clear divisions that help navigate this lengthy manuscript.[7]

---

7. It should be made clear that I will not utilize my own subgrouping as an interpretive tool, only a referencial one—i.e., referencing the fact that a certain discussion is

1. Introduction: Chapter 1 provides an introduction to the purpose of Kingdom. Traherne outlines the reason that he is writing a treatise on the nature of the Kingdom of God. He defines his task as one which will "look into the Causes of this Kingdom," namely the efficient, material, formal and final causes of the Kingdom.

2. Rationale: Chapters 2–4 explain why we must meditate on Creation in order to interpret the causes of the Kingdom.

3. Ultimate Cause: Chapters 5 and 6 are devoted to God as the ultimate cause of Creation.

4. Efficient Cause: Chapters 7–16 discuss the efficient causes of the Kingdom, including an outline of God's attributes, and a discussion on natural, moral and Divine Goodness.

5. Material Causes: Chapters 17–30 discuss the material causes of the Kingdom. It is worth noting that this section makes up the majority of *Kingdom*. The fact that the largest section of *Kingdom* is devoted to the material causes of the kingdom suggests Traherne's scientific interest in the material nature of creation. It also affirms the value that Traherne places on the way in which contemplating creation's material nature helps the human perceive the ultimate significance of creation and our role in it.

6. Formal Cause: Chapters 31–39 discuss the kingdom's formal cause. This section contains Traherne's discussion of the relationship between the Love of God and creation, and the way in which that love is revealed by the relationality among creatures. The love of God is demonstrated in the services that a creature renders to their fellow creatures.

7. Appendix: Chapters 40–42 provide a kind of appendix to the document. After considering the ultimate, efficient, material and formal causes of creation, Traherne ends by considering the way in which Image of God is embodied in human beings. This "appendix" outlines the importance of human perception in its created and fallen state.

This outline suggests that Traherne preserves the rather theologically conservative manner of rooting the ultimate, efficient and formal causes of

---

located within Traherne's section on material causes. Denise Inge has ventured a similar kind of subdivision in her description of *Kingdom* in Inge, *Wanting Like a God*. Inge uses subdivisions to outline a very general description of *Kingdom*. While I believe her division to be completely adequate, I add a few extra divisions, given the focus of my study.

creation in the attributes of the Creator. After opening with his rationale, he explains that the Love of God is the ultimate cause of all being. But God's Wisdom, which "will not suffer Omnipotence to be Idle,"[8] efficiently motivated God to create. And out of God's Goodness, the material causes of creation must necessarily and naturally be good. It is for that reason that the section on the material causes of the Kingdom focus on goodness as a natural, communicative attribute of creation. It is in this section that I will begin this study of Traherne's own study of *The Kingdom of God*.

The Optics of Light and Life: Shifting Our Gaze from Telescopy to Microscopy

The Gospel of John opens with these words.

> In the beginning was the Word, and the Word was with God, and the Word was God. He was in the beginning with God. All things came into being through him, and without him not one thing came into being. What has come into being in him was life, and the life was the light of all people. (John 1:1–4)

The symbol of the Eagle is often used as a symbol for the fourth Evangelist because it depicts John's high and lofty poetic language. However, Thomas Traherne does not interpret John's prologue as a retreat to the lofty heights of poetic metaphor or a cognitive transcendence to a rational truth about the Creator. Traherne believes that light is the matrix of a real communication between the Creator and Creatures. God's life is the light which actually animates creation. With this text, Traherne sees the significance of the way in which light continues to communicate God's goodness throughout creation.

Even as a poet, Traherne wrote that he did not wish to teach a way of apprehending knowledge through "curling metaphor," but rather through naked sense.[9] He frequently associates the human *telos* with the naked sense of sight. His poem "Fullnesse" suggests the way in which the naked sense of sight helps us achieve the "Perfect" fullness of human being.

> That Light, that Sight, that Thought,
> Which in my Soul at first He wrought,
> Is sure the only Act to which I may

---

8. Traherne, *Kingdom*, 283.

9. This concept of the naked sense, or naked intelligence that could perceive God without the need of metaphor is considered in Traherne's poem, "The Preparative" (Traherne, *Centuries, Poems, and Thanksgivings*, 2:20).

> Assent to Day...
> My Power exerted or my Perfect Being,
> If not Enjoying, yet an Act of Seeing.[10]

Achieving our human purpose depends in part upon an act of "seeing" "That Light." Stephen Clark has shown that this kind of "optics" was a familiar, but complex trope in seventeenth-century poetry. Often, the naked, or "gymnosophistical," sense represented the bare intellectual or spiritual sight. It was the kind of rational, noetic seeing that was stripped of all our human senses, as in the case of Plotinus, Descartes, and Herbert.[11] However, as was in the case with Donne, the naked sense of sight often referred to the actual kind of phenomenal "feeling" that occurred when we employed our senses in the apprehension of self-evident or common truth.[12] With these diverse possibilities in mind, Traherne's use of the concept of naked senses needs to be better understood. In *Kingdom*, Traherne explores the subject of optics in an empirical, rather than rationalist way. He uses contemporary theories of light to explain the optical theory that informs his view. I will demonstrate that his "naked sense" of sight is not simply a disembodied, noetic, interior gaze.

The theme of optics was a central issue for most scientists of the sixteenth and seventeenth centuries. The technology of the telescope allowed Galileo and Tycho Brahe to map a new cosmology. With the telescope, astronomers could watch the movement of planets around the sun and triangulate the infinite distances that accommodates the procession of the stars. After observing their movement more precisely, Kepler's mathematical calculations revealed that planets did not respect the Divine notion of a perfect circle at all. Rather, their orbital processions were elliptical. When scientists broke the safe confines of the Divine circle, Nicolson suggests one of Traherne's great accomplishments was his lack of fear in the face of this new infinite reality.[13] He embraced the possibilities that this new telescopic vision offered, and turned his theological and philosophical gaze towards notions of the infinite, and related his understanding of consciousness and rationality to this new telescopic vision of cosmology.[14] According to his

---

10. Traherne, *Centuries, Poems, and Thanksgivings*, 2:1.

11. The complexity of the "naked sense" is explored in Hedley and Hutton, *Platonism at the Origins*, 45–46.

12. Hedley and Hutton, *Platonism at the Origins*, 58.

13. Nicolson, *Breaking of the Circle*.

14. As mentioned in the introduction, this thesis represents the path that Balakier and Kuchar follow in Blevins, *Re-Reading Thomas Traherne*. And as mentioned above, Akers also follows Nicolson's thesis in his reading of Traherne's *Kingdom*. See Akers "From the Hexaemeral."

embrace of the new cosmological infinity, studies of Traherne's rationalist affinities, such as Balakier and Kuchar, as well as works by Clement,[15] Salter[16] and Wade[17] that focus on Traherne's mysticism interpret his use of the "naked sense" of sight as the metaphorical, noetic kind of spiritual gaze that is a "mirror" of the optics of the telescope. However, in *Kingdom* there is another kind of optics at work—microscopy.

Robert Hooke wrote *Micrographia*, the first book on light microscopy, in 1665.[18] This date is significant. Because Traherne died in 1674, and *Kingdom* includes quotes from Theophilous Gale's *The Court of Gentiles* which was written in 1669, Jan Ross has dated the text between 1670 and 1674.[19] *Kingdom* was written between five and ten years after Hooke's *Micrographia*. Because *Micrographia* was one of the first books published by the Royal Society, and was immediately well known, it is certain that Traherne was familiar with his theories. I have not found a reference to Robert Hooke anywhere in his writings, nor have I found any use of the word "cell," which Hooke coined for biological use when looking at cork through his microscope.[20] But Traherne certainly refers to the growing science of light microscopy. Chapter 29 is titled "Of life in particular: And of its several Kinds; of the life of Plants, of Beasts, of Men, of Angels." Microscopy is the method that Traherne invokes for considering the nature of life in the Kingdom. It is worth noting this passage in its fullness:

> How great a lover of life God is, and how greatly he delighteth in it, we may see by this, he made all the Elements for the sake of Life. the Earth, the Air, and the Seas Contributing to those that liv on Earth: But it more appeareth by his filling evry one of these with life in themselvs, not suffering any to be destitute of Inhabitants. Whose Senses and Affections are Great and Marvellous, whose Hostes innumerable, whose lives no less Beautifull, and Pleasant, then Profitable and Miraculous. The Earth, even beneath its Surface is filled with Inhabitants. Frogs, Moles, Worms, Ants, Addars, Woodlice, Spiders, Bettles, Askars, Dormice, with Innumerable others which dwelling in those Blind Cavernes, shew the Vertue of his Power, who makes them breath in a fixed Element, even as fishes live in a fluid one; with which his Wisdom shineth also, which maketh these as the basests

15. Clements, *Mystical Poetry of Thomas Traherne*.
16. Salter, *Thomas Traherne*.
17. Wade and Parker, *Thomas Traherne*.
18. Hooke, *Micrographia*.
19. Traherne, *Kingdom*, xxi.
20. Hooke, *Micrographia*, 116.

Dregs: and Refuse of Animals to Beautify the World in their Place and Station, by setting off the Glory, and lustre of the other Creatures. . . . Evry man's Memory, and Experience Witnessing Enough to Convince him of the Infinit Plenty of lives God hath Created. I shall only Note, that Mettal upon Mettal is in Herauldrie absurd, but living Creatures upon living Creatures, and many Hundred sometimes Conceald upon one is a token of the Value, and Amiableness of Life, as those Myriads of Imperceptible Movers are, that by the Help of the Microscope are found.[21]

First, this passage demonstrates that Traherne's focus in *Kingdom* is on the geocosmic level.[22] In the wake of the "broken circle," he does not retreat into the infinity of the heavens or the heavenly forms of Neo-Platonism. He makes a geocosmic turn and asks his reader to see the "Vertue" of God's power through the variety and interrelatedness of creation and its elements. This is not a "naked sense" which denudes the soul of its bodily perception in order to peer into the depths of rational consciousness. Rather, he calls the faithful to turn their phenomenal eyes and attention towards the actual forms of life that exist outside of themselves. The microscope allows us to see a multitude of "Imperceptable Movers" that contribute to the "Amiableness of Life." Clearly, he has symbiotic mutualism in mind as opposed to parasitism. Microscopy recalls his "Memory and Experience" of seeing the way that the "basests Dregs" and "Refuse of Animals" beautify the world. Even microscopic works reveal God's Goodness, and among them, the ultimate goodness of life is revealed. One primary concern of this text is to explore the means by which all creatures, down to the microscopic works, communicate Divine Goodness through material means.

Traherne's goal of explaining the ultimate and efficient causes of creation is to demonstrate that God's Goodness is the primary attribute revealed in creation. He writes at the beginning of this section on the material causes of the *Kingdom* that "The Works of God are Wisdom and Goodness Embodied as it were in Effects."[23] This notion of God being embodied in creation is not hyperbole. In the quote above, he affirms that God fills "evry one of these with life in themselvs, not suffering any to be destitute Inhabitants." Each being is filled with the Life of God. For his explanation of how this happens, we turn to the concept of light in his interpretation of John, 1.4, "What has come into being in Him was life and the life was the Light."

21. Traherne, *Kingdom*, 420.

22. The term geocosmic stands in distinction from the term "macro-cosmic," meaning the celestial realms. I am bringing this term forward from its usage in the previous chapter.

23. Traherne, *Kingdom*, 340.

Traherne often paraphrases passages of texts from memory. Not surprisingly, he often remembers them incorrectly. Such is the case with this passage from John. Traherne actually inverts the causality between light and life. The Greek passage recorded in chapter 19 reads, "Τὸ φως ἡ ζωή," which he translates, "The Light was the Life of Men." His Greek is translated correctly, however, he began with an inaccurate version of the Greek. John's prologue reads "Τὸ ζωή ἡ φως," which translates as "the Life was the light." While slightly embarrassing, this transpositional faux pas is ultimately inconsequential. Traherne's logic suggests that the life of God is emitted as light. That light supplies life when it shines upon creation. From the perspective of the Divine source, life is the original, and light is the derivative. But from the perspective of the creature, light gives life. So, regardless of whether life is light or light is life, the causal relationship is a matter of perspective. Ultimately Traherne is not concerned with the causality between light and life. His aim is to suggest the relationship that exists between light and life. This passage from the prologue of John's Gospel forms part of the empirical basis of Traherne's moral theology. Light helps reveal the ultimate significance of life.

Goodness Is the Relationship between Light and Life

"When the Sun Manifesteth the Glory of God, it is thus an Embleme of the Blessed Trinity."[24] Traherne suggests that the Sun is an image of the Trinity because it is at one time the source of light and the fountain of it, just as God is the source of Goodness and the efficient fountain of it.[25] However, the Sun is not only a metaphor of God's life, the Sun is "the light of the World, and next under God, the only Publick Instrument and Wellspring of Life unto all the Creatures."[26] Traherne makes a clear distinction between the essence of God and the essence of creation. He is not suggesting a radical monism such as the kind Baruch Spinoza deployed,[27] whereby God's being might be mingled with that of the Sun. Traherne relies on a causal relationship between God's being and act, but insists on a clear distinction between the two. In his *Ethicks*, Divine Goodness is "proper only to GOD," and "Invisible in its

---

24. Traherne, *Kingdom*, 360.
25. Traherne, *Kingdom*, 356.
26. Traherne, *Kingdom*, 356.
27. In his *Ethics*, Spinoza writes: "There can be or be conceived, no other substance but God," which is his support for his claim "that no substance can be produced or created by anything else. Furthermore, in Proposition 14 we showed that apart from God no substance can be or be conceived, and hence we deduced that extended substance is one of God's infinte attributes" (Spinoza, *Complete Works*, 225).

Essence, but Apparent in its effects."[28] He writes that "In GOD, [goodness] is that infinite and Eternal Act from which all other Goodnesses spring."[29] The works of God reveal the inherent Goodness of God in the world, not God's actual essence as such. In *Kingdom*, Traherne spends a good deal of time and space affirming that God's Wisdom and Goodness are the two Divine attributes which "will not suffer Omnipotence to be Idle." However, while affirming the wonder of God's act of creating *ex nihilo*, he confirms that "Even God's word Effected it without a Transmutation, imparting nothing of itself thereunto."[30] But, while there is no mutability of God's essence, Traherne's term "life" implies creation's real participation in the Creator.

He defines life as "so Mysterious, and Miraculous a Being, and So Sublime in order of Nature" that "its Material Cause is almost Impossible to be understood."[31] However, he spends several pages providing us with a definition. Because the final goal in life is to "see" God and enjoy his Divine presence, life "is founded in perception, for whatsoever is able to Apprehend, liveth."[32] He posits that *"Life is an Abilitie to Apprehend, and Move."*[33] A living being is able to perceive its surroundings, and then act according to the reality which it perceives. Traherne classifies plants as having "being, and Life, and Reason"[34] because they are able to apprehend the position of the Sun, and move accordingly. This definition of life is significant for his moral theory, as it suggests that "life" is something separate from being. A rock is, but it is not alive. In one passage, Traherne conveys this claim by observing that even though God made the heavenly and earthly Kingdom, and beautified it with:

> Woods, and Corn, and Herbs and flowers, which he underlayd with rich and Precious Minerals; tho he had given all kind of Influences, Virtues, and Odors to these, yet had they all been useless both to GOD, themselves, and us, had no Life been Created.

---

28. Traherne, *Christian Ethicks*, 79.
29. Traherne, *Christian Ethicks*, 78.
30. Traherne, *Kingdom*, 282–83.
31. Traherne, *Christian Ethicks*, 409.
32. Traherne, *Christian Ethicks*, 409.
33. Traherne, *Christian Ethicks*, 409.

34. Reason is another category that is introduced in this quote. Traherne has a bifurcated notion of reason. Limited reason is movement based on physical or instinctual motions, and illimited reason results in moral actions or movements. Therefore, plants qualify as having life and limited reason, although not illimited moral reasoning. See Traherne, *Christian Ethicks*, 490.

> Without life Even God himself could not have seen them, nor could anything else have enjoyed them.[35]

We see here that "life" is something material that God created to equip a creature to be aware of itself and perceive other beings. The purpose of "life" is that created beings can apprehend God and other creatures, and communicate with one another:

> Figures, and colours, and Smels, and tangible Qualities, are all foreiners, and Strangers, to the Nature of God: but life is a Domestick Propertie of his Essence. It is the first Thing in him, wherof any Creature participates wherein all that Communicat with him, are beyond Measure Superior to the other Creatures: Had not this been created, the Sun had been Dross, light Darkness.[36]

Without sensible qualities "God himself could not have seen [creatures], nor could anything else have enjoyed them." These physical qualities of being are "foreiners" to God's nature, *per se*. But the ability to "sense" those secondary qualities of a creature is a "domestic property" of God's very "Essence" which is to enjoy the "Virtues" of creation. A being has this "Life" when it can perceive figures, colours, smells and tangible secondary qualities of other beings. So our ability to perceive the "Influence" of other creatures is the "first Thing" of our participation in God's activity. Beings communicate their "Virtues" to one another. "Seeing" other creatures in the way God's act of creation intended, that is to say to be alive, is to perceive the secondary qualities of other creatures.

This point is fundamental to being able to locate Traherne among the moral theories of his day. Traherne suggests being alive, which is to say being a creature, is related to that creature's ability to perceive the influences and virtues of other creatures by means of the senses. This theory is a very long way from the notion that the "naked sense" is a dualist, disembodied rationalist mode of "seeing," and Rationalist moral theories. Against Descartes's notion that "being" can be confirmed by isolating a person's internal, rational cogitation from the distraction of the body's outward sensibility, Traherne affirms that being alive (indeed "Life" itself) is constituted for the purpose of sensing the "Influences" and "Virtues" of other beings. And against the emergence of Kantian modes of moral theory, which we will continue to explore in later chapters, Traherne affirms that this kind of sensory perception is one of the first acts of our participation in the Creator.[37] Our

---

35. Traherne, *Christian Ethicks*, 416.
36. Traherne, *Christian Ethicks*, 416.
37. Allchin has explored this theory in Allchin, *Participation in God*; Allchin et al.,

moral movements are a response to that which we sense in other beings. Continuity between our nature and the moral order is a fundamental aspect of what it means to be a "living" creature. For that reason, the sensory way in which a creature actually perceives the qualities of other creatures is morally significant. Remembering Eliot's theory about the great disassociation of the senses that was taking place in this age, Traherne maintains a close association, or continuity, between our natural senses and moral motivation in the very definition of "life."

Because "life" is formally given so that we may apprehend the Divine, and the material definition of "life" is defined by a being's ability to "apprehend and move," therefore the formal and material cause of life are the same. "Life therfore, in my Apprehension is so Simple a Being, that its Material Cause, and Form are one."[38] Traherne equates Life (which is the Divine formal cause of being able to perceive the "Virtue" of other creatures,) to Light (which is the material cause of our being able to physically perceive the influence of those creatures) based on two points. He knows the Sun's material light is one vehicle by which our living, corporeal, nervous systems actually perceive other beings.[39] But Traherne also knows that the Sun's material Light is an elemental component of the material cause of Life itself. To understand that claim, we will return to the quote from above, that the Sun is "the light of the World, and next under God, the only Publick Instrument and Wellspring of Life unto all the Creatures."[40]

Chapter 20 is devoted to operations of the Sun. Traherne writes that the Sun is "the Efficient cause of Minerals," and its beams "impregnate the Earth."[41] This means that sunbeams create minerals that nourish life in the depths of the earth. He goes on to affirm that:

> The Sun extendeth not to the Heavens and to the Earth only, to Mountains, Valleys, Wildernesses, Elements, Minerals, Vegetables, Meteors, Animals, or Living Creatures; but to the Souls of Men, and to the Holy Angels . . . Sabean Spices, and

---

Profitable Wonders. However, both were written prior to the discovery of these manuscripts, which, in my opinion, impact our understanding of his moral theory far more than any previous texts.

38. Traherne, *Kingdom*, 409.

39. Traherne deploys an informed understanding of the relationship between light and the nervous system when he suggests that apprehension is the result of "tangible Qualities affect the Nerves, and Stir the Fibres that are Rooted in the Brain, and communicat their Impressions by Motions of the Nerves, or Spirits there" (Traherne, *Kingdom*, 409).

40. Traherne, *Kingdom*, 356.

41. Traherne, *Kingdom*, 356.

Precious Stones, Amber, Balm, Oyl, and Wine, and Gold; and all the Rareties of the Earth and Heaven. The Air being made Susceptible of Sounds and Melody it self, by these latent Beams wherwith it is enspirited. And by these the Sun appeareth to, and toucheth the very Soul.[42]

Traherne boldly claims that the Sun is the centre and fountain for the "Impregnation, Information, and Life of the Whole and for the Light, Glory, and Splendor of it."[43] As an explanation of the material cause of life, Traherne presents a kind of proto-genetic stellar theory of life that is remarkably consistent with modern physical chemistry and astronomy. He learned these theories in their nascent forms from the scientists of his day. In *Kingdom*, Traherne paraphrases a passage from Gale's commentary on the physics of Grotius, the pan-sophism of Comenius, and the mathematics of Euclid. Gale writes "evry Natural operation of Bodies Known to us, is either an Action of Fire, or depends upon it. Possidonius of old defined a Star, to be a Body Divine."[44] Traherne fully comprehends the significance of the theory that stars generate the elements of life.

> It may Easily be Granted, that that Light which was Scatterd over the Hemisphere, and Expanded the three first Days of the Creation, was contracted into the Body of the Sun, the fourth. Whose Particles being Infinitly Small, and Volatile, no sooner touched one another in that Glorious Centre, but they Immediately reflected with unconeivable Violence: Drawing in a Train of Æther after them, which from all Parts meeting in the centre, is Enkindled, and Ejected:[45]

Today we know that all of the natural elements of life can be traced to the atomic activity of stars, specifically the elements that are ejected from the death of stars. The material "stuff" of life is found in stellar nurseries, and is

---

42. Traherne, *Kingdom*, 356.

43. Traherne, *Kingdom*, 350.

44. Traherne includes an extended portion of Gale, *Court of Gentiles*, in two sections (Traherne, *Kingdom*, 376–77). The first quote begins on page 376 and runs from line 13 until line 52. The quote that I refer to is from the second section, which begins on page 377 and runs from line 60 until line 72. Jan Ross has determined that these extended paraphrases come from Gales, *Court of Gentiles*, 69, 338. It is important to separate the two portions of extended quotes, however, because between them, Traherne inserts his own commentary, which I have called his "catalogue of 'Modern Divines and Philosophers.'" Because Traherne often inserts paraphrases from other writers without citation, recognizing Traherne's use of Gale in this particular section helps us to discern Traherne's own thoughts on the stellar theory in Traherne, *Kingdom*.

45. Traherne, *Kingdom*, 377.

communicated to beings by a star's natural activity. Sentient "Life," as created by God for the purpose of perceiving, pervades human being "As the Solar Particles abide in all the Parts of the Body, not under the Notion now of Light, but Life."[46] Of course, Traherne did not have physical chemistry in mind when he claimed that the Sun impregnates creation with life and "information" about other creatures. His claim that light is a material cause of communicating morally significant information about life is rooted in two contemporary scientific theories about light and the atom. The next two sections will explore these theories respectively.

The Material Basis of Traherne's Theory of Light and Life: Gassendi or Hooke?

The claim that the Sun is a material cause of communicating "information" about "life" accords with the seventeenth-century debate between two competing optical theories. While any stellar theory necessarily relates to telescopic astronomy, the significance of Traherne's theory is actually based on the microscopic effect of light. Light microscopy was one of the newest scientific developments in Traherne's lifetime. As demonstrated above, Robert Hooke made scientific history by observing creatures at the cellular level. But he was not only interested in what he saw through his new technique of light microscopy. He was also interested in how he was able to see. In *Micrographia*, Hooke posited a new theory regarding the movement of light. Hooke proposed that light travelled in waves. His wave theory challenged Pierre Gassendi's existing theory that light was made of corpuscles of particulate matter.[47] I will show that the basic difference between Gassendi's particle theory and Hooke's wave theory of the motion of light actually has a significant impact on Traherne's moral theory.

In *Kingdom*, Traherne names Gassendi among his catalogue of "Modern Divines and Philosophers."[48] This reference reveals Traherne's familiarity with Gassendi's particle theory or at least the reception of his theory. Gassendi's theory states that light is a particle of matter which has mass. According to his observation that shadows respect the line between a source of light and an object (and generally light does not bend around objects), he maintained that light travels at predictable angles. In an age prior to the mechanical laws of motion codified in Newton's *Principia*, Gassendi knew

---

46. Traherne, *Kingdom*, 355.

47. For an excellent resource on interpreting Gassendi's theories of light, matter, and atomism, see Fisher, *Pierre Gassendi's Philosophy and Science*.

48. Traherne names Gassendi as "Gassendus" (Traherne, *Kingdom*, 377).

that physical particles travel in predictable, linear movements. Because light travelled from its source, or could be reflected, in predictable linear movements, he therefore logically concluded that light must be a physical particle. Gassendi adopted Epicurean theories of the atom to define these "particles." On this basis, he proposed that a secondary quality such as colour was physically carried by an atom of light, and the perception of that colour was generated by an atom of light actually striking the retina.[49]

Within Traherne's lifetime, Robert Hooke proposed an alternative to Gassendi's particle theory. Contrary to Gassendi, Hooke did not observe light travelling in straight lines. He noted that when objects are observed through a source of hot air, the image will "wave much like the sea."[50] Unlike a single particle in motion, a wave of light can bend and distort. So following the idea that space was filled with fluid called "ether," he proposed that light travelled through the fluid as a wave. Hooke's innovation moved optical theories beyond simple angles of reflection and attempted to explain the reason light refracted through media of varying density, including warm air, wind, and water.[51]

Unfortunately for Hooke, the elemental precision and mechanical laws of the physical sciences relegated the concept of "ether" to the past. For that reason, and because Newton decided to adopt the particle theory of light, Gassendi's theory was preferred throughout the eighteenth century. Newton espoused the particle theory of light based on his belief that refraction could be explained by forces exerted on a particle. He incorrectly suggested that refraction could be explained by the fact that denser substances had more gravity and therefore caused the path of the particle to bend.[52] Further studies by Max Planck and later Albert Einstein would prove that Newton was not correct about the forces that cause the refraction of light particles, and so today we have a *melange* called the "particle wave" theory.[53] But regardless of Newton's theoretical mistakes, Gassendi's particle theory exerted more "gravity" within the optical debate. Traherne followed his lead, and the notion of light particles made a significant impact upon his moral theory.

49. Fisher provides a clear explication of Gassendi's thought in context in Fisher, *Pierre Gassendi's Philosophy and Science*, 33–35.

50. Hooke, *Micrographia*, 232.

51. Hooke, *Micrographia*, 232.

52. Cantor provides an excellent summary of Newton's optical theory and the impact it had in the eighteenth century in Cantor, *Optics after Newton*.

53. Thanks largely in part to Planck's constant and Einstein's theory of relativity, we now believe that both theories provide accurate information about the behavior of light under certain conditions. And while it is anachronistic to suggest Traherne had anything like relativity in mind, he utilized parts of Gassendi's and Hooke's theories.

Inspired by this inductive optical debate, Traherne conducted his own optical experiment, which is worth relating in its full length. His record of his observation demonstrates his scientific method as well as his adoption of the particle theory.

> As in one Instance more, which is Mysterious and Miraculous I will name. Studying the Nature of Light. And falling upon some Discoveries there, I Evidently saw that if Light were the thing I conceived it to be, wheras a Candle seemeth to reflect but in one part of the looking Glasse, on which it shineth, Its flame is visible in all. And going to trie, I found it so, which is very Strange; for no flame appeareth to any Ey, but in one place. But to many Eys, in many, of which I was not aware till I then Saw it in its Causes. For the Idea being in evry Part of the Beams of Light, and the Beams falling upon evry Part of the Glass; the Idea will in evry part be Expressed: But the Lines of Incidence being observed in the Reflexion; the Severall Beams com off Severall Ways, and are seen only by Severall Eys. Evry single Ey seeth but one Idea; the rest that others see, or may see, are to it unseen; because nothing is Seen, but what Enters the Ey; and all, but one, flie away to several places. I am tedious here, but the Benefit will be Endless. For upon the Knowledg of these thing, we are able Intelligently to have Communion with God; to admire his Art; and See his Skill; to Adore his Wisdom, Goodness and power; to delight in the Methods and proceedings of his Work:[54]

Through his own study of "the Nature of Light," Traherne was testing his theory of what he conceived light to be. Based on "lines of incidence being observed in the Reflexion" of light, he determines that while the light emanates from a single source in many directions, the eye perceives only one beam of light. That is, one particular particle of light that has been reflected in a predictably straight line. By focusing on the lines of reflection, and the nature of individual beams, Traherne is operating with Gassendi's particle theory of light, as opposed to Hooke's wave theory. However, what is more important for Traherne, and for our study, is that he believes a particle of light carries the "Idea" of the original source. Traherne believes that "knowledge" of this idea has great theological significance for communing with God and perceiving goodness and wisdom.

The notion that particles of light carry the idea of an object is based on Gassendi's theory that the particles of light are actually atoms. Traherne affirms that "particles of Light" are not "Shadows and Images, but things

---

54. Traherne, *Kingdom*, 385.

of themselvs, Substances being imparted in their own Essential Parts and Spirits."[55] He writes:

> The particles of Light being infinitly volatile, as Particles divided to the Bottom of their Capacitie will Necessarily be, flie back from the Parts on which they fall with Inifinit Speed. . . . And because they are Innumerable and Infinitly Small, being thereupon infinitly formable into any Figure, and continuing in the order in which they leave the last Place, they contain in themselvs the Idea of their Object. Which they last Smote, and from whence they last came: which cannot possibly be broken in the Way between the object and the eye.[56]

After striking a creature, these atomic particles of light are imprinted with some physical aspect of that creature's "figure." Upon reflection, the atom carries with it the idea or "Essential Parts and Spirits" of that creature which it struck.[57] The atomic particle of light actually "communicates" the secondary qualities or "essential spirits" of a creature to other creatures. This particulate behavior of light enables a creature to perceive another creature, and thereby enter into the kind of communion that is the purpose and definition of being alive. It is the material basis for Traherne's scientific and theological understanding of how light gives life to objects.

I have shown that Traherne roots his concept of life and light in Gassendi's particle theory. But his explanation of how "Light was the Life of Men" also depends upon Gassendi's atomic theory. Embracing the theory of the atom was not something a theologian of the seventeenth century would have done without very good scientific and theological reasons. Therefore, it is noteworthy that the atom plays a significant role in Traherne's moral theory.

The Shape of the Atom

The first real atomic theory was recorded by the Epicurean poet Lucretius in *De Rerum Naturam*. In this poem, Lucretius theorizes that the world is created out of the collision of atoms.[58] His materialist notion of life suggests beings are created by the movement of atoms, and beings are morally atomized. That is, moral motivation is the result of atomic movements. This

---

55. Traherne, *Kingdom*, 382.
56. Traherne, *Kingdom*, 381.
57. Traherne, *Kingdom*, 382.
58. Titus Lucretius Carus, *De Rerum Natura*.

theory was present in the early empirical movement of the fifteenth century, and would become the hallmark of David Hume's skeptical empiricism in the eighteenth century.[59] During the seventeenth-century atomistic philosophies such as that of Thomas Hobbes seemed to be supported by the scientific observations of Royal Society members, including Gassendi and Hooke. The perceived atheism of these atomic theories seemed to threaten Christian systems of moral theology. For that reason, atomic theories of the New Philosophy were roundly condemned by theologians and moralists of the late renaissance.[60] Stephen Clucas concludes that the volatility and atheistic liberty of the atom's movement was the significant cause of unrest in the sixteenth and seventeenth century. The notion that a free radical could exist threatened to unravel the order that God established out of chaos.[61] This fear of chaos and discontinuity marks the majority of the theological criticism waged against the atomic theories of the New Philosophy. Clucas cites Donne's fear of the "New Philosophy which 'calls all in doubt'" and atomizes the universe. Donne feared that atomism would cause the universe to:

> Crumble out againe to his Atomies,
> 'Tis all in pieces, all cohaerance gone;
> All just supply, and all Relation:
> Princes, Subject, Father, Sonne, are things forgot.[62]

Fear of the radical instability of matter led many writers to resist the claims of scientists. Poets and divines feared the very dissolution of creation back into chaos so much so that atomic dissolution played an important role in Milton's notion of hell.[63] If material causes were linked to atomic motion, then there was no basis for a theological notion of metaphysical purpose

---

59. Hume's "bundle theory" will be explored in chapter 5.

60. Watson explores the impact that theories of the atom had upon late renaissance poetry and art, particularly in his chapter "Ecology, Epistemology and Empiricism" in Watson, *Back to Nature*, 3–35.

61. Clucas, "Poetic Atomism and Scientific Imagination," 327–40.

62. Grierson quoted in Clucas, "Poetic Atomism and Scientific Imagination," 328.

63. Clucas cites Milton's verse: "A dark Illimitable Ocean without bound. Without dimension, where length, breadth and highth And time and place are lost, where eldest Night And Chaos, Ancestors of Nature, hold Eternal Anarchie, amidst the noise Of endless Warrs, and by confusion stand, For hot, cold, moist and dry, four champions fierce Strive here for Maistrie, and to Battel bring, Their embryon Atoms; they around the flag, Of each his faction, in their several Clanns, Light-armd or heavy, sharp, smooth, swift or slow. Swarm populous, unnumbered as the Sands, Of Barca or Cyrene's torrid soil. Levied to side with warring Winds, and poise Thir lighter wings. To whom these most adhere—Hee rules a moment: Chaos Umpire sits. And by decision more imbroiles the fray By which he reigns: next him high Arbiter Chance governs all" (Milton, *Paradise Lost*, 2:891–910, quoted in Clucas, "Poetic Atomism and Scientific Imagination," 331).

of life, communion, social and political cohesion. Just as theologians feared the chaotic instability of matter, many feared the atomistic nature of democratic liberty could lead to significant moral and political instability. Clucas demonstrates multiple examples of seventeenth-century theologians and moralists who equated the political chaos of the Civil War with atomistic dissolution.

As a staunch royalist and priest of the Anglican Church of the Restoration, one might expect Traherne to reject Gassendi's atomic theory based on its political implications, as well as moral ones. But where most theologians and moralists saw the atom as a threat to the mystery of God, Traherne saw it as a way to explain the mystery of Divine communication of Light and Life. He employed all the scientific knowledge that he had learned from the "Epicureans and Atheists."[64] He affirms that "there is a Shadow of reason at least in their Arguments."[65] He was also sure that theologians have nothing to fear from the inductive pursuit of the material causes of nature, for "if their Discourses, were true no Detriment can accrue to Religion thereby."[66] In the end, God certainly has nothing to fear from empirical pursuits of science. Beside a marginal gloss that reads, "Of the Power of Examining Gods ways," he wrote "Neither is it Boldness in the Soul, to make such Enquiries, but a Modest confidence of his Infinit Excellencey, that it will Endure the Test."[67]

Against the strong trend of theologians in his day, Traherne believed that the material causes of creation should be explored. He dedicates the whole of chapter 17 to the theory of the Atom. It is called "Of the Matter of the univers. Matter is the very Dreg, and filth of Nature. Divested of its uses. But the Matter of God's Kingdom most Glorious. A treatice of Atoms." As the title suggests, Traherne spends the first part of this chapter convincing the reader that the material matter of creation, even with all of its wonderful qualities and different accidents, is by itself "filth" and "the very Dreg" of nature unless it is understood according to its efficient cause. The material "stuff" of life is only "alive," that is perceptive and morally motivated, in relationship to the "Light and Life" of God. But first Traherne demonstrates that the atomic "stuff" of life is common to all beings.

Traherne writes "All Matter without its Form is but one."[68] Matter, Traherne affirms, "may be divided, till we come to Parts Absolutely Indivisible."

64. Traherne, *Kingdom*, 349.
65. Traherne, *Kingdom*, 349.
66. Traherne, *Kingdom*, 369.
67. Traherne, *Kingdom*, 274.
68. Traherne, *Kingdom*, 341.

The atom is the "Seed of Corporietie," and "the first Matter of the univers."[69] Because of its fundamental status, Traherne suggests that the atom provides a basis for material unity among the great diversity of creatures. Note here the atom is a source not of radical dissolution. The atom provides the material basis for a common nature shared by all creatures. "Simplicitie" is the term for that common nature. Beside the marginal heading "The properties of An Atom. Its Simplicitie," Traherne writes:

> an Atom is most Simple and uncompounded, Immutable and Incorruptable, and by a Multitude of these, in quite, or in Motion, are all the Bodies made in Heaven and Earth, all Operations in the World being by them accomplished. Its Simplicitie is Such, that it is wholy divested of all first, second and Third Qualities, utterly voyd of Figure and colour. For Figure is made by an Extension of Parts, colour by a Reflexion of Light. Elementary Qualities by a various Composition of Many Atoms, producing Heat or Cold or Moysture, or Driness, according to the Combination, union or Kind of Operation, wherein they meet.[70]

We see in this quote that Traherne believes the atom is the smallest, immutable building block of matter. Today we know that the atom can be further separated, and that its constituent parts contribute to the qualities of the atom itself. However, it is clear that Traherne understood something rather profound about the nature of an atom. He maintained that the properties of an atom require a relationship to display their qualities.

Unlike Donne, More, and Milton, Traherne did not hesitate to suggest that a particular gathering of "loos and free,"[71] individual, immutable atoms has something to do with the nature of a being's purpose. Unlike the theologians named above who denounced the theory of atoms for fear that the free radical nature of atoms threatened dissolution and chaos, Traherne embraced the possibility of dissolution as that which differentiated life, death and resurrection. When a being died, the "loos and free" atoms dissolved. However, against the likes of Descartes,[72] Traherne believed that "Time and Continuance are not the Principles of Individuation, but unitie

---

69. Traherne, *Kingdom*, 342.
70. Traherne, *Kingdom*, 343.
71. Traherne, *Kingdom*, 345.
72. In his study of Descartes, Keith Ward demonstrates that Descartes defines the self as the continuation of mental "substances" over a duration of time. Therefore, resurrection does not necessarily depend on the continuation of matter or the reconstitution of it, only the continuation of the mental substance, soul, or even memories throughout time. See Ward, *More Than Matter?*, 64–80.

of Matter and Form." A body can die and the unity of its atoms dissolve, but after a time if the "Same Matter, and the Same Spirits united together in the same maner," they would compose "the very same object, that was before their Dissolution."[73] With this idea, Traherne interprets the Mystery of the Resurrection. When Jesus died, his "being" discontinued in time. But when the same Spirit returned to the same matter, the resurrected Jesus was the same being. It is questionable whether this would be the case according to Descartes's intellectual notion of individuality.[74] According to Cartesian rationalism, the Spirit could have returned to any dead body and been Jesus.[75] This is philosophically interesting, but the significant point to take away from this excursus is to note that the physical and relational arrangement of the atoms themselves is part of the "Principles of Individuation."[76] Traherne believes that an individual's inherent qualities are made possible in part by the unique physical shape of a conglomeration or community of atoms.

In the above block quote, Traherne suggested that the atom itself is not the source of first, second or third qualities of creatures, such as shape, colour and heat, respectively. He assumed that the unity of diverse atoms gives a creature these qualities. We now know that secondary qualities of matter, such as colour, smell, and temperature or tertiary qualities such as moisture and heat require a composition of atoms, compounds, proteins and amino acids, or to be more exact, atoms grouped in cells, to display those phenotypic qualities. Robert Hooke was the first to appropriate the word "cell" for its modern biological use.[77] He used it to describe the cork which he viewed through his microscope. Even though microscopy had not reached the stage at which human beings could see the atomic level, Hooke's writings demonstrate that seventeenth-century scientists theorized cells were made up of groups of atoms. Various atoms unite into a form of matter, a cell, which has the capacity to communicate information about their being to another group of atoms. The relationship between various atoms in a cell expressed the basic qualities of life.

Traherne also believed that the expression of an individual's qualities relied on a collective unity of many atoms. Traherne referred to these

73. Traherne, *Kingdom*, 354.

74. Thiel, *Early Modern Subject*.

75. I refer again to Ward, where he demonstrates that while temporal gaps in the body, and even a different body are acceptable, the continuity of mental substance or memory is the defining feature of personhood in the Cartesian view. See Ward, *More Than Matter?*, 64–80.

76. Matar explores this theme in Matar, "Individual and the Unity."

77. Hooke, *Micrographia*, 116.

groups of atoms or cells as "Visible Monads."[78] He believed that "Implicit Roundness is their [the atoms'] Conceivable Figure."[79] Being round, "visible monads" must "meet unequaly in their Conjunction, and are the occasion of Pores and of the different Sizes and figures"[80] of a being's constituent parts. These different "Sizes and figures" are unique to each group of atoms, and are therefore the source of a being's material individuality.

That unique "figure" of an atom provides its "colour by a Reflexion of Light" as well as "Elementary Qualities by a various Composition of Many Atoms, producing heat or Cold, or Moysture, or Driness, according to the Combination, union or Kind of Operation, wherein they meet."[81] A being's unique primary, secondary and tertiary qualities depend in part upon the unique arrangement of these cellular "monads." Indeed, the various phenotypic qualities of a creature have everything to do with their unique genetic and biological chemical structure. Developmental biology reveals that gene expression and cellular differentiation depend on the location of a cell within an embryo. All of the cells of a fertilized egg are identical until the blastocyst reaches a certain size. Only then do the cells differentiate in accordance with their proximity to other cells. Cells at one end of the fertilized blastocyst receive chemical cues about their location within the organism and their genes express the characteristics that cause them to develop into the brain and spinal column. Likewise, cells on the other end of the blastocyst organize into the soft tissue of the fetus. According to developmental biology, we do know now that the unique location, chemical composition and molecular structure of a tissue allow it to "communicate" with other tissues and utilize its inherent capacity to fulfill its biological purpose. The unique properties that a cell expresses depend on the relative position of compounds, and groups of atoms which form tissues.

Of course, Traherne did not have chemical or cellular theories to support his hypothesis about the communication that occurs between atomic compounds. His theory is based on the unique "Pores" that lie between groups of atoms. Meditating on that interstitial space, Traherne poses a question and answer:

> Why is it an Universal Canon, and Rule of Nature that all Bodies Should be Porous: But that they may receiv the Influences of Heaven And the Assistances inspired by other creatures and communicat themselvs after the Manner of the Deitie, to all that

---

78. Traherne, *Kingdom*, 346.
79. Traherne, *Kingdom*, 346.
80. Traherne, *Kingdom*, 346.
81. Traherne, *Kingdom*, 343.

is about them? Evry thing being the End of its own Operations, and the cause in some Measure of others Enjoyments![82]

Pores are the space in which a discourse occurs between "Material Spirits and the Nature of Light."[83] By reflecting through these microscopic interatomic spaces, light is able to communicate the information and life that is unique to a particular arrangement of "Visible Monads." A particle of light is able to pick up the unique idea, or "Essential parts and spirits" of the creature which it "last Smote."[84] Pores are the staging areas for the communication of the creature's unique qualities.

> For the Particles of Light that are immitted into their Pores, when united to the Particles of the Thing, which they loosen, are in all vital Wights, and Vegetables, by a Balsamick Humor, wherin they are Invested, united to the Subject: And when ever they breathe out in the Humor wherin they are cloathed, or any Particle of it, so much of the very Body and Substance, Soul and Spirit, of the vegetable or Animal is parted with: yet this it doth for the Enlargement of itself, and Benefit of others, Night and Day, which Nevertheless by the Ministrie of the Same Spirits, or others Succeeding Continualy, is repaired. And thus the Creature is wholy Communicated from the Very Centre of evry Part and Assignable Particle in him, yet is wholy Initre and wholy continued: Imitating God in that particle.[85]

From the pore, the particle of light carries the unique secondary and tertiary qualities of the creature and communicates them to the being which receives the particle of light. Such a communication of the nature of the "Body and Substance, Soul and Spirit" that animals and vegetables share is a communion by which the whole creature is shared for the beneficence of others. Traherne writes:

> I dare not Insist too much upon Physical Speculations, but this I shall say; such Atoms are Rightly called Animal, and Vital Spirits in Men and Beasts, because they are the Instruments of Life and Motion, of Animation, Concoction, sence, etc. And Spirits

---

82. Traherne, *Kingdom*, 350.
83. Traherne, *Kingdom*, 349.
84. Traherne, *Kingdom*, 381.
85. The word "Wight" here is an error preserved from the manuscript; Traherne obviously intended to use the word "Weights." Traherne uses the phrase "dead weights" to describe irrational creatures, such as plants, or creatures "without life," such as minerals, and "living weights," which are rational, moral creatures, such as human beings and most animals (Traherne, *Kingdom*, 382).

they may be call to wit, Material Spirits, bec. They are the Mean between Immaterial Spirits, and Material Bodies.[86]

While atoms express the inherent qualities of a creature's unique material and immaterial being, they are also the material "Medius Terminus for Common Union"[87] between all creatures. All "necessary" and "moral" beings, "dead weights" and "live weights," creatures with "limited" and "illimited" reason, plants, animals, minerals, earth and water who share common, atomic elements of life can communicate in this way. This joyous communion also occurs via a common cause:

> The Sun extendeth not to the Heavens, and to the Earth only, to Mountains, Valleys, Wildernesses, Elements, Minerals, Vegetables, Meteors, Animals, or Living Creatures; but to the Souls of men, and to the holy Angels: Communicating itself, in all the Joy it occasions to their understanding. . . . And by all these the Sun appeareth to, and toucheth the very Soul.[88]

The deep exchange of the "life" and "information" of our creaturely nature is the morally significant first step in our participation in the Creator. This participatory exchange is made possible, in part, by the light of the Sun.[89] Understanding his optic and atomic theory, we can now make sense of Traherne's interpretation of John's prologue, and the relationship between light and life. While many Traherne scholars recognize Traherne's embrace of atomic science,[90] no one has yet realized the impact that his embrace of empiricism has on our understanding of his moral theory. With that goal in mind, we will now explore two processes by which this communicative communion occurs.

---

86. Traherne, *Kingdom*, 349.
87. Traherne, *Kingdom*, 349.
88. Traherne, *Kingdom*, 356.
89. Traherne, *Kingdom*, 416.
90. Akers has provided one of the most focused studies of Traherne's theories of the atom. But again, Akers emphasis is on Traherne's cosmology. He uses Traherne's fascination with the atom as a means to demonstrate the importance of the Sun as that which generates atoms. However, he does not suggest the atom's significant role in Traherne's moral theory. Akers's analysis of this them can be found in Akers, "From the Hexaemeral," 188.

Communication of Information and Life Occurs through Exhalation and Transpiration

Today, we would describe the manner in which creatures "communicate information" at the atomic level by describing the endocrine or the autonomic nervous system. While Traherne demonstrates only a basic awareness of the existence of nerves,[91] he explained communication with observations of the water cycle and basic nutrient cycles. In one instance, he invites his reader to observe. He asks us to "single out any Sand upon the Sea shore."[92] He knows that this sand is made up of constituent elements that may be dissolved. Some of the elements "mingle" with the water, some are carried in the air, and some dissolve into the earth. We know this element to be sodium. He asks us to follow the molecule that dissolves into the earth. As the molecule passes through the nutrient cycle, it will "leav the Residue to [the] Several Fortunes" of those creatures to which it is communicated. He writes that this mineral can end up residing in a root, a seed, or "breath up at last into a Spire of Grass, be Eaten by a Beast, assist in the form of Nourishment, and pass into Flesh" which can be eaten by a human, and "become part of his [flesh] for a considerable season." From our bodies it can be evaporated or exhaled into the air. From the air, it can be born up by the Sun, and "absorpt into that Fiery Vortex, Glittering there, and assisting as a Part of that Flaming Globe." From the sun, the sodium will be reflected in a beam of light whose "Influence" will be sent to the Moon or to the Earth where it may enter into a fish. "There it may Act, and minister among its Fellow (The Animal, Material and Vital Spirits)." Eventually it will be communicated into an oyster where it becomes part of a pearl which finds its way to a lady's neck or become part of a King's crown or sceptre.

Traherne affirms that such an atomic compound has the "Liberty" to be communicated via any number of paths. However, its dissolution and free radicalism does not threaten chaos. He is confident that the "circulation" of these atoms through the water and nutrient cycle is the very process that nurtures life between creatures. It is part of the process by which creatures communicate life, or commune with one another and God's will for life. In

---

91. Traherne writes: "For tho we may shew the Way how objects are Applied to the Organs of Sense; how Sounds do Enter the Eare, and Smite upon the Drum; How Figures, and colours Enter the Ey and are Represented upon the Retina, in the Brain, or carried by the optick Nerv to the Fancy. . . . Finally, how tangible Qualities affect the Nerves, and Stir the Fibres that are Rooted in the Brain, and communicat their Impressions by Motions of the Nervs or Spirits there" (Traherne, *Kingdom*, 409).

92. Traherne, *Kingdom*, 349.

chapters 23 and 24 of *Kingdom* he names two such processes[93] by which "all Visible and corporeal Beings" communicate. The outward and superficial means of communication is called reflexion. The inward communication of Spirits and Interior qualities is called Transpiration.

Reflexion is the more basic of the two processes. It occurs by the simple reflection of light previously outlined in this chapter. A particle of light enters into the pores of a being. The particle has the "capacitie" to collect the "Idea of their Object." Then that particle reflects, carrying that information to the eye of the observer, where the quality is deposited and perceived as a "naked" sense. The Sun's light drives this optical process of communication, which is synonymous with sight.[94] Transpiration, however, is the process of communication that results from the influence of the Sun's heat. It is the more complex and morally significant process of the two. Among a being's unique secondary and tertiary qualities that we named above, Traherne mentions "moysture" and "Driness." Moisture is a significant quality because water is the medium for transpiration.

In an experiment which demonstrates the "Attractiv power' of fire,[95] he observes the way heat has the ability to move, attract, or conduct certain natural qualities. He ignites a piece of plain paper and places it into a cup. He then turns the cup over into a dish of water. He observes that instead of the fire repelling the moisture of the water, it creates a vacuum which draws the water up into the cup. The fire then collects parts of the water into steam, which transpires in the air. From this experiment he concludes that heat has the power to drive processes of transpiration, and affirms the role of the Sun's heat in the water cycle and nutrient cycles. The heat of the Sun warms bodies and causes them to transpire moisture. In the same way that light particles can carry an idea from the atomic pores of one creature to another, heat can cause moisture to transpire essential, vital, or material spirits between creatures. Chapter 26 catalogues the way heat drives the water cycle, which communicates life and information among seas, rivers, trees, herbs, minerals and precious stones. The sun's heat causes "liquefaction" by which chemical parts of creatures are dissolved and carried away into the waters of the rivers and seas where beasts of the air, sea and field drink their fill.[96] The transpired nutrients are precipitated onto the fields and mountains where

---

93. Chapter 23 marks the point at which Traherne stopped editing his document. I do not think this is qualitatively significant in terms of the content of the text, but it does mean that there are more spelling and textual errors in the document. See Traherne, *Kingdom*, 376.

94. Traherne, *Kingdom*, 381.

95. Traherne, *Kingdom*, 378.

96. Traherne, *Kingdom*, 396.

they nourish vegetation of every kind. Apples, pears, nuts, cherries, dates, figs, olives, currants, cloves, sugar, nutmegs, cinnamon, cider, lemons, oranges, nectarines, raspberries and many more benefit from the ministry of "these Spirits" which have transpired.[97] Even minerals inhale and exhale the "juices" that communicate life between creatures.[98]

Chapter 24 catalogues many examples of "liquefaction" and transpiration. On earth he observes how moss on a tree's bark, the "hoariness" of mouldy bread, the drying up of ponds, the odours of spices, the evaporation of sweat from the skin, the withering of leaves, and the atrophy of tissues in the bodies of old men who appear to wither "into Skeletons" all demonstrate the transpiration of "Spirits." In each case, the Sun causes bodies to desiccate and expire.[99] On the macro-cosmic scale, the sun causes the "Abundant Vapors of Earth and Sea" to transpire from the mighty oaks and cedars into the heavens and back down to earth in the form of rain, dew, hail, and snow.[100] On the grandest scale of all, Traherne returns to his theory of stellar procreation by observing the "transpirations of Greater Bodies."[101] The "Influences of the Stars" begins when these great orbs breathe out the material stuff of life to the Earth. He believes that "were it not for the Influence of the Sun and Stars, all the Pores of the Earth would be quickly Empty."[102] But the Sun's transpiring is the material power station which continues to circulate life. He suggests that if the Sun failed to exhale:

> All the Influences of the Moon would fail, the very Effusion of the Springs, and Rivers Ceas; All Animation and Vegetation be at a Stand; all Communication of Smels, and Properties, and figures, and colours, perish. The Air it self would vanish, And a vast Chaos, or desolate Gulph appear between Evry Creature, and its Neighbor. Wheras now there is an Incessant Trade, and free Commerce between them, they Shake Hands and Mingle Rayes at all Distances, and are Sweetly united in a fair Correspondence.[103]

There is much to learn from this beautiful quote. It reiterates the point that while most theologians feared the free radical motion of atoms as a sign of

---

97. Traherne, *Kingdom*, 398.

98. Traherne, *Kingdom*, 398.

99. These examples are from a catalogue of transpiration in chapter 24 (see Traherne, *Kingdom*, 383).

100. Traherne, *Kingdom*, 383.

101. Traherne, *Kingdom*, 384.

102. Traherne, *Kingdom*, 384.

103. Traherne, *Kingdom*, 384.

chaos, Traherne asserts that if atoms ceased their circulation, a vast chaos would ensue. Rather than a threat to creation's order, the communication of these radicals is the process by which God maintains and nourishes the created order. Secondly, Traherne affirms that all creatures participate in this cycle of transpiration. All creatures shake hands and freely trade "Rayes" with one another. This communication is what creates the relationships that hold the "Gulph" or chaos at bay.

The "free Commerce" of "Rayes" occurs among a community of creatures who constantly communicate "so much of the very Body and Substance, Soul, and Spirit of the vegetable or Animal" from which it parts to its neighbour. The "fair Correspondence" of these "Influences" naturally happens "for the Enlargement of itself, and Benefit of others Night and Day."[104] The vision of a communion of vital, material spirits leads Traherne to invoke Eucharistic language. "Those other Rays that com by Transpiration" lead to a communication of substance and Soul that results in a "Wonderfull and Happy Exchange" that can "teach us Humilitie and Admonish us of that unitie; and Reciprocal officiousness, that ought to between us."[105] Absorbing the vital, material spirits of another creature reminds us of our unity, teaches us humility and leads us to reciprocal moral acts. Transpiration creates a morally significant communion.

In Traherne's concept of Transpiration, the Sun is "the cause and Fountain of all Emanations: wherby all Beings Exchange themselvs for each others Sake to one another, and are united together."[106] For Traherne, this is the "Key and Clew of Nature's Labyrinth."[107] He claims that "upon the Knowledg of these things, we are able Intelligently to have Communion with God; to admire his Art; and See his Skill; to Adore his Wisdom, Goodness and power; to delight in the Methods and proceedings of his Work."[108] God's Wisdom and Goodness are woven into the very processes that sustain creation, and by entering into these relationships, we are participating in a morally significant communion.

Traherne's optical and atom ic theories became part of his moral theory that was rooted in the material nature of creation. Creatures have the capacity to communicate life through their natural physical forces and biological cycles. That relational, physical communion is the means by which living beings are able to perceive the presence of other creatures, and respond with

104. Traherne, *Kingdom*, 382.
105. Traherne, *Kingdom*, 382.
106. Traherne, *Kingdom*, 381.
107. Traherne, *Kingdom*, 383.
108. Traherne, *Kingdom*, 385.

moral movements. In this way, Traherne can "meet with the Epicureans, and Atheists."[109] But in order to understand the theological significance of this moral theory, we must also understand his critique of the "Epicureans and Atheists." After briefly considering Traherne's critique of Thomas Hobbes, we can then construct a complete picture of Traherne's moral theory in *The Kingdom of God*.

Against the Atheists: Traherne's Critic of Skepticism

Kingdom reveals that Traherne was making an innovative contribution to the moral theology of his age by highlighting the role that sensory perception of natural, empirical processes played in theological ethics. Such an analysis suggests Traherne was an early moral empiricist. However, up to this point, we have been concerned with the empirical aspects of his moral theory. We have only focused on the sections of *Kingdom* related to the material causes of communion in God's Kingdom. In order to understand Traherne's critique of the empirical "Epicureans and Atheists" we will now turn to the sections on the Efficient and Formal causes of the Kingdom.

While Traherne is certain that the natural communication of creatures contributes to the moral fabric of the Kingdom, Traherne is equally certain that "The King him self is a Part of the Kingdom."[110] Throughout *Kingdom*, Traherne wages criticism against "the atheists" for their inability to see that truth. Not to see that "κοίνούν ένοιον," which Traherne defines as a "Common Apprehension Engraven in evry Soul," is the root of "all Folly, and Impietie."[111] Traherne writes:

> All Atheism, Infidelitie, and pronfaness is Introduced, Skepticism, and Ignorance, and Dimness and Error are continued in the World for want of this one Observation.[112]

Chapter 1 of *Kingdom* is titled, "OF GODS Kingdom: that it is but one Monarchy, tho consisting of Several Territories. A Digression Concerning its Incomprehensibleness." Traherne's empirical study of creation is predicated on the metaphysical unity of "Heaven and Earth as parts of the same Empire."[113] The several territories of the Kingdom include the heavenly and created realm with its national, political and municipal realms full of "Various

109. Traherne, *Kingdom*, 349.
110. Traherne, *Kingdom*, 341.
111. Traherne, *Kingdom*, 327.
112. Traherne, *Kingdom*, 327.
113. Traherne, *Kingdom*, 256.

Clymates, Tongues, Countries, commodities, Customs and Polities."[114] By a marginal gloss that refers to Ephesians (Eph 2:12–14, 16–22), he paraphrases Paul's words. Christ "is our Peace, who hath made both one, and hath broken down the middle Wall of Partition between us."[115] Because in Christ Jesus, the partition between heaven and earth has been broken, earth and heaven are one "Household of God." "Jesus Christ himself being the Chief Corner Stone, in whom all the building fitly framed together, groweth unto an Holy Temple in the Lord: In whom ye also are built together for an Habitation of God through the Spirit. Nay, we are neerer yet: We are Members of his Body, of his flesh, and of his Bones."[116] The reconciliation of heaven and earth creates a "body" at peace. The very nature of the Kingdom of God embodies the concept of diversity in unity. In an age that suffered the tragedies of political conflict, this emphasis has obvious political consequences. However, Traherne does not base his notion of God's Kingdom on any political theology.

Sixteenth-century theologians tended to root their discussion of the Kingdom of God within some version of the two kingdoms doctrine, in order to justify their version of Christian political orders that were ushered in during the Reformation. Theological formulae were often used to justify a particular view of the Christian state, prince or principality. For instance, Luther deployed creation theology to suggest that the three orders of Church, family and state were rooted in the design of God's Kingdom. In the wake of the English Civil War, Traherne certainly did not hesitate to use theological proofs in defence of the monarchy and his national church. As the son of a royalist family growing up in the loyalist stronghold of Hereford during the Civil War and an ordained priest of the restoration, Traherne pledged his loyalty to the Church of England a year before the act of uniformity of 1662 made any such loyalty necessary.[117] There are many passages within his poetry[118] and *Select Meditations* that sing the praises of England's restored monarchy. The fact that his political theology can be so easily detected in other writings makes its absence from *Kingdom* very notable. In *The Kingdom of God*, Traherne acknowledges the temptation to invoke a

---

114. Traherne, *Kingdom*, 256.

115. Traherne, *Kingdom*, 265.

116. Traherne, *Kingdom*, 265.

117. The evidence shows that he was episcopally ordained in 1660 and installed at Credenhill in 1661, prior to the Act of Uniformity of 1662. See Traherne, *Centuries, Poems, and Thanksgivings*, 1:xxxvii.

118. For instance, Traherne wrote a beautiful poem singing the praises of Restoration England entitled, "A Thanksgiving and Prayer for the NATION" (Traherne, *Centuries, Poems, and Thanksgivings*, 2:320).

doctrine of creation or Christology towards a baptism of the political realm. When outlining what he means by the term the Kingdom of God, he writes:

> We might speak here concerning God's Legal Kingdom, in the Estate of Innocency; concerning the Kingdom of Grace in its various Dispensations under the Law and gospel; as also Concerning the Kingdom of Glory.[119]

There are various places which refer to the way in which the political realm can show the glory of God. But in *Kingdom*, he concludes "this is not the Time for these things. All that I shall observ is, that we are in the Kingdom of God even now."[120] Traherne's purpose in writing *Kingdom* is not partisan. Any debate about the redemptive nature of various political dispensations misses his point because God's creatures are already in the midst of the reconciled Kingdom of God.

The reason for this perspective is self-evident. Traherne is reacting against the social and political atheism that has developed in his century. Specifically, he critiques a Hobbesian political and social ethic.[121] In this text from *Leviathan*, Hobbes writes:

> Desire of knowledge, and arts of peace, inclineth men to obey a common power . . . and consequently protection from some other power than their own. . . . Fear of oppression, disposeth a man to anticipate, or to seek aid by society: for there is no other way by which a man can secure his life and liberty. . . . To this war of every man, against every man, this also is consequent; that nothing can be just. The notions of right and wrong, justice and injustice, have there no place. Where there is no common power, there is no law: where no law, no injustice. . . . Justice and injustice are none of the faculties neither of the body nor mind. If they were, they might be in a man that were alone in the world. . . . The passions that incline men to peace, are fear of death; desire of such things as are necessary to commodious living; and a hope by their industry to obtain them. And reason suggesteth convenient articles of peace, upon which men may

---

119. Traherne, *Kingdom*, 264.

120. Traherne, *Kingdom*, 264.

121. Matthew Akers recognizes this point in his analysis of Kingdom in Akers, "From the Hexaemeral," 141. More generally, the relationship between Traherne and atheism has been the subject of many volumes of Traherne scholarship, from early works by Gladys Wade right up to the more recent, such as Denise Inge and Jane Ross's editorial work on the new manuscripts. See Traherne, *Kingdom*, xiv.

be drawn to agreement. These articles are they which otherwise are called the Laws of Nature.[122]

There are many critical nuances to observe when interpreting Hobbes's political theory, but his view of human nature is significant.[123] Seventeenth-century critics understood that Hobbes perceived human nature to be selfish. Hobbes professed there is no metaphysical moral source, and so replaced natural law with the law of nature. We can see in the quote above that according to the law of nature, a selfish human being seeks political society solely to amass the power needed to protect life and property in the war of "man against man." Whether in war or peace, there is no such thing as justice, except what the political society agrees will be just. But for Hobbes, peace is not a state of being or a reality. His social theory assumes nature exists in a state of conflict.[124] He believes that a state of peace is discontinuous with our nature, rather we must invoke political sanctions against our nature to maintain peace. Peace is only the effect of a social or political covenant that constrains our nature. In a section of his *Ethicks* devoted to the virtue of "Gratitude," Traherne critiques *Leviathan* on this point:

> It is a great mistake in that arrogant Leviathan, so far to imprison our love to our selves, as to make it inconsistent with Christ towards others. It is easie to manifest, that it is impossible to love our selves, without loving other things: Nature is crippled (or if it has her feet, has her head cut off) if Self-preservation be made her only concern: We desire to live that we may do something else; without doing which life would be a burden. There are other principles of Ambition, Appetite, and Avarice

---

122. Hobbes, *Leviathan*, 106.

123. Zagorin, *Hobbes*. This volume of critical essays does well to demonstrate that it is important to read Hobbes in isolation from his critics which have, since the seventeenth century, transmitted several assumptions about his ethical theories. First, that selfishness defines the nature of human beings. Secondly, regarding Hobbes's atheism, that there is no moral source beyond the human's will for self preservation. Of course, Hobbes professed a belief in God and denied the charge that he was an atheist. And if Hobbes's theories were the product of his observation of the social and political reality, then his theory of sociality and political covenanting might not be atheistic or antimetaphysical, but a kind of early social scientific analysis of politics. However, as we are engaged in a study of Traherne, this nuance is anachronistic. Traherne believed Hobbes to be a complete atheist who embraced a perspective on human nature and natural law that completely stood against his Trinitarian metaphysical view of the nature of the Creator and creation.

124. John Milbank suggests that those who base their social theories on the presumption of conflict embrace an "ontology of violence" as opposed to an ontology of peace. See Milbank, *Theology and Social Theory*, 278–79.

in the Soul: And there are Honours, and Pleasures, and Riches in the World.[125]

Here Traherne recoils against the Hobbesian view of human nature. He completely rejects Hobbes's notion that the desire to seek social justice and peace is rooted in the desire for self-preservation. He agrees that human nature is inclined to love ourselves. But he believes Hobbes's "great mistake" is to believe that it is "impossible to love ourselves, without loving others." If we act solely for self-preservation, we are acting out of "Ambition, Appetite and Avarice" or other "principles." But if we act according to those vices, we are not actually loving ourselves. True love is an active agent that cannot be simply selfish. Traherne believes when the desire for society is merely derivative of a human being's will for self-preservation "Nature is crippled (or if it has her feet, has her head cut off)." The selfish love at the core of Hobbes's theory is not the love of self that is human nature.

The natural integrity between a creature's love of self and love of the other is rooted in the integrity that exists between the God's essence as Love and the God's activity as Creator. Traherne's term for this natural integrity is "Simplicitie." In chapter 12 of *Kingdom*, he demonstrates that Love is simply the origin of all that is. God's love must be externally creative, for if God's nature is to love, then there must be a beloved something. Having created that beloved something, God in turn enjoys it, or is pleased by it. To create something so that you can enjoy it is inherently an act of self love. However, that specific act of self love is not selfish. It is not separate from the act of loving the object, because the object is loved. Traherne posits,

> indeed the Love of himself and his Creatures are not two things in GOD, but one; for there is no Diversity in Simplicite. . . . Because he loves himself, he loves them, and in loving them he loves himself. For he loves them, that himself whom he loves might be delighted in them.[126]

In this quote Traherne makes the point that God's simple essence is natural and active love. There is no selfish or disinterested act of love, for all acts of true love are inherently interested in the relationship between the lover and the beloved.[127] On a finer point, "diversity" is a reference to a diver-

---

125. Traherne, *Christian Ethicks*, 261.

126. Traherne, *Kingdom*, 310.

127. Traherne's notion of Simplicitie calls us to reconsider the theory of agape and eros in Nygren, *Agape and Eros*. Of course, many theologians have challenged Nygren's theory in recent years, including John Milbank and Tuomo Mannermaa. But perhaps Traherne can contribute to the discussion, which is to demonstrate that such a division between selfish love and selfless love is to follow a Hobbesian notion that there can

sity among the intentions of a loving act. The great diversity of mutually interested relationships that can be observed between creatures proves the infinite nature of love's simplicity. The differences between individuals

> are Reconciled in its Nature with Infinit Sweetness, being Various Differences, intended in Simple unitie. The Unitie is Indivisible, yet includeth diversities innumerable. And Evry diversity is a Several face, or Appearance of Beauty, and Evry Appearance an Infinit Realitie, and Evry Realitie a Glorious delight to all Spectators. And Evry delight in all the Creatures, its own Enjoyment, both as it is their delight, and the Mirror, wherein it discernes its own Realitie. All Wisdom, and Goodness, and Holiness, and Peace, and Blessedness, and Reason, and Beauty, and Variety, and Simiplicity and purity are in it.[128]

Here Traherne undermines Hobbes's view of nature. Hobbes posits an ontology of violence in which diverse beings naturally compete in a war of man and seek social relationships to preserve our life and property. Against Hobbes's violent narrative of nature, Traherne posits an ontology of peace.[129] Diversity is the means through which mutually interested relationships benefit the health of creation which was wrought by love and shows peace, reason, wisdom and goodness. For Traherne, peace is a natural continuation of our created "nature." Violence is the aberration from that "nature." Creations of a Creator who is "infinitly Lovly" are so "prone to lov" that "Joys and Affections will be Excited between them!"[130] Based on the ultimate "Simplicitie" of God's loving nature and its creativity, Traherne rejects the foundation upon which Hobbes bases his theory of human nature. He outlines his theological proof in his section devoted to the formal cause of nature.

---

even be such a separation among love's activity. Traherne's notion of Simplicite seems to challenge the entire basis of that theory.

128. Traherne, *Kingdom*, 312.

129. For Milbank, the ontology of violence is a mythical narrative that should be challenged with a compelling witness to the abiding ontology of peace (Milbank, *Theology and Social Theory*, 279). I will demonstrate that Traherne suggests this ontology of peace can be discerned from the nature of creation.

130. Traherne, *Centuries, Poems, and Thanksgivings*, 1:35–36.

The Formal Cause of the Kingdom: Love Is Nature's Form

Against the materialism of Thomas Hobbes, Traherne makes the morally significant claim that creation's nature is to love. To support that claim, one section of *Kingdom* outlines Divine Love as the formal cause of creation's diversity. The section begins with these words:

> The Matter alone cannot answer the Efficient Cause of the World, nor in Excellency be Equal to the End, yet may we Hope for more in the Form, and Perhaps find out the Glory of the Efficient and Final Cause, in the Perfection of the same. The Glory of Matter is that it is Capable of all those Formes which infinit Wisdom is able to devise, that it is wholy subject to Almighty power, and apt, and ready for all these uses, which infinit Goodness can appoint unto it. If the uses to which all Matters are applied, be the Best, and Most Glorious of all that are Possible, we shall Easily Conclude, that the Most Excellent of all Imaginable Formes is due to the Universe, and rightly ascribed unto GODS Kingdom.[131]

If the glory of God's love is demonstrated in creative diversity, then the diversity of creatures must reveal the glory of diversity in unity.[132] By Hobbes's estimation, creation is selfish, which either means that there is no formal reality of Divine Love, or that love or peace is not revealed in creation or a continuation of it. Traherne finds this atheistic notion philosophically inconceivable. But he also believes Hobbes's estimation to be empirically short-sighted. He observes God's love in the myriad ways that a diverse creation mutually relates, and in the way human beings socially relate. Chapter 31 begins with the title, "Of the Formal Cause of God's Kingdom, which is the Manner of its Constitution, much to be sought in the Order, Measure, and use of all his Creatures, and in their Mutual Relation to him, and Each Other."[133] The title alone suggests nature is constituted as a mutually cooperative ecology. But one passage in chapter 31 demonstrates this life giving, relational nature. It is worth reading in its fullness:

---

131. Traherne, *Kingdom*, 428.

132. Traherne writes: "Lov is never Seen, but in its operations. God therfore being Incorporeal Is seen in his Works: And the World is the Glorious Body, which he hath assumed to make himself Famous. Nor only to make it Known, that he is: but to make it Known what he is" (Traherne, *Kingdom*, 400).

133. Traherne, *Kingdom*, 428.

> GOODNESS and Lov are absolute Beings, yet is Nothing in the World more Relativ then they. Were the Sun Divested of its Relations, to the Earth, and Seas, to the Stars and Skies, to Birds and Beasts, and Fishes and Men, and Angels what would it become? Take away its Relation to Trees and Herbs, you abolish a part of its Goodness. Take away its Relation to God, you remov it all. Its Emanations and Influences make it Good, and if it be not Good to other things it is good for Nothing. It relateth to God, and me, and thee, and evry Thing, and in all Its Relations to GOD and Me, it relateth unto thee, and in all Relations unto all, it relateth unto Evry one. So doth the Kingdom, wherin the Sun is but a base and Inferior Light, and a Shadow only of what is more Divine. It is more Mine, and more precious to me, then if twere mine alone; Because it is evry ones it is my Perfect Joy, being infinitly Beautifull in its Relation to GOD, to God the Father, to GOD the Son, and to GOD the Holy Ghost. More good abundantly because of its Communication of it self to this Angel, to that Seraphim, to the other Cherubim, to Evry Saint and Holy Creature, whom I love, as I lov my self; and the more good, the more I enjoy it. What can be more, it relateth wholy unto all, all Its Influences come to all, and occasion Joys and Praises, and Hallelujahs, and Graces and Affections, and Vertues, and good Works in all, and for all. And all are Trees to bring forth fruit and Stars to Shine, and Seas and Gardens, nay and Suns and Kingdoms; And I to Enjoy them.[134]

Amidst the diversity of individual interests, love reconciles the one to the many in an ecological unity. Nature's mutuality is the image, or icon of God's form of love active in nature. The mutual benefit of creatures in a healthy, properly constituted relationship is a hallmark of a healthy ecosystem. Today, organisms are said to provide ecological "services" for the health of an ecosystem. Traherne knows we can see examples of life giving, mutual acts of love, "If we look upon the Services of this Kingdom, and the Relation which it bears to other Beings."[135] He rejoices in seeing God's love active in the health of an ecosystem. He writes:

> How great a lover of life God is, and how greatly he delighteth in it, we may see by this, He made all the Elements for the sake of Life. The Earth, the Air, and the Seas Contributing to those that liv on Earth: But it more appeareth by his filling evry one of these with life in themselvs, not suffering any to

---

134. Traherne, *Kingdom*, 431.
135. Traherne, *Kingdom*, 429.

be destitute of Inhabitants. Whose Senses and Affections are Great and Marvellous, whos Hostes innumerable, whos lives no less Beautifull, and Pleasant, then Profitable and Miraculous. The Earth even beneath its Surface is filled with Inhabitants. Frogs, Moles, Worms, Ants, Addars, Woodlice, Spiders, Beetles, Askars, Dormice, with Innumerable others which dwelling in those Blind Cavernes shew the Vertue of his Power, who makes them breath in a fixed Element, even as fishes live in a fluid one; with which his Wisdom shineth also, which maketh these as the basest Dregs: and Refuse of Animals to Beautify the World in their place and Station, by setting off the Glory, and Lustre of the other Creatures.[136]

God's love of life is revealed by creation's natural social tendency towards unity in diversity. Our social nature is evidenced by the observation that even the "basest Dregs" are affectionate and pleasant companions who contribute to the life of all other creatures. Traherne writes that God's love "is the Foundation of a more Glorious super structure, which without Societie it cannot be crowned with." That sentence is tortured with an odd syntax, but he elaborates.

He explains that "The Necessity of companions shews that Riches are ordained by Nature for higher and further Ends, then our sole subsistence. Self is the End, but not the sole End of a Man's Enjoyments." And to make his point even more strongly, Traherne writes that the "Desire of Nature" is to be loved, but also "to see ones self the caus of others Satisfactions," and "to Enjoy their Dependance on us, and our selves as the Authors and possessors of their Felicitie."[137] Inter-dependence is part of our nature. The necessity of companions and our desire to contribute to the flourishing of their life are part of our nature. In our desire to be interdependent, attributes such as beauty, harmony and peace flourish. This formal causality is the basis upon which:

> all Religion, and Right Reason is founded: for Want of which, All Atheism, Infidelitie, and profaneness is Introduced, Skepticism, and Ignorance, and Dimness and Error are continue in the World for want of this one Observation. Had it not been for this Rule, that the most lovely things were most to be beloved it had been Indifferent with God, whether he had Created or no. Tho not to Creat was an Infinit Evil, it would Not be Material: Tho to Creat in a perfect Manner was infinitly Good, it would not be lovely: There had been no Lov of Good or Evil in the World. To

---

136. Traherne, *Kingdom*, 420.
137. Traherne, *Kingdom*, 443.

Lov a grain of Goodness as much as it deserves, is Just. . . . All Nature is unanimous in carrying Power to the most Excellent Actions.[138]

Moral acts of beauty, justice and peace are those that are formed through a creature's ability to perceive the inherent goodness of another creature. Nature communicates its natural goodness in a manner that can motivate moral action. "All Nature is unanimous in carrying Power to the most Excellent Actions." If we perceive creation's natural communication, we will be carried towards "most Excellent Actions" in response to its natural benefits and needs. Traherne believes the angels are able to see this glory in creation, and this is the reason that "The Seraphim so continualy Cry Holy, Holy, Holy Lord God of Hosts. Heaven and Earth are full of the Majesty of thy Glory. Because the Love of righteous Actions is the fountain of all their Blessedness."[139] The "κοίνον ἕνοιν" or "Common Apprehension" is the "stable rule, a fixt Principle, an universal Law in the Nature of things" that "Good is to be Beloved, and Evil must be Hated."[140] Contrary to Hobbes, the universal law of nature is not a desire to associate for the sake of self preservation, but a desire to see the nature of goodness in each creature and respond with justice. To act contrarily to this law of love is the deviant exception to the stable rule of nature.

Love is the stable law of nature. Traherne praises love for two pages, which are best summarized by two examples. Love "Makes Wars to Ceas"[141], and is "The Mother of Peace."[142] He affirms "Lov is the Fountain of all peace and Securitie in the World,"[143] against the skeptical atheists who demand that political consent for the sake of the common defence is the only true source of justice and peace. Traherne contests Hobbes's moral theory for being built on a false premise that neither justice nor peace are natural realities. However, he does not divorce himself from Hobbes's empiricism *per se*. This chapter has demonstrated that Traherne believes we can learn about the causes of nature from the biological and physiological empiricism of "the Epicureans and Atheists."[144] This is so because Traherne knows there is moral content to perceive from the communication that transpires among creatures' interdependent relationships. The next section will focus on the

138. Traherne, *Kingdom*, 327–28.
139. Traherne, *Kingdom*, 327.
140. Traherne, *Kingdom*, 327.
141. Traherne, *Kingdom*, 438.
142. Traherne, *Kingdom*, 438.
143. Traherne, *Kingdom*, 435.
144. Traherne, *Kingdom*, 349.

efficient causes of the Kingdom which give shape to the virtues that can be discerned in communion with nature.

On the Efficient Cause of the Kingdom: Justice and Goodness are Divine Attributes

Traherne chooses to address the "atheism" of Hobbes's political theory not on the basis of political theology, but through the concept of "nature" upon which Hobbesian theories stand. It is for this reason that an account of justice is almost missing from *Kingdom*. I am not aware of any study regarding Traherne's understanding of justice, and I believe that he never intended to dwell on the subject. In the Cornell edition of *Ethicks*, the topic of justice occupies a mere 4 out of 285 pages. In this most systematic study of moral philosophy, he made a conscious decision to move justice from its traditional place among the cardinal virtues.

> THO following the common Course of Moralists, in our Distribution of Vertues, we have seated *Justice* among the Cardinal *Moral*; yet upon second Thoughts we find reason to reduce it to the number of *Divine* Vertues, because upon a more neer and particular Inspection, we find it to be one of the Perfections of GOD, and under that notion shall discover its Excellence far more completely, then if we did contemplate its Nature, as it is limited and bounded among the Actions of Men.[145]

Traherne believes we cannot perceive justice within our human or political nature. We might speculate that the kinds of injustices he saw during the siege of Hereford at the age of twelve led him to doubt Hobbes's notion that justice could ever be derived from a political contract. He acknowledges that "PARTICULAR Justice is conversant in the Distribution of Rewards and Punishments" and that the political realm relies on the exercise of distributive and commutative justice. However, he immediately lists cases in which the influence of unjust economics corrupts the exercise of political and civic functions from the King, to soldier, to priest, to tradesman.[146] Justice is a Divine attribute. And more importantly for our purpose, God's justice is itself a derivative of a greater Divine attribute which is, God's Goodness.

> THE foundation of his Righteous Kingdome, and of the Room prepared for his Eternal Justice to act in, is infintely deeper, and must in other Discourses more full and copious (on that Theme)

145. Traherne, *Christian Ethicks*, 94.
146. Traherne, *Christian Ethicks*, 96.

be shewn. And to those we refer you. All we shall observe here is, that this Punitive Justice beings GODS infiinte Zeal whereby he vindicates his abused Goodness: His Goodness must of necessity proceed it.[147]

The Kingdom is the material result of a simple, efficient act of Goodness, and all notions of justice are predicated on God's Goodness. In the previous section I considered the quote, "To Lov a grain of Goodness as much as it deserves, is Just. . . . All Nature is unanimous in carrying Power to the most Excellent Actions."[148] Justice is the act of loving each creature according to its perceived inherent goodness. Traherne writes:

> Besides this, there being an innumerable Multitude of Things to be belovd, all with a Lov proportionable to their place, and Kind in Measure; when we are Exact and Just in our Returns, an Endless Beauty arises from the Varietie and Greatness of the Objects, in the Lov of him, that Embraces them, to accomplish which, and to be Cloathed with which, is his peculiar Glory.[149]

Because justice is proportional to the peculiar goodness of each creature in "their place," justice is therefore not a mere product of a social contract. Justice relates to our ability to perceive the natural goodness of God in the "peculiar Glory" of each part of creation. A living being acts justly when it perceives a creature's goodness, and is moved to love that part of creation for the "service" that it provides in its place. This concept fits nicely with his definition of life, which is that a living being is that which perceives another creature's communication and responds with a moral movement. It also raises the question of means and ends. Does Traherne base his notion of Justice on the inherent goodness of a creature, or some metric of "services" that a creature provides? He turns to the teaching of St. Augustine to clarify his point:

> I know that to use and to Enjoy are words having a different Signification. For according to St. Augustine, the Means are used, the End is Enjoyed.' In which sense Treasures are never Enjoyed, because they are the Means only to a further End. But the Essence of God is an Act so pure, that to use and Enjoy in him are one.[150]

---

147. Traherne, *Christian Ethicks*, 98.
148. Traherne, *Kingdom*, 327–28.
149. Traherne, *Christian Ethicks*, 435.
150. Traherne, *Christian Ethicks*, 439.

He will not be distracted by the temptation to calculate usage value of the kind codified by John Locke a few decades later.[151] Traherne allows for no such confusion between ends and means. He suggests that the entire concept of justice is based on perceiving God's goodness that is naturally present in the creature. Unlike justice which can only be fully perceived in its Divine form, *Ethicks* demonstrates how Goodness has divine, moral, and natural forms.

He admits that Goodness "is a hard matter to define," but he summarizes that "it is something like *a willing Conformity to the Interests and Affections of his fellow Creatures*."[152] An act is morally good when it is done in response to the interests or well being of another creature. In Traherne's words:

> To Act upon Great and Mighty Principles, in a vigorous free and Generous Manner . . . increases the Measure of Moral Goodness: but its Perfection is seated in a Loyal Respect and Perfect Gratitude to GOD almighty. Who, by being infinitely Good to us, has infused and created such a Goodness in the Soul, that its principal Joy and Delight is to please him. For tho all Creatures consult themselves & their own Preservation, yet the force of Gratitude upon and Ingenuous Soul is very powerful.[153]

Here again, we see that Traherne does not allow for self-preservation to be the defining characteristic of our nature. On the contrary, moral goodness is perfected when our actions motivated by gratitude for our infused goodness, which is to say our natural goodness.

He defines natural goodness as "the Aptitude of Corporeal Beings, to produce such profitable and healing Effects as the enjoyer desires."[154] He describes this natural goodness as a "natural fitness," or a "*Fatal* Necessity" which is present even among "Dead Agents." In *Kingdom*, Traherne elaborates on the difference between necessary beings and living beings, or as he refers to them, "necessary weights" and "living weights." "Necessary weights" are those creatures which are amoral. They may or may not be able to perceive other beings, but they cannot choose to act. According to these

---

151. A good summary of Locke's calculations of usage value as it relates to land and labour can be found in Haddad, "Property Rights," 19–31; Miller, "Property and Territory," 90–109; Russell, "Locke on Land and Labor," 303–25. Most of the articles themselves deal with the notion of usage value and justice as presented in the primary text, Locke, *Two Treatises of Government*.

152. Traherne, *Christian Ethicks*, 79.

153. Traherne, *Christian Ethicks*, 79.

154. Traherne, *Christian Ethicks*, 78.

categories, minerals would be considered dead, necessary beings because they can not perceive and act only out of a necessary reaction to natural forces. Plants, birds, fish, most insects and mammals are counted among the "living weights." The "living weights" are those moral beings who possess "life" as defined above.[155] A living being can perceive the fact that there are other creatures in their space, and make a moral "movement" or judgement based on the fact of the other being's presence. Of the group of living weights, plants and certain insects are living, but necessary beings. They can perceive the actions of other creatures, but their responses are yet mere reactions to natural motions. On the contrary, birds, certain insects, and mammals including *homo sapiens* perceive other creatures, and can reason a moral response.[156] For now, the significant point is that whether one is a dead necessary being, a living necessary being, or a living moral being, Goodness is the nature of all creaturely being because Divine Goodness is the efficient cause of that creature. All beings, whether they are "Dead Agents" or "living weights" have a certain inherent agency in so far as they communicate that God given, natural goodness.

In *Ethicks*, Traherne cites God's goodness as the efficient cause of everything. He writes, "THIS *Divine* Goodness is the first Perfection of the efficient Cause of the Worlds Creation, which of necessity derives an immediate Excellency into all the Creatures, because it is the most Communicative and active Principle that is."[157] Creation is the result of Goodness, which is "a *Living* and *Eternal Act* of free and undeserved Love."[158] Goodness is the attribute by which God "communicates all his Powers and Perfections with pleasure."[159] All other powers and perfections of God's attributes are communicated by God's goodness. That is not to say that goodness is God's most important attribute. Traherne lists Knowledge, Love, Truth, Wisdom, Righteousness, Holiness, Justice and Mercy among the Divine virtues. But Traherne's point is that the means by which we can know any of these Divine attributes is because God communicates. Communication is an efficient function of God's goodness. A loving God could love from afar, but a Good God is compelled to transform that love into a fountain which communicates that love. Goodness is God's "communicative and active principle."

---

155. Traherne, *Kingdom*, 411.

156. There is a further distinction to be made among living, moral beings which relates to those who have limited versus illimited reason. This distinction will be important for the discussion about communication below.

157. Traherne, *Christian Ethicks*, 80.

158. Traherne, *Christian Ethicks*, 79.

159. Traherne, *Christian Ethicks*, 81.

From this notion of Divine Goodness, Traherne derives his understanding of nature's inherent goodness. The efficient act of God's goodness necessarily derives "an immediate Excellency into all the Creatures," the necessity being "the Perfection" of moral goodness, which you will recall is "conformity to the Interests and Affections" of "fellow Creatures."[160] Natural goodness is an inherently social virtue which seeks the welfare of other creatures, and the means by which creatures communicate their social intentions. "Tis that by which all Creatures Communicate themselves to others Benefit, all Living Creatures affect others, and delight in doing Good unto them."[161] That is not to say that we do not have free will to do otherwise. Chapter 8 confirms his belief that free will is precisely the means by which we make evil decisions that do unjust violence against the goodness of creation. But our awareness of injustice is based on our knowledge of God's goodness.

Because creation was made by an efficient act of Goodness, creatures are naturally good. Natural goodness is communicative, and seeks the welfare of other creatures. Dead, living, necessary and moral creatures all communicate and receive communication through reflexion and transpiration. Living, necessary creatures will perceive fellow creatures and respond to their physical presence. Living moral creatures will perceive their fellow creature, and respond with a moral movement that is relative to the good which they perceive in their fellow creature.

Perceiving Goodness in Creation: The "Optics" of an Ontology of Peace

The Goodness of God is the foundation for Traherne's belief that creation is naturally good. As we have considered ultimate, efficient and formal cause of creatures, and the transpiration of their material spirits, we have already noted Traherne's observations about the good nature of individual creatures and ecosystems. Creation bears witness to the simple goodness where creatures seek the complacency, or peaceableness of life through their mutual service to one another. Traherne believes this peaceable goodness can be perceived among the non-human parts of creation, between the non-human and human parts of creation, and within human society. Because the Kingdom is full of examples of God's goodness, so, too, is *Kingdom*. The space of this thesis does not allow for a full record. I will demonstrate the point through one key example.

160. Traherne, *Christian Ethicks*, 79.
161. Traherne, *Christian Ethicks*, 78.

Chapter 25 of *Kingdom* begins with what Denise Inge calls Traherne's catalogue of creation.[162] It begins with a hypothetical story about an an alien from the celestial sphere who visits earth and witnesses our society for the first time.[163] Traherne imagines the being lived in the body of the Sun or the ether of space and knew "nothing but the Azure skie, and face of Heaven."[164] He speculates about what this alien would see upon his first visit to earth, and how he would perceive the nature of Earth's creatures. This scene is worth considering in its fullness as it tells us a great deal about what Traherne saw when he observed human nature, and the nature of society. First, we will consider the section devoted to the individuals within creation:

> Should he be let down on a Suddain, and see the sea, and the Effects of those Influences he never Dreamd of; such Strange Kind of Creature; Such Mysteries and Varieties; such distinct Curiosities; Such never heard of colours; such a New and Lively Green in the Meadows; such Odoriferous and fragrant Flowers:; such Reviving, and Refreshing Winds; such Innumerable Millions of unexpected Motions; Such Lovely, Delicate, and Shady Trees; So many Brisk and Beautifull, and melodious Birds; Such Fluent Springs; and silver Streams; Such Lions and Leopards, and foure footed Beasts; such innumerable Companies, and Hosts of Insects; Such an Ocean of Fishes, Whales, and Syrens, surprizing him in the sea; Such Kidneys of Wheat in the Fat, and abundant Valleys; Such Quarries of Stone, and So many Mines, and Mettals in the Hills: Such Fruits and Spices; such Robes and Attires; So many kinds of Gems and Precious Stones; Such cities, and villages; Such Multitude of Boyes and Girles in the Streets; such Men, such Beautifull Women upon Earth; Such Intelligent and sagacious spirits; Such High, and Heavenly Minds; Such Divine, and all Commanding Souls; such a Gradual Ascent from Sands to Spires of Grass, from Grass to Insects, from these to Birds, from Birds to Beasts, from Beasts to Men, from Earth to Heaven: Such Dominion over the living Creatures; such combinations of States, and Common Wealths; Such Kingdoms and

---

162. Inge, *Wanting Like a God*, 299.

163. Marjorie Hope Nicolson observed that part of the crisis of the "new philosophy" in the seventeenth century relates to the notion of space as an infinite realm. Not only did this create a problem for those theologians who maintained that the earth was the centre of a revolving universe. The notion of an infinite universe raised the question of the possibility of other worlds, and therefore, other creatures. It proved difficult for many to reconcile the notion of human beings as the crown of creation with the possibility that there may be other, unknown forms of life. Traherne was not only unafraid of this possibility, he positively embraced it.

164. Traherne, *Kingdom*, 388.

Ages; Such Bookes, and universities; such Colleges and Libraries; Such Trades and Studies; Such occupations and Professions; Such Retirements and Devotions; Such Altars and Temples; such Holy Days and Sabbaths; such vows and prayers; such Joys and Pleasures; Such Solemnities, Songs and Praises; Such Sabbaths, Holy Days Sermons, Sacraments and Ministers; Such Histories and Records; such Arts and sciences; such Oracles and Miracles; Such Prophesises and Visions; such Virtues and Graces; such Sufferings and persecutions; Such Deaths and Martyrdoms; such Love and fidelity; such Faith, and Hope, and Desire; Such obligations and Lawes, Such Duties and Examples; Such Rewards and Punishments; He would think himself faln into the Paradise of God.[165]

This alien visitor would see the miracles of our social nature, and the communication that occurs by way of the influences and exhalations between creatures. The visitor would be amazed to see the Sun's beams "Stretching out their Rayes like fingers, and feeling at their Fingers ends so many thousand Glorious Objects, the Air, the Clouds, the Rain and Dew, the Seasons of the yeer; All with these Conspiring So fitly together, for the carrying on of one common End, the Happiness of evry Mortal."[166] We read again that the feeling and seeing rays of the sun communicate the paradise of God among its creatures, to the point that the visitor would imagine that "Heaven It self is under their feet!"[167]

Casting his eyes upon aspects of human society, the visitor would be in awe of agriculture, sex, childrearing, sport, and cooking. In all these activities, the visitor would think, "How Rich are they to Each other, how Divine and Precious in all their Ways!"[168]

> Their Dancings and their Feasts, their Coronations are Delightfull; their Caresses and marriages are Sweet, and Joyfull; Their Amities and friendships, their Contemplations and Studies, all are Divine, in a Lively Disguise; they are Angelical.[169]

In everyday society, Traherne sees the empirical evidence for natural goodness all around him. But in order to support his claim to the presence of an ontology of peace he reaches beyond the confines of his age and retrieves the perspective of the Church Fathers, namely St. John Chrysostom. The

165. Traherne, *Kingdom*, 388.
166. Traherne, *Kingdom*, 389.
167. Traherne, *Kingdom*, 389.
168. Traherne, *Kingdom*, 390.
169. Traherne, *Kingdom*, 390.

marginal gloss in line 25, chapter 4 refers us to "S. Chrysost. Homil. 2 in Matth." He paraphrases St. John Chrysostom's second homily on Matthew to announce that "Peace upon Earth, and Good will towards Men is evry where sounded forth by the material Accents of all the Creatures."

While Traherne clearly heard peace and good will sounded forth from "material accents of Creatures," he also heard the horrible sounds of Civil War from his childhood. He knows the pains of war and injustice in human society, and the fact of predation in the non-human creation.[170] But he knows these are privations of our natural goodness. He makes the point succinctly:

> Thus the Design is layd in his Kingdom: and if it failes in the Issue we may thank our selvs, for bereaving our Souls of so Glorious an Attainmnet by our own Wickedness; which without a Barbarous Abuse of Libertie, an Odious Crueltie against our Selvs, and Horrid Ingratitude against God, Could never be.[171]

Even while acknowledging the reality of human privation, Traherne was not swayed by any atheistic notions that the nature of human being was somehow violent or individualized. The design of the Kingdom, which reflects unity in diversity is a direct effect of God's simple, peaceable essence. Traherne writes that:

> [God's] Beauty is not the Effect, but the cause of his operations: And yet if we should say, it is the Effect, we should not Lie, for it is begotten of it self: It is unbegotten in the Father, begotten in the Son and proceeding in the Holy Ghost. His Beauty being an Essence, arising, and Springing of its own Pleasure, and the Cause of all other Beauty whatsoever. His Greatness, and power depends on the Beauty of his Kingdom, as the Excellency of the cause depends on the Effect. . . . He that Exceeds himself is greater then he that is in him self alone. He that is out of Himself, and in himself together, is greater then he that is shut up, and confined, abiding in himself alone. God is Infinite in himself and in his Kingdom too. He is wholy out of himself; as well as wholy in himself. I may say, He poured out himself, when he proceeded to his Work And that GOD himself is the Life, and Beauty of the Same. Who is as Great in the Holy Spirit; as in the first Person of his Eternal Essence. As Great in his Kingdom, as

---

170. Traherne, *Centuries, Poems, and Thanksgivings*, 1:3–4.
171. Traherne, *Kingdom*, 401.

in himself: Since His Holy Spirit Intirely proceedeth from him, and really dwelleth in all the creatures.[172]

Human "being" is rooted in the loving relationality of the Holy Trinity, which reveals the beauty of diversity in unity. Traherne had eyes to see how creation's diversity contributed to the health and growth of all creatures within natural ecosystems, including human society. The way he presents the notion of difference demonstrates his strong held belief that an ontology of peace underwrites all of creation and actually inspires all creatures. A "naked" perception of the Divine peaceableness is possible because the Spirit really dwells in all creatures.

Compelled by their natural participation in this goodness, creation communicates the peaceableness through the natural circulation of vital spirits. Living, moral beings enter into a real communion with one another when they perceive the communication of each inherently good being, and the inter-dependent nature of each creature, mineral, plant and animal, serving one another in their ecological place. This peaceable communion with other creatures leads to moral movements in living, reasoning, moral beings such as humans and some animals.[173] Such is the empirical nature of Traherne's moral theory.

Our empirical, creaturely, sentient communion is morally formative. This notion provides the empirical and theological basis for maintaining the epistemological importance of human sensibility.

Ethical Implication of Empiricism and the Role of the Senses—between Ants and Angels

Beginning with chapter 39, *Kingdom* ends with two chapters dedicated to embodiment and the importance of the senses. One of Traherne's great poems, "Thanksgiving for the Body," sings the praises of all five human senses.[174] After considering the empirical aspects of Traherne's moral theory, we can understand the reasons he praises bodily senses. Our ability to perceive communication, and respond with a free and appropriate moral movement that gives just honour to the perceived creature is "the Image of God."[175] The "Image of God" refers to the continuity between God's Goodness and the goodness of our nature. He writes, "For he made us his Image in power, that

---

172. Traherne, *Kingdom*, 453.
173. Traherne, *Kingdom*, 409.
174. Traherne, *Centuries, Poems, and Thanksgivings*, 2:214.
175. The notion of the *Imago Dei* is taken up in Traherne, *Kingdom*, 456.

we might be capable of Making our Selvs So in Act, and that with Infinit pleasure." Traherne provides examples of these free moral acts, and they are all responses to the perception of a sensory motion such as the sweetness of a melody, the fragrance of perfume, the smoothness of a touch.[176]

Chapter 40 is titled "That the Image of God in a Body, is yet something higher then one purely Spiritual, or incorporeal. Of the Reason why Visible Things were made: Their Use, and Glory." It suggests that it is was better for God to put the *imago dei* into a material creature rather than an incorporeal, spiritual one. He prefaces his explanation with the obvious objection "what Service can Material Things do to Spiritual?" Why would Wisdom and Goodness compel God to create corruptible and untrustworthy matter to bear his image? He answers his question by suggesting, "The difficulty was his allurement; being Infinitly wise, he Contrived a Way to Surmount their Incapacitie, and overcome the Barrenness of their Nature."[177]

The way that God overcame the barrenness of matter was to enliven it with senses and a soul.[178] Traherne uses pages to describe the senses, and outline the manner in which material organs are the conduits between material beings and the soul.

> For tho we may shew the Way how objects are Applied to the Organs of Sense; how Sounds do Enter the Eare, and Smite upon the Drum; How Figures, and colours Enter the Ey and are Represented upon the Retina, in the Brain, or carried by the optick Nerv to the Fancy. . . . Finally, how tangible Qualities affect the Nerves, and Stir the Fibres that are Rooted in the Brain, and communicat their Impressions by Motions of the Nervs or Spirits there.[179]

Be it pain or pleasure, Traherne knows that humans perceive "the Motion, and Concurrence that is made between them, that is the Proper object of Sence and its immediate Material Cause."[180] The perfume is not what smells, but the sweetness of the perfume is an effect that is communicated. "The Real Effect of that cause [is] in the Organ" that is "Inherent" to a sentient creature.[181] The motions of qualities reflected or transpired from other creatures communicate impressions which are perceived by "the Organs of Sense."

---

176. Traherne, *Kingdom*, 457.

177. Traherne, *Kingdom*, 481.

178. Traherne discusses the relationship between rationality and the soul at length in Traherne, *Seeds of Eternity*.

179. Traherne, *Kingdom*, 409.

180. Traherne, *Kingdom*, 485.

181. Traherne, *Kingdom*, 485.

He concludes "there would be no Sweetness in the World; were it not for Organs and perceptions."[182] Finally, this "perception makes a judgement."

There is nothing novel about this process of perception, which would separate him from a rationalist like Descartes. However, Descartes asserts that the moral moment exists in the time it takes for a mind to pass judgement on a perception.[183] The moral moment is sequestered in the cognitive activity of the brain. The moral judgement is a rational process that hinges on the cognitive analysis of the sense. In other words, if a person can cognitively recreate the interaction in their mind, it is as morally significant as if the interaction had physically taken place. For that reason, if you can think it, it was as good as real and morally significant. Traherne's concept of the moral moment is qualitatively different from this rational process. For Traherne, one living creature's moral judgement cannot be divorced from another creature's act of communicating vital spirits. Perception necessarily occurs in the proximity of another body. Traherne's poem states:

> Pure Bodies, or Pure Spirits we with ease
> May apprehend; but Such Mixt things as these,
> Which neither Bodies, nor yet Spirits are,
> And yet are both, are more Sublime, and Rare.
> How Matter should perceiv, or feel, or see,
> Is as Miraculous a Mysterie as
> Nature can Afford. Yet in a Beast
> These Powers are, and are in Beasts the least . . .
> But yet are all Subservient in their Kind,
> Unto the Higher powers of the Mind,
> And on the pow'rs (on which they all attend,)
> In operation, Nature, use, depend.
> Two Natures in one Person must unite,
> That common sence might fill them both with Light,
> For he must hav a Body with a Mind,
> By Wisdom Infinite, in one Conjoyned:
> Without which union Common Sense Can't Live
> because its nature's wholy Relative.[184]

He agrees that pure bodies and pure Spirits are easy enough to imagine. But dismissing purely rational, Cartesian thought experiments as lacking

---

182. Traherne, *Kingdom*, 485.

183. René Descartes expounds this notion of the moral moment in his Fourth meditation (Descartes, *Meditations*). For a full defense of Descartes's view and a critical look at the moral implications of his notions of embodiment, I recommend Ward, *More Than Matter?*, 18–70.

184. Traherne, *Kingdom*, 484.

"Common Sense," the mixed human body, the embodied spirit, is more sublime and rare. The two natures, body and mind "must unite That common sence might fill them both with Light." The body's ability to perceive, feel or see is the miraculous mystery. He affirms that the rationality of our mind is "wholy Relative" to our body's ability to sense other beings around us. Remembering the title of chapter 40, "The Image of God is something higher than purely spiritual or incorporeal," Traherne believes that reason is not and cannot be purely rational. The "Image of God" respects the continuity between the Goodness of the Creator and the goodness of creation. This is the blessed mystery of human nature. He writes:

> that which I Shall chiefly close this Chapter with, is a Reflexion of the Excellency of the five senses, whose office it is to represent all sensible Objects, and effects to the common power of Perceiving, as the office of that is to represent them to the Understanding. All the Pleasures, and Delights in the world depend upon them.; all Harmonious Sounds, Beautiful Sights, fragrant Odors, Delicious Tastes, alluring Tongues, and pleasing Contacts, are conceived in the sense, that is formed, and framed by the union of Life, and Matter. And how excellent Man is, that by Nature is the Engine of all these, we may more fully discern by considering the Vast and powerfull Degrees of Pain and Pleasure, of which Sence is capable, which without Sence could not be in the World.[185]

He follows this with a list of all types of illnesses and torture that human beings experience here on Earth as in hell. While this catalogue of pain seems depressing, he uses it to make a significant point about joy. Our ability to sense pain and suffer torments in this life are often seen as proof of our fallen nature. Human suffering is a source for lamentation and grief over our human condition. However, our ability to sense pleasure and pain, and make a moral response, is a source of joy for Traherne. This embodied moral sense is the very aspect of our being that places human beings somewhere between Ants and Angels. That is to say, humans were created somewhere between necessary beings and heavenly beings. This scheme is perhaps the most significant aspect of Traherne's moral theory.

First consider the ant. Ants were one of Traherne's favourite animals to observe. They make an appearance in *Kingdom*, and they also receive an entire entry in Traherne's incomplete encyclopedic manuscript, *Commentaries of Heaven*.[186] The Ant is the archetype of a living, necessary being.

---

185. Traherne, *Kingdom*, 487.
186. Traherne, *Commentaries*, 93.

Traherne believes that "an Ant is a more Glorious Creature then the Sun; for they Know themselvs, and are Sensible of the Light, and of the Comfort of their lives:"[187] The ant is counted among the living beings that can perceive communication from their surroundings and respond accordingly. As a living being ants "really feel The Benefit, and the pleasure that doth accrue from union and communion."[188] They are a very social animal. However, Traherne also believes that while ants are alive, they are not moral beings. They only make "necessary" movements, according to the material stimulation that they sense. So, ants have all the senses of human beings, and fully participate in the reflexive and transpirational communication of creation. But they lack the reason to judge a moral response.

On the other end of the spectrum of living beings, we find angels. Traherne writes of angels:

> Angels have a Lov truly Infinit to the Deitie, and so hav the seperat Souls of Men. But Angels which hav no Bodies, cannot have those Sentiments, which arise from the Mistion of the Blod and Spirits In their various Repercussion against the vessels of sence and Motion. All their Affections are without sence, purely Intellectual, and to us (as yet) incomrehensible. They have no Vessels wherein to reposit the Effects of Reason. Their Joy therfore and Lov is Spiritual, So is their Hope, and fear, and sorrow. The Angels are not capable of Corporeal Torments in Hell, nor Material Joys in Heaven. In themselves they are incapable of Corporeal Joys. Yet certinly they render to all Things their Due, and their Thoughts beings Consonant to right Reason, are affected with them. Wherfore they must be capable of Spiritual Passions. Could they not fear, and griev, they could never Rejoyce; and without Joy there could be no felicitie.[189]

The life of Angels is purely rational. In a Cartesian world, where rationalism was emerging as a response to the atheistic materialism of empiricist moral theories, pure rationality was often seen as a moral ideal. However, Traherne's poem demonstrates that rationality is not the goal in his moral theory. First, Traherne writes pure rationality is an incomprehensible impossibility for humans. Furthermore, far from being a moral goal, pure rationality is actually a state of moral deficiency. A purely rational being such as an angel lacks something. In their pure state of rationality Angels are excluded from knowing joy and felicity.

187. Traherne, *Kingdom*, 410.
188. Traherne, *Kingdom*, 412.
189. Traherne, *Kingdom*, 489.

Traherne believes the fallen state of mortal sensibility is not merely a privation from a heavenly state. It is a super-added state of blessedness. Traherne explains:

> For Eternity, and Glory, and Wisdom, and Goodness, and Power may be conceived by us, as well as by them [Angels], even without our Senses. Since therfore our Senses are without Impediment, superadded to our Inward, and Spiritual powers, it seemeth that our Humane Nature is more then Angelical, because we have one Way more then they, to feel, and Enjoy all Objects, Visible, and invisible, and their Way in like manner.[190]

Human nature is superior to that of the Angels because we can feel the joy that comes from being able to sense creation's communication. Traherne admits that, in the first creation, Angels were more "Secure" (and humans were "more Hazzardous"), humans are also capable "of more Compassion, and of Standing with Greater Glory then they."[191] In this way he turns our fallen nature into our very blessing. Humans are capable of freely practising virtue, while Angels are not.[192] This is why the final chapter of *Kingdom* is titled, "That it was better to be made in a State of Trial, then immediatly placed in the Throne of Glory."[193] The created territory of God's Kingdom is fallen and does threaten the perception of pain. Yet the possibility of feeling is the very gift that moves us to moral actions and the ability to know the joy of responding to goodness.

The fact that our moral motions depend upon the complex of sense and reason makes Traherne refer to our created bodies as "this Wonderful Posie there being bound up in him the Excellencies of all Created Beings."[194] He believes that humans are not alone in receiving this blessing of sensibility. All created beings have some share in that which makes for life, reason and morality. But Traherne notes that "Plants hav being, and Life, and Reason, but not sence. Man hath all, Beings with the Planets, Life with the Plants, sence with Beasts, and Reason with Angels."[195] Regarding the human's moral and sensible constitution, he further believes:

---

190. Traherne, *Kingdom*, 489.

191. Traherne, *Kingdom*, 490.

192. Clearly, Traherne chooses to leave behind the mythology of angels that was placed into the popular imagination by John Milton's *Paradise Lost*. In other places, Traherne does refer to the fall of the angels. See Traherne, *Kingdom*, 490.

193. Traherne, *Kingdom*, 495.

194. Traherne, *Kingdom*, 490.

195. Traherne, *Kingdom*, 490.

> Should we take evry Affection apart, and Shew what a Marvellous Addition of Life, Sence being added doth put into it, we should seem to move the Jealousy of Angels, and provoke them to Envy. But the Angelical Nature is so Divine, and Gracious, and it participates so much of the Eternal Goodness, that having on Will and Pleasure with God, it is their Joy and Delight to see our Perfection.[196]

Traherne seems to be invoking 1 Peter 1:8–12.[197] He delights in the thought that the joy of being able to apprehend God in creation through our sensibility is something that the Angels long to see. Our ability to sense God at work in the creation's communion makes the Angels jealous of our fallen "perfection." In his *Centuries*, Traherne affirms this paradox by proclaiming "God made man more by making him less."[198] Humanity's moral nature is bound to our sensibility. We can not achieve the fullness of our human identity as a living, moral being in any other state. It is for this reason that Traherne begins his *Ethicks* with the statement:

> Above all, pray to be sensible of the Excellency of the Creation, for upon the due sense of its Excellencey the life of Felicity wholly dependeth. Pray to be sensible of the Excellencey of Divine Laws, and of all the Goodness which your Soul comprehendeth. Covet a lively sense of all you know, of the Excellency of God, and of Eternal Love; of your own Excellencey, and of the worth and value of all Objects whatsoever. For to feel is as necessary, as to see their Glory.[199]

---

196. Traherne, *Kingdom*, 490.

197. "Although you have not seen him, you love him; and even though you do not see him now, you believe in him and rejoice with an indescribable and glorious joy, for you are receiving the outcome of your faith, the salvation of your souls. Concerning this salvation, the prophets who prophesied of the grace that was to be yours made careful search and inquiry, inquiring about the person or time that the Spirit of Christ within them indicated when it testified in advance to the sufferings destined for Christ and the subsequent glory. It was revealed to them that they were serving not themselves but you, in regard to the things that have now been announced to you through those who brought you good news by the Holy Spirit sent from heaven-things into which angels long to look!" (1 Peter 1:8–12).

198. This notion was the subject of Newey, "God Made Man Greater," 227–41, which found inspiration in Robert Ellrodt's study of the metaphysical poets. "Le sentiment religieux s'y exprime souvent avec un accent d'humilité qui n'est pas l'accent habituel de Traherne [The religious sentiment often expresses itself with an accent of humility that is not the habitual accent of Traherne]" (Ellrodt, *L'Inspiration personnelle*, 264, translation mine).

199. Traherne, *Christian Ethicks*, 6.

Conclusion

Traherne ends *Kingdom* by summarizing the relationship between morality and the natural state of creation. He writes that God could have created his Image "in an immediate state of glory" wherein the "Beauty of Goodness" would have been immediately seen. However, in that state all beings would have been "necessary" just as Ants and Angels, and therefore not be free to be moral. To be confined, as the Angels are, to necessary glory would not allow our participation in Joy. Our moral world, therefore, is integrally related to our human sensibility. In this construct, Traherne would never agree with the atheistic empiricists that moral judgements are only the result of motion any more than he would agree with the rationalists that morality could ever be realized in an act of pure rationality. Traherne rejoices in suggesting that the edification of a moral being is rooted in the fact that a living being depends upon a physical, transpiring, communicative relationship with other creatures that are participating in creation's goodness.

The empirical optical, atomic, biological and physical theories of his day made a significant mark upon Thomas Traherne's moral theory. My reading of *Kingdom* affirms the thesis of K. W. Salter that Traherne was not simply a mystic.[200] He certainly saw with his mind's eye. He does record seraphic visions of joy. But while he saw with rational and spiritual clarity, his moral theory is not based on an act of mysticism or rationality. On this basis I disagree with Neef,[201] Kuchar[202] and Balakier[203] that Traherne's notion of the self is related to a mere psychological or Vedic state of rational consciousness.

Finally, I can argue against the claim raised by Carol Marks that Traherne offered nothing to the age of ethics in which he wrote.[204] She may feel this is the case for Traherne's *Ethicks*, which was the object of her study. However, a close reading of *Kingdom* reveals the contrary. Traherne was developing a complex moral theory unlike those belonging to the moral theologians of his day. He was not a Neo-Platonic, proto-Rationalist who retreated into metaphysical poetry to defend against the advance of Hobbesian atheistic empiricism. By daring to incorporate scientific notions derived

---

200. Salter, *Thomas Traherne*. This thesis can also be found in Clements's ground breaking study of Traherne's mystical tendencies, and is broadly confirmed by my reading of *Kingdom*. See Clements, *Mystical Poetry of Thomas Traherne*.

201. DeNeef, *Traherne in Dialogue*.

202. Blevins, *Re-Reading Thomas Traherne*.

203. Blevins, *Re-Reading Thomas Traherne*.

204. This is a reference to Mark's quote that framed the discussion of Traherne's ethical contribution in chapter 2.

from Baconian empiricism into a Trinitarian system of moral epistemology, Traherne was constructing a Christian theory of moral formation that affirms the embodied, sensory reality of our created nature. His theory seems to warn against both moral extremes that would develop in the next century—Hume's skeptical empiricism and Kant's transcendent rationalism. As we will see in the next chapter, Traherne's caution, as well as his daring, offers a voice to our contemporary notions regarding the role of ecology in the moral formation of children.

3

Retirednes
Understanding the Principles of the Perceiving Child

Introduction

THE MORAL THEORY OUTLINED in *The Kingdom of God* suggests that the moral life of a living being can be shaped by participating in a sensory, communicative relationship with other creatures. The goal of the next three chapters is to demonstrate how Traherne applies that moral theory towards methods of moral formation. "Retirednes" is one such method that has ethical and pedagogical implications for the moral formation of human beings, particularly that of children. Two of the new manuscripts, *Inducements to Retirednes* and *Seeds of Eternity or the Nature of the Soul* will serve as the primary context for this reading.

I begin by demonstrating how his moral theory informs his practical theology of retiring among creation. I will show that Traherne bases his belief in the morally efficacious benefit of "retirednes" on three concepts; (1) human principles, (2) interest, and (3) the nature of the created objects that we behold. This chapter will then focus on the first concept. I will discuss the human principles by which Traherne believes human beings perceive our creation's communication, and focus specifically on the concept of wonder as a significant principle of childhood. A comparison with French phenomenologist Maurice Merleau-Ponty will demonstrate the consonance that exists between Traherne's understanding of the epistemological significance of our relationship with nature, and the contemporary phenomenological movement. I will support the claim with research in developmental psychology that suggests a child's relationship to creation is morally significant. This comparison will highlight a major implication of Traherne's moral theory. If human beings can naturally perceive moral knowledge through a wondrous exploration of creation, then children are equally capable to enter into this kind of morally formative communion.

The Child as Moral Philosopher

Chapter 2 ended with Traherne's thought experiment about a foreigner who visits the earth. It is the first time that the "stranger" experiences the social nature of our life. The "stranger" is able to perceive knowledge that is naturally communicated between creatures by physically entering into our world. By engaging their senses in a physical relationship with this creation, "Thus would a Celestial Stranger be Entertained in the World."[1] And by it, the stranger is "able to See the Original, and the End of things."[2] The stranger would be amazed to see the Sun's beams "Stretching out their Rayes like fingers, and feeling at their Fingers ends so many thousand Glorious Objects, the Air, the Clouds, the Rain and Dew, the Seasons of the yeer; All with these Conspiring So fitly together, for the carrying on of one common End, the Happiness of evry Mortal."[3] The stranger would feel the rays of the sun communicating the reality of this paradise of God among its creatures, to the point that the stranger would imagine that "Heaven It self is under their feet!"[4] This visitor would be amazed at the beauty of our social nature, and the communication of goodness that occurs by way of the influences among creatures.

The passage raises a question regarding perception. After exploring Traherne's moral theory, we can understand that creatures communicate goodness through their natural communion and communication. In the example, we can see that Traherne is equally sure that the "stranger" can use their naked senses to perceive the goodness that exists in this communion. But Traherne is not only illustrating an idea about the communicative nature of other creatures. He is making a statement about the perceptive nature of human beings. After all, the "stranger" in Traherne's thought experiment is not actually an extra-terrestrial being. At the end of the passage Traherne reveals that he knows this "stranger" to our world and it is a child.

> I know a Stranger upon Earth in his Infancy that thought the Heavens more Sublime then Saphires, and the Stones in the streets more pleasant then fine Gold. The Fields laden with Delights, more Rich then Carbuncles, and the Meadows for Divine, then if Covered with Emeralds. The univers appeared a Sphere of Joys, and Immortal Glories:[5]

1. Traherne, *Kingdom*, 390.
2. Traherne, *Kingdom*, 390.
3. Traherne, *Kingdom*, 389.
4. Traherne, *Kingdom*, 389.
5. Traherne, *Kingdom*, 391.

Traherne often figures his childhood personnage as "a stranger." After being orphaned around the age of four, he was adopted from his Herefordshire country life Uncle who lived in Hereford city. He felt like a stranger to the adopted urbane life of Hereford and London. He records that living among the riches of the urban environment and learning to value jewels and baubles of urban society made him a "stranger to the shining skies."[6] Traherne's trope of the child philosopher in his Centuries and poetry is well established. However, in light of my new reading of his moral theory as expressed in the new manuscripts, I will revisit this concept and demonstrate why the child is the philosopher *par excellence*. I will show that Traherne's theory about moral epistemology and the nature of human perception is at the heart of the child's morally significant relationship to creation.

Traherne's third century of meditations contains an autobiographical account of his childhood. He famously recalls:

> Certainly Adam in Paradise had not more sweet and curious apprehensions of the world than I when I was a child.[7]

As a child, Traherne perceived the world with a natural curiosity that was equal to that of Adam, the consummate "stranger," who knew creation through direct, sensory communication. A child can know the world in this way because they engage their natural, sensory wonder. As living, moral beings, children are born with the ability to apprehend communication of goodness in creation and consequently can be formed by the perception of that knowledge. It is for this reason that Traherne believes Christ's word about becoming a little child:

> is deeper than is generally believed. It is not only in a careless reliance upon Divine Providence, that we are to become little children, or in the feebleness and shortness of our anger and simplicity of our passions, but in the peace and purity of all our soul. . . . So these things would appear to us only which do to children when they are first born. . . . God in His works, Glory in the light, Love in our parents, men, ourselves, and the face of Heaven: Every man naturally seeing those things, to the enjoyment of which he is naturally born.[8]

There are several key concepts contained in this passage which I will explore over the next few chapters. "Carelessness" is one. The "nature" or "naturally

---

6. This phrase is from Traherne's poem, "The Apostacy" (Traherne, *Centuries, Poems, and Thanksgivings*, 1:96).

7. Traherne, *Centuries, Poems, and Thanksgivings*, 1:6.

8. Traherne, *Centuries, Poems, and Thanksgivings*, 1:113.

born" abilities of "every man" is another. First I will focus on the statement that creation can "appear to us" in ways that they appear "to children when they are first born." In other words, creation can appear to us as when we are strangers who first encounter creation. I will demonstrate that Traherne believed young children perceive through their senses, in much the same way that child psychologists and educators describe a child's perception of their environment. Traherne believes that the things we perceive through our sensory relationship to creation are morally significant for our Christian moral formation.

This makes sense for one who frequently paraphrases St. John Chrysostom, and refers to his brother Gregory of Nyssa, and his sister Macrina.[9] In the sermon, *An Address on Vainglory and the Right Way for Parents to Bring Up Their Children*, Chrysostom progresses through each of the five senses. He demonstrates how the child's sense of sight, hearing, taste, touch and even smell play an important role in helping a child develop into a peaceable creature of God as opposed to a vainglorious individual. The senses are the gates of the city[10] in which the tripartite soul spirit, appetites and reason reside.[11] Chrysostom felt overexposing a child to baubles, fineries, *richesse*, and even violence of urban life skews the child's ability to sense true glory. This kind of tutelage caused the child to pursue "vainglory" which resulted in creating an unnatural "man-child." Alternatively, he urged parents and tutors to guard the "city" by strengthening the gates, which is to say keeping their senses trained on true glory. This kind of tutelage would allow the child to both utilize their natural sensibility which is capable of grasping the moral significance of what it means to be a creature.[12] Chrysostom writes, "The man-child has lately been born. His father thinks of every means, not whereby he may direct the child's life wisely, but whereby he may adorn it and clothe it in fine raiment and golden ornaments. Why dost thou this, O man? Granted that thou dost thyself wear these, why dost thou rear in this luxury thy son who is as yet still ignorant of this folly? For what purpose dost thou put a necklet about his throat? There is need for a strict tutor to direct the boy, no need for gold." The tutor who honours the true glory of a child helps them direct their senses to that which is truly glorious. "In

---

9. Traherne, *Seeds of Eternity*, 239.

10. Laistner and Chrysostom, *Christianity and Pagan Culture*, 137.

11. Laistner and Chrysostom, *Christianity and Pagan Culture*, 142. Interestingly, Traherne refers to the writings of Chrysostom's brother and sister in his manuscript *Seeds of Eternity or Nature of the Soul*, in which Traherne critiques the sufficiency of Aristotele's thesis on the tripartite notion of the soul. It is a concept that Chrysostom readily employs.

12. Laistner and Chrysostom, *Christianity and Pagan Culture*, 93.

this matter the tutor and attendant must exercise the greatest care. Show the boy other fair sights, and thou wilt steer his eyes away from those others. Show him the sky, the sun, the flowers of the Earth, meadows, and fair books. Let these give pleasure to his eyes; and there are many others that are harmless."[13] According to Chrysostom, a continuity exists between the nature of creation and the pursuit of moral knowledge.

Traherne agreed children needed a tutor who could teach the true glory, or moral identity of being human in continuation with the goodness of creation. After his own education he felt:

> That childhood might itself alone be said
> My tutor, Teacher, Guide to be,
> Instructed then even by the Deitie.

His childhood allowed him to engage the forests and fields of Herefordshire with his senses, which:

> taught me that I was concerned in all the world : and that in the remotest borders the causes of peace delight me, and the beauties of the earth when seen were made to entertain me : that I was made to hold a communion with the secrets of Divine Providence in all the world.[14]

The child's entrance into that wondrous communion with creation is "the beginning of Gifts, the first thing which God bestows to every infant, by the very right of his nativity."[15] These perceptual "Gifts" are part of his belief that human nature is naturally pro-social which he maintains against Hobbes. These "gifts," not original sin, are passed on through our natural birth. Even in light of the Arminian Controversy[16] he does not shrink from this interpretation of original sin:

> our misery proceedeth ten thousand times more from the outward bondage of opinion and custom, than from any inward corruption or depravation of Nature : And that it is not our parents' loins, so much as our parents' lives that enthrals and binds us.[17]

---

13. Laistner and Chrysostom, *Christianity and Pagan Culture*, 111.
14. Traherne, *Centuries, Poems, and Thanksgivings*, 1:123.
15. Traherne, *Centuries, Poems, and Thanksgivings*, 1:57.
16. Associating Traherne with the influences of Arminianism is often the preferred way of citing contemporary influences on his belief regarding sin. This thesis is explored in Marshall, "Thomas Traherne," 161–65.
17. Traherne, *Centuries, Poems, and Thanksgivings*, 1:115.

Distracting a child's senses towards adult, vainglorious "opinion and custom" is a privation that spoils the child's native ability to perceive knowledge about our true nature. In this regard, Traherne recapitulates Chrysostom's notion of sin as it relates to the moral status of children.[18] Chrysostom urges the telling of the stories such as Cain and Abel to demonstrate the dangers of privations such as jealousy. After the child is able to recount the story, he urges the parent to say to their child, "Thou dost see how great a sin is greed, how great a sin it is to envy a brother."[19]

Traherne displays a similar notion of sin as a privation that is exacerbated by our love for the "preternatural" luxuries and customs of urbane life.[20] Our jealous fetish for this kind of urbane society is the source of the earth's "Curses Briars and Thorns. Hence flow all their Rapines Discontentments Wars and Miseries. An Evil Ey, Envy, Repining, etc. being the Effects only of Conceited Poverties."[21] The "Dumness" and "Blindness" which obscures our "naked" capacity to see aright is a "misery," and a "fall" that "arises naturally from the greatness of your sin."[22] Teaching a child that preternatural things are valuable is a sinful attempt to recreate a vainglorious "man-child" by denying the child access to the moral epistemology that creation communicates. To make the point positively, a child's moral formation should be accomplished in continuation with their knowledge of creation and their natural place in it. He laments the time in his own early childhood when his capacity to perceive knowledge of creation was obscured by the influence of a "bad education":

> The first Light which shined in my Infancy in its primitive and innocent clarity was totally eclipsed: insomuch that I was fain to learn all again. If you ask me how it was eclipsed? Truly by the

---

18. This thesis follows closely the work of O. M. Bakke on various notions of children in the early church, namely that of St. John Chrysostom. See Bakke, *When Children Became People*. Traherne's doctrine of sin was the subject of Grant, "Original Sin," 40–61. In this thesis, Grant debunks the notion that Traherne did not have a strong doctrine of sin; rather, he had a doctrine of sin that relates more to that of Irenaeus than that of Augustine. In light of the current topic on childhood, I would add that his Irenaean doctrine of sin is therefore congruent with Chrysostom's doctrine of sin, specifically as it relates to the moral status of children.

19. Laistner and Chrysostom, *Christianity and Pagan Culture*, 104.

20. Patrick Grant has explored Traherne's concept of sin in Grant, *Transformation of Sin*. He suggests that, against his critics, Traherne does have a strong concept of sin. It is simply not an Augustinian concept of the biological transmission of sin, which was found more in the Puritanical circles of theology. Grant attributes an Irenean concept of sin to Traherne's theology.

21. Traherne, *Inducements to Retirednes*, 25.

22. Traherne, *Inducements to Retirednes*, 58.

customs and manners of men, which like contrary winds blew it out: by an innumerable company of other objects, rude, vulgar, and worthless things, that like so many loads of earth and dung did overwhelm and bury it: by the impetuous torrent of wrong desires in all others whom I saw or knew that carried me away and alienated me from it: by a whole sea of other matters and concernments that covered and drowned it: finally by the evil influence of a bad education that did not foster and cherish it.[23]

His university education did the exact opposite that the "tutor" should. A "bad education" codified the epistemological split between "knowledge," and the child's perception of the "Light." He indicts this kind of education with his own fall into what he calls the "Apostasy" that made him "a stranger to the shining skies."[24] He believes a proper education should hold together what Philip Sherrard calls a single, unified science.[25] He knew that the methods of teaching "knowledge" were being bifurcated in the education of his day. During this time, Traherne is clearly yearning to recover a unified way of knowing. Unfortunately during his undergraduate years, which began at the age of 15, nature was silent.[26]

Traherne's first ordination papers were signed in 1656, prior to the Restoration, by several prominent Puritans of the day.[27] However at the age of 21 he was too young to serve. While he waited to turn the canonical age of 24 he was installed as rector of St. Mary's Church near Credenhill in the forests of Herefordshire where he grew up.[28] He passed these years in his beloved country parish prior to returning to Oxford in 1656 when he studied for his master's degree. During these intervening years, he seems to have claimed a theological perspective that helped him recover the "Infant Ey" of his childhood. Gladys Wade attributes his breakthrough to the influence of the Platonists.[29] But I demonstrated in chapter 1 that this particular recov-

23. Traherne, *Inducements to Retirednes*, 110.

24. Traherne, *Inducements to Retirednes*, 114–15.

25. Sherrard quoted in Cutsinger, *Not of This World*, 146.

26. Traherne records this silence in his poem "Solitude" (Traherne, *Centuries, Poems, and Thanksgivings*, 2:98).

27. Wade and Parker, *Thomas Traherne*, 62.

28. The details of these years between his undergraduate study and his episcopal ordination in 1661 are notoriously difficult to reconstruct, in part due to conflicting records regarding the financial support given to him by the Commonwealth. We can be certain that his episcopal ordination occured in 1661, and between 1657 and 1661, the Herefordshire forests around Credenhill afforded him the opportunity for recovering his "sight." See Traherne, *Centuries, Poems, and Thanksgivings*, 1:xxiv, xxxvii.

29. Wade and Parker, *Thomas Traherne*, 218–19.

ery was more likely due to his ability to synthesize an inductive, Paracelsian engagement with nature into a mature moral theology.

The moral significance of a sensory perception of creation was missing during his "Apostasy," abetted by his "bad" education. But in an age that sought to divide the senses from moral knowledge, and sequester them in the new science, Traherne had learned the ways in which creation naturally communicates. He remembered perceiving that communication of goodness in his childhood. His reentry into the forests of Credenhill confirmed his theological anthropology of the child and helped him experience that communion which for which he yearned. He recorded, "When I came into the Country, and being seated among silent Trees, had all my Time in mine own Hands, I resolved to Spend it all, whatever it cost me, in Search of Happiness, and to Satiat that burning Thirst which Nature had Enkindled, in me from my Youth."[30] This recovery must have been the answer to his prayer to "become, as it were, a little child again that I may enter into the Kingdom of God."[31]

Nurturing our native, living, moral capacity to perceive this communication became a "clue" in helping his parishioners recover their natural human capacity to perceive the goodness of God's peaceable Kingdom.

Following Nature's "Clew"

The Kingdom of God outlined the natural communication "wherby all Beings Exchange themselvs for each others Sake to one another, and are united together."[32] A creature's participation in that "Wonderfull and Happy Exchange" can "teach us Humilitie and Admonish us of that unitie; and Reciprocal officiousness, that ought to between us."[33] Creatures transpire "vital" and "matcrial spirits" within the parameters of that physical relationship. When a living, moral being perceives that communication, it teaches humility and "influences" a reciprocal moral act. The spatio-temporal relationship is a morally significant communion. Since transpiration compliments our native sensibility, it is the key to understanding how creation can communicate the moral order of God's Kingdom. Traherne identifies this concept as the "Key and Clew of Nature's Labyrinth."[34]

---

30. Traherne, *Centuries, Poems, and Thanksgivings*, 1:136.
31. Traherne, *Centuries, Poems, and Thanksgivings*, 1:111.
32. Traherne, *Kingdom*, 381.
33. Traherne, *Kingdom*, 382.
34. Traherne, *Kingdom*, 383.

He claims that "upon the Knowledge of these things, we are able Intelligently to have Communion with God; to admire his Art; and See his Skill; to Adore his Wisdom, Goodness and power; to delight in the Methods and proceedings of his Work."[35] Creation communicates moral knowledge that is necessary for our development into our true glory as living, moral, human beings. By understanding this "clue" to his moral theory, we can better understand why he so passionately urges his readers:

> By an Act of the understanding therefore be present now with all the creatures among which you live; and hear them in their beings and operations praising God in an heavenly manner. Some of them vocally, others in their ministry all of them naturally and continually. We infinitely wrong ourselves by laziness and confinement. . . . You are never what you ought till you go out of yourself and walk among them.[36]

The "clue" to becoming that which human truly is, which is to say moral creature, you must "go out of yourself and walk among them." The term "Clew" leads us to another of Traherne's late manuscripts, *Inducements to Retirednes*. There he suggests "Nothing is more Expedient then that in our Retirement, we Should first find out the Clew that leads us into those Hidden Labyrinths, and those Rules by which we may make it Evident, that we can certainly Know."[37] By "retiring" among nature, we exercise the "key" or "clue" to perceiving the kind of moral epistemology that is woven into the fabric of creation.[38]

The Location for "Retirednes"

As the title promises, the treatise *Inducements to Retirednes* urges its readers to retire into God's creation in order to perceive the moral epistemology that underwrites creation. The manuscript is divided into five sections. Sections one, two, three and five each begin with an abstract. The abstract of the first section summarizes the purpose of *Inducements*. The bold script reads:

> In this Introduction the pious Soul is Invited unto Retirement from the World for the better Introversion of Spirit to Consider and enjoy those Devine Objects heer presented, and delineated to it: For Every thing Rests most Composedly in its Proper place,

---

35. Traherne, *Kingdom*, 385.
36. Traherne, *Centuries, Poems, and Thanksgivings*, 1:94.
37. Traherne, *Inducements to Retirednes*, 29.
38. Traherne, *Kingdom*, 499.

and the Soul of Man is not in its Proper place, till it be sweetly disposed and Composed for Devine Enjoyments.[39]

Before getting to the main point of this chapter regarding perception, we must understand Traherne's use of the term "World." The abstract reads, the soul must retire "from the World for the better Introversion of Spirit," and retire "in its Proper place" to perceive creation's communication. On the face of it, it appears that Traherne is advocating turning away from the physical world, and retiring into the recesses of the mind. In other texts, he does utilize cognitive retreats in the exercise of reason that span time and space. For instance, when he receives news from a far away land he retreats into his mind to imagine that separate spatial reality.[40] Traherne also imagines the stories from Scripture in order to comprehend their import.[41] However, Traherne implies the exact opposite when he induces humans to retreat from "the World" in this treatise.

In *Inducements*, Traherne refuses to divide the Kingdom into physical and mental states. Traherne uses the term "abroad" to describe the courses of life, mental or physical, where we exercise the active life. He explains that participating in an activity that allows us to exist in our proper place, or according to our proper function, brings us "home." The distinction between "abroad" and our "proper place" is not temporal. For example, "Bees fly abroad to make honey, but they eat it at home."[42] For the bee, making honey and eating honey happen in the same temporal realm. Even the bee's work abroad, which includes pollinating other plants, is virtuous and life giving to others. However, home is where the bee's life is nourished. In this way, the term "the World" does not refer to some temporal reality as opposed to a spiritual or mental reality. The term "the World" refers to our life "abroad." So, when Traherne induces us to retire "from the World," he is calling us to return to our proper place where we can be nourished as the living, moral creature that we are. Our proper place is in nature, away from the preternatual world:

> What is more Easy, then for a man to withdraw Him self, that He might intermeddle with all Wisdom? . . . The Millions of men are upon Earth, and Angels in heaven; yet God hath made the World so Wide, that there are Resting Places enough wherin we may retire. . . . Were Men Wise, to know the Glory which

39. Traherne, *Inducements to Retirednes*, 5.
40. This idea is conveyed in his poem, "News" (Traherne, *Centuries, Poems, and Thanksgivings*, 2:88).
41. Traherne, *Centuries, Poems, and Thanksgivings*, 1:124.
42. Traherne, *Inducements to Retirednes*, 20.

> might there be Enjoyed, those Solitary Places would be only visited, Shops and Taverns be left Solitary. Insomuch that had not God made the World Exceeding Vast, a man should scarce hav no Room to be alone. But now the Market is so filled with Cares and People, and so many Shady Groves and Lovly fields are quite Empty; (as the Fall of Angels (according to som mens Opinion) made room for Men) the Negligence of many, is the Advantage of a few.[43]

It is important to keep in mind that he is not demeaning the spiritual value of our work "abroad." Like the bees, the occupations of our daily lives can equally be opportunities for the communication of virtues, or "communion." Traherne writes our daily life abroad is full of:

> the Joys and Pleasures, that may be Tasted by Angels, yet such is the frailty of our Corrupt Estate, that we may Surfeit on these. Which we then do, when we are Distracted by them from the Lov of God, or Disturbed in the Enjoyment. It is true indeed, that where we can reconcile them, with our union and Communion with God; they are in themselvs Desireable, as a Great Part of the End of our Creation. For Man is made a Sociable Creature, and is never Happy till His Capacities are filled with all their Objects, and his Inclinations have attained their proper Ends. But these Objects are Wide and many, their fountains are Dispersed, and lie abroad: they cannot therefore but in Retirement be at once Enjoyed. Truly Acquired, they are Worthy of God. But the Sweetness of them lies much in their Causes. For it consists in the Contemplation of those Noble Things, we hav don in the Atchievment: And cannot well but by recollected Thoughts within, be Enjoyed. To gain a Confluence of Praises by Surreptitious Means, is to Wear a crown and Scepter that is Stoln. The Noble Paths of Honor and Vertue are found in Retirement.[44]

The joys of our life's work are reconciled "with our union and Communion with God," because they are both "Part of the End of our Creation." By nature, we have the "Capacities" to contemplate the Love of God as a cause of creation while we engage in our society with the world and with God. He knows that to say otherwise would be to disregard the Christological truth of the life and ministry of Jesus, as well as the redemption of our life. However, Traherne's caution is due to the fact that he knows our life "abroad"

---

43. Traherne, *Inducements to Retirednes*, 10.
44. Traherne, *Inducements to Retirednes*, 11–12.

can equally be a distraction and temptation from our proper work.[45] Even the temptation to beneficent activism can be a temptation which deviates us from our proper place.[46] Traherne is clear that the holy life can not be mere activism. Nor can life be mere contemplation.

In the end, Traherne is laying out a fairly straightforward notion of the balance between the active and contemplative life that is driven not by beneficence, but the desire to participate in the communication of divine knowledge that reveal "The Noble Paths of Honor and Vertue." He understands that the Christian life exists in a continuum between meditation and action. He actually calculated a ratio of retirement to work by using a formula that he derived from the life of Christ.[47] Because Jesus spent thirty years preparing for a three year ministry, Traherne ambitiously suggests that

---

45. The market places, temples, government buildings, and palaces and the interactions that happen there are, for Traherne, "Occassions of Offence," full of "Yong mens' Debaucheries, Widdows Tears, Covetous Mens Oppressions, Rabschecha's Blasphemies, the Oaths, Ingratitudes, and Impudences of men; which so much hurt a Tender Soul." When we are distracted by "Things unprofitable" then we are arrested from our capacity to know true knowledge. Traherne records: "Among those Things which withdraw us from Retirement, I shall not name Splendid Houses, Crowns and Scepters, Gold and Pompous clothes; nor Feasts and Palaces: The outward Carcase which appears unto Children: But the Ends of them, for which they are Esteemed: Their inward Sweetness, which is the Soul and Spirit, unseen by the Vulgar World: A long Influence upon other Souls; a deep Interest in a Multitude of Affections; Honor and Power acquired therby; Delightfull Intercourse, and Mutual Enjoyment; Zeal and Admiration; Dominion, Greatness, Highness and Glory. these are Joys and Pleasures, that may be Tasted by Angels. Yet such is the frailty of our Corrupt Estate, that we may Surfeit on these. Which we then do, when we are Distracted by them fro the Lov of God, or Disturbed in the Enjoyment" (Traherne, *Inducements to Retirednes*, 11–16).

46. Traherne cautions that our "deep Interest in a Multitude of Affections" that result from being a good friend, spouse or political leader may distract us from the Love of God. He cautions that "to giv is the Greatest Sensuality in the World, and to be Doing Good, the Highest Epicurism." He acknowledges the gravity of good intentions coupled with the snare of Epicurean delight often stifle us from apprehend the proper goal of "retirednes." He acknowledges that "Tenderness and Compassion, which moveth us to yeeld to others, by way of Pity and Compliance, is, not Seldom, a Snare that Captivats. Where it overthroweth the Strength of Judgement, it vilifies the Person, and Weakens the Man" (Traherne, *Kingdom*, 486).

47. While the main body of the manuscript contains references to this calculation, the marginal gloss is equally as instructive. Recorded in the editorial script, designated as "Script B" by Traherne's editor, Jan Ross, Traherne writes: "Tho: our Saviour would not Enter into his Prophetical Office, till he was 30 yeers of Age (the Age in which the Jews admitted their priests) yet had he not designd to make Retirement Exemplar onto us, he could have as well lived in publique Exposures as in private humble Retirement; and being we are to Imitate him in all his Imitable perfections, How Easy as well as happy and safe is it to Imitate him in this" (Traherne, *Inducements to Retirednes*, 13). See also footnote 15.

we should pass our life in retirement versus action by a staggering ratio of 10:1.[48] While this equation is ambitious by most metrics, suggesting a balance between the active and contemplative life is neither unique nor outstanding in theology or ethics. This middle way is a position taken by the Church fathers, Aquinas, and the Anglican divines. In particular, the model for many of Traherne's concepts about the Church and the life of faith seems to be Richard Hooker, who Traherne calls "that Glorious Beam of the English Church."[49] Traherne relies on Hooker's conception of the active and contemplative life to make a larger epistemological point. Following the passage quoted above, Traherne praises Hooker for recognizing the way in which creation, if properly perceived, is a spokesperson for the Creator. He says by

> wading into the spring and fountain of Laws, and digging neer unto the root of things, hath some Sage and important Maxims which he casteth up like Sparkling jewels. Speaking of the first and Eternal Law, which is the fountain of all Laws, he saith, The Being of God is a Kind of Law to his Working; for that Perfection which God is, giveth Perfection to that he doth. Whereupon he observeth, that that, and nothing els is done by God, which to leave undone were not so Good: that there was never sin committed, wherin a less Good was not preferred before a greater: and that the Works of Nature do always aim at that which cannot be bettered. These Seeds being Scattered so near the root of Perfection, these Principles so closely laid in the foundation, these Ingredients giving a Tincture to the very Well-Head of all Demonstration, must needs be of General Concernment in all the streams, as fitly applicable to all Particulars. The uses then and the Services of the Stars may be treasured by these.[50]

Hooker's position is one in which scripture, tradition and creation are all epistemologically significant. There exists a continuity between scripture, tradition and creation, between nature and grace. His position, which would come to be understood as the *via media*, provides Traherne with a

---

48. Traherne cites many examples of public life that depend upon a ten fold period of preparation: "When we consider the Great Skill that we stand in need of, and the Abundance of Work that we hav to do; our Saviors Example may seem more Eligible: whose Proportion of Retirement, was ten yeers, to one of Exposure. For the Term of His Concealed Life was Thirty full yeers, and that of His Publick less then Three. He Spending ten parts of His Time in Secret towards God, that He might spend one profitably among men. Not but that he was able much Sooner to hav gon abroad: but this he did for our Example" (Traherne, *Inducements to Retirednes*, 13).

49. Traherne, *Kingdom*, 369.

50. Traherne, *Kingdom*, 369.

theological precedent to view creation as a source of moral knowledge.[51] Traherne writes of the epistemological connection between scripture, tradition and creation:

> Since therfore Nature requireth Gratitud, which is so Beautifull in the Beauty of Nature we see the verity of Religion, and in the verity of Religion the Beauty of the same. Gods infinite Bounty being the foundation of all.[52]

Traherne did not simply rely on Cambridge Platonism in order to construct his "latitudinarian" concept of creation. His moral philosophy was rooted in a doctrine of creation that was present in the Church catholic from the fathers, through Aquinas, Hooker, and the Anglican Church of the restoration. Traherne's doctrine of creation affirms that the Holy Spirit enlivens creation, and communicates through it. God's essence is "All in all, and therefore All in us."[53] He proclaims, "O what an Individual Union ought there to be between Him and us, who is wholy within us!"[54] Traherne is so certain that God's goodness is the efficient nature of creation that "He [God] is wholy evry where: and so Beautifull, that He is evry where ours, and wholy ours."[55] When we enter into natural, transpirational communication with other creatures, we "see the verity of Religion" in the "Beauty of Nature." We are participating in a real communion with Divine goodness. So if we retire from the preternatural "World" to our "proper place," which is "out of yourself" and "among" creation, we can "Know," or perceive that goodness.

Returning now to the quote presented above, Traherne states that when we retire in our proper place we are privileged to communicate with "Devine Objects" that are "heer presented" in nature. Traherne reassures

---

51. That is, if the *via media* is to be assumed as a viable thesis. There is ongoing debate about the appropriateness of the concept of via media to describe sixteenth and seventeenth-century Anglican theology. The debate regarding whether via media is an historicist, anachronistic evaluation continues in the writings of Stephen Sykes and Henry Robert McAdoo. See McAdoo, *Anglican Heritage*. However, the point that will be made here is that with regard to nature and grace, scripture and reason, Traherne's moral theology is as closely aligned to that of Richard Hooker as it is to the latitudinarians. Like Hooker before him, Traherne was not trying to make any qualitative distinction between the kind of knowledge transmitted by scripture, law, grace or nature. In his experience, meditating on Scripture and contemplating creation communicate knowledge of God's goodness.

52. Traherne, *Inducements to Retirednes*, 34.
53. Traherne, *Inducements to Retirednes*, 6.
54. Traherne, *Inducements to Retirednes*, 6.
55. Traherne, *Inducements to Retirednes*, 6.

us that "to see that which is Infinit and Eternal, is the priviledge of His Creatures."[56] When God's creatures are properly positioned among creation, their natural or native ability to perceive natural goodness is the manner in which they "see" the goodness of God active in creation. With this we have arrived back at the central thesis of this chapter regarding the nature of perception that operates in Traherne's moral theory.

Morality Exists "Out of Yourself"

By insisting that human beings need to spend time retiring amongst creation in order to apprehend knowledge of goodness that comes from God through creation, Traherne embraces the notion that our senses play an important role in our perception of moral epistemology. At the end of the third section of the *Inducements*, Traherne paraphrases Psalms 8 and 9, beginning with:

> When I consider the Heavens which thou hast made, the Moon and Stars which are the works of thy fingers. What is an that Thou art Mindfull of Him or the Son of man that Thou visitest Him. Thou hast made Him a little lower then the Angels, that Thou mightest Crown him with Glory and Honor.[57]

Trahrene recapitulates the notion that human beings are actually blessed to be created a little lower than the purely rational, amoral angels. Precisely because we are located between the ants and the angels, we are moral beings. As I demonstrated in chapter 3, it is part of our joy that makes the angels jealous. If we were completely rational beings such as the angels, we would cease to be moral beings. Our ability to "sense" is part of the "glory" of human beings. Our status as a living, moral creature depends upon whether we can ever say that we "Know," that is perceive, the nature of another one of God's creatures so that we can respond with a moral movement. Our sensual state of being a little lower than the angels is a joyful, positive, constructive aspect of our moral status. Traherne claimed that God made humans greater by making us less.[58] This point is significant because it places Traherne's moral theory squarely between two competing philosophies of his day, rationalism and empiricism, which both threatened to disassociate sensibility from moral epistemology.

---

56. Traherne, *Inducements to Retirednes*, 5.
57. Traherne, *Inducements to Retirednes*, 23.
58. Traherne, *Centuries, Poems, and Thanksgivings*, 1:121.

I have shown that Traherne felt this division left both rationalist and empiricist positions morally and conceptually impoverished. In light of the belief that our created nature is continuous with the moral order, both Hobbes and Descartes unnecessarily leave behind critical aspects of any reasonable moral theory. Traherne understood the dangers of this philosophical divide, and knew that it resulted in a "bad education" that denied children the fullness of the "truth" and knowledge of our identity as human creatures that is revealed in our morally significant relationship to other creatures.

The Cartesian, or rationalist, method of "knowing" relies on the mind's cognitive ability to represent an object. For instance, by thinking about our experience of creation, the rationale mind is capable of conceiving God's will for creation. It is true that many of Traherne's writings slip into this rationalist, representationalist mode as he explores the relationship between the senses and "common sense."[59] However, unlike Descartes's method which excluded the senses in order to achieve a purely rational knowledge, Traherne's method of "retiredness" suggests the perception of moral epistemology can begin with the senses. Traherne's notion of "retirement" outlines this "other" method of apprehending the moral epistemology. Traherne clearly makes this point in the short, but comprehensive quote that was introduced above:

> By an Act of the understanding therefore be present now with all the creatures among which you live; and hear them in their beings and operations praising God in an heavenly manner. Some of them vocally, others in their ministry all of them naturally and continually. We infinitely wrong ourselves by laziness and confinement. . . . You are never what you ought till you go out of yourself and walk among them.[60]

---

59. Traherne initially writes, "I Shall not insist on the Nature, and perfection of this common Sense, nor Methodicaly treat of the fancy, and Memorie; only Shew that the fancy is the Power of Imagination, that is an Interior Abiliti, to Creat, or raise, at least to use, and Govern all Images, as it self pleaseth, in the Mind, proposing the Ideas of any Thing possible, or Actual, present, or Absent to the Common Sense, and affeting the Mind therewith, as if it were present. And that the Memory is a Power of reviving ideas, that were in the fancy or common Sence before, representing them anew in Relation to Time past" (Traherne, *Kingdom*, 487). However, he concludes this notion with the statement, "But that which I Shall chiefly close the Chapter with, is a Reflexion of the Excellency of the five senses, whose office it is to represent all sensible Objects, and effects ot the common power of Perceiving, as the office of that is to represent them to the Understanding."

60. Traherne, *Centuries, Poems, and Thanksgivings*, 1:94.

Our "Act" of understanding is based on being among creatures so that we can "hear them in their beings and operations." In the quest to perceive this "heavenly" communication, we "infinitely wrong ourselves" by confining ourselves to cognitive loneliness. You can become what you are, which is a fully live, moral human being by going "out of yourself and walk[ing] among them." Here is a significant observation. The perception of this kind of moral knowledge happens outside of our self. In other words, it is not generated in our minds as a result of Cartesian rational intellect.

On the other hand, Traherne is equally as sure that communion is based on the interaction between two beings, and is more than the impression derived from simple sense perception, as is the case with "dead weights," or "necessary beings." This makes his theory quite distinctive from the moral empiricism of Hobbes, which would come to fruition in the writings of David Hume a century later as a reaction to Cartesian rationalism. Hume eventually championed the notion that all of our moral actions are derived from the influences of our senses, meaning there are no objective moral beings there to perceive, we merely make judgements based on our sensory perceptions. We do what is benevolent, right, beautiful or good, based on the collective influence of our sensory perception of various properties of those beings we interact with. Hume writes,

> An action, or sentiment, or character is virtuous or vicious; why? Because its view causes a pleasure or uneasiness of a particular kind. In giving a reason, therefore, for the pleasure or uneasiness, we sufficiently explain the vice or virtue. To have the sense of virtue, is nothing but to feel a satisfaction of a particular kind from the contemplation of a character. The very feeling constitutes our praise or admiration. We go no farther; nor do we enquire into the cause of the satisfaction. We do not infer a character to be virtuous because it pleases: But in feeling that it pleases after such a particular manner, we in effect feel that it is virtuous. The case is the same as in our judgments concerning all kinds of beauty, and tastes, and sensations. Our approbation is imply'd in the immediate pleasure they convey to us.[61]

In the empiricists' world, there is no actual "virtue" to be discerned from our relationship to another being. There is only a moral deliberation that we make regarding how we feel when we come in contact with that being and it sets off a "bundle" of reactions in our body. This describes Hume's "bundle theory" of moral sensibility.[62] According to this empiricist theory, an object

---

61. Hume, *Moral Philosophy*, 78.
62. See a discussion of Hume's theory in Dicker, *Hume's Epistemology*, 31. There is

is only a vehicle for causing us to deliberate on virtues and vices. The object itself does not necessarily have any inherent moral significance in itself or value to us. The creature is valued for its influence, not for the inherent virtue of being a creature. Hume summarizes this point in his *Treatise of Human Nature* when he writes:

> I may venture to affirm the rest of mankind, that they are nothing but a bundle or collection of different perceptions, which succeed each other with an inconceivable rapidity, and are in a perpetual flux and movement. . . . There is properly no simplicity in it at one time, nor identity in different; whatever natural propension we may have to imagine that simplicity and identity. . . . They are the successive perceptions only, that constitute the mind; nor have we the most distant notion of the place, where these scenes are represented, or of the materials, of which it is composed.[63]

In this empiricist view, there is no actual moral epistemology to be perceived, there are only moral judgements to be made about the way we feel about sensory input from the presence of other creatures. Hume took this approach because he was trying to combat the Cartesian notion that there were objective truths that were rationally self-evident. Against rationalism, Hume states that he has:

> objected to the system, which establishes eternal rational measures of right and wrong, that 'tis impossible to shew, in the actions of reasonable creatures, any relations, which are not found in external objects; and therefore, if morality always attended these relations, 'twere possible for inanimate matter to become virtuous or vicious.[64]

In critiquing the Cartesian rationalist moral theory, Hume extends his empiricist theory to its logical conclusion. There can be no objective morality because if there were, then he would have to concede that even inanimate creatures had moral significance.

Of course, thoroughgoing empiricism and rationalism both collapse into the same idea. Both theories are concerned with how a human being comes to "know" herself and make moral judgements, and so they compete

---

also a fine discussion of the bundle theory in it's larger philosophical context in Miller, *Topics in Early Modern Philosophy*. As well, there is a fine treatment of this theory from the context which begins with the epistemological transition from scholasticism to Cartesian thought in the early modern period in Thiel, *Early Modern Subject*.

63. Hume, *Treatise of Human Nature*, 188.
64. Hume, *Moral Philosophy*, 78.

over the degree to which our moral knowledge is the result of our physical interaction, or our rational thought. For different reasons, both theories fundamentally ignore the moral significance of the object that we perceive. Here we see the single greatest contradistinction between Traherne's moral theory and the two dominant moral theories which were developing in his lifetime. Traherne based his moral theory on the fact that all creatures, animate and inanimate were replete with moral significance because they all necessarily communicate the natural goodness that is the effect of the Creator's Divine goodness in action. In his theistic moral theory, moral epistemology is perceivable because each creature we encounter is morally significant.

Against empericism, Traherne affirms that there is moral knowledge to be perceived from creatures which have inherent, objective value. And against rationalism he affirms that the actual body of human, moral beings must be in some real communion with those other morally significant objects in order to perceive its fullness. The perception of moral epistemology is a social experience. Moral beings, both humans and non-human creatures, are social beings, neither purely rational nor selfish. As a human being, it is your glory that you must "go out of yourself" to perceive moral goodness.

Perceiving the Moral Significance of Creatures

Traherne's theory displays a great deal of prescience regarding the impoverished consequences of the epistemological split that was occurring within his lifetime. The split between Descartes and Hobbes became a gulf between the Hume and Kant. We currently live in an age that is attempting to bridge this epistemological divide and return to an awareness of the moral unity and richness that exists between sensibility and rationality. The philosophical discipline of phenomenology grew in large part as a response to the bifurcated view of moral epistemology, and human perception.

Operating on our side of the epistemological divide, Maurice Merleau-Ponty prefaces his book *Phemonology of Perception* with simple claims about the insufficiency of scientific empiricism and rationalism. He recognizes that "science," meaning the knowledge of myself and the world, is not simply

> the outcome of the meeting-point of numerous causal agencies which determine my bodily or psychological make-up. I cannot conceive myself as nothing but a bit of the world, a mere object of biological, psychological or sociological investigation. I cannot shut myself up within the realm of science. All my knowledge of

the world, even my scientific knowledge, is gained from my own particular point of view, or from some experience of the world without which the symbols of science would be meaningless.[65]

Our agency and our identity as beings is defined by more than a "bundle" of senses, because we always already interpret our perception of sense data with "symbols" that are based on our situation in relationship to the world that we are interpreting. Merleau-Ponty reminds us that:

> Scientific points of view (*Les vues scientifiques*), according to which my existence is a moment of the world's, are always both naïve and at the same time dishonest, because they take for granted, without explicitly mentioning it, the other point of view, namely that of consciousness, through which from the outset a world forms itself round me and begins to exist for me. To return to things themselves is to return to that world which precedes knowledge, of which knowledge always speaks (*la connaissance parle toujours*), and in relation to which every scientific schematization is an abstract and derivative sign-language, as is geography in relation to the country-side in which we have learnt beforehand what a forest, a prairie or a river is.[66]

Here he identifies a fundamental flaw in empirical philosophy. Sentient, moral beings always approach nature consciously. We do not simply respond to sense data, because as sentient, moral beings we receive and interpret that data "for me." Empiricism is naïve because it overvalues the data itself, and denies the complexities and contingencies of the relationship to the one who is actually perceiving nature.

However, on the opposite side of the epistemological divide, Merleau-Ponty feels the rationalists overestimate the role of consciousness in their epistemological theory. In the rationalist perspective, which was epitomized in Traherne's lifetime by Descartes and later expanded by Kant, the mind, or the *cogito* is the location of perception. The rational idealists, or "intellectualists" (*l'intellectualiste*) as Merleau-Ponty often calls them, suggest that we only know something to be true if we experience ourselves as consciously perceiving the knowledge.[67] When you are consciously aware of your own existence as a being, then you "know" that you exist. Only by an act of consciousness can we truly "know" that any being exists at all. So, the world

---

65. Merleau-Ponty, *Phenomenology of Perception*, ix. The French original is found in Merleau-Ponty, *Phenomenologie de La Perception*, 9.

66. Merleau-Ponty, *Phenomenology of Perception*, ix.

67. Merleau-Ponty, *Phenomenology of Perception*, x.

must be recreated in the mind before we can ever "know" it. Merleau-Ponty summarizes it this way:

> Analytical reflection starts from our experience of the world and goes back to the subject as to a condition of possibility distinct from that experience, revealing the all-embracing synthesis as that without which there would be no world. To this extent it ceases to remain part of our experience and offers, in place of an account, a reconstruction.[68]

In this rationalist scheme, knowledge of the world is the product of that analytical reflection that happens at a distance from the influences of our sensory experience. Our mental conception of the world can be done apart from our embodied experience of it, and without our mental reconstitution of the world, we can not know that it exists. Merleau-Ponty demonstrates that this kind of analytical reflection "believes that it can trace back the course followed by a prior constituting act and arrive, in the 'inner man'—to use Saint Augustine's expression—at a constituting power which has always been identical with that inner self. Thus reflection is carried off by itself and installs itself in an impregnable subjectivity, as yet untouched by being and time."[69] Epistemological knowledge, and therefore moral knowledge, is discontinuous with our corporal nature.

Rationalists believe that our cognitive analysis, or "noetic analysis" as Husserl named it, has the power to constitute our knowledge of reality.[70] If knowledge depends on our "noetic" construction of reality, then natural phenomena, non-human animals and their environment for instance, are morally insignificant. There is nothing to be learned from our physical relationship to other beings that we can't construct in the recesses of our inner mind.[71] In this analytical scheme, phenomenal beings have no inherent moral agency, being, or value until we rationally determine their importance to us. By participating in the One, Platonic *Nous*, our noetic "cogito" decides what beings are morally significant and therefore we determine what relationships are universally, epistemologically significant.[72]

68. Merleau-Ponty, *Phenomenology of Perception*, x.

69. Merleau-Ponty, *Phenomenology of Perception*, xi.

70. Merleau-Ponty rightly points out that Husserl struggled with the concept well into his late years, but adopts it and deploys it in his own critique of rationalism. See Merleau-Ponty, *Phenomenology of Perception*, xiii.

71. Merleau-Ponty, *Phenomenology of Perception*, xiii.

72. Kant would extend this notion to suggest that we can only know something to be morally significant if it can be classified as a categorically imperative, meaning, that knowledge can be universally applied to all situations. This is best demonstrated in chapter 2 of Kant, *Groundwork of the Metaphysic of Morals*, 49–79.

The problem with this noetic scheme is that other creatures really do exist whether or not we think of them as existing. "The real is a closely woven fabric" of beings in time which is "the natural setting of, and field for, all my thoughts and all my explicit perceptions."[73] For phenomenologists such as Merleau-Ponty, the rational causality does not make sense. It is not our thoughts that constitute reality, rather, the real, natural "fabric" of being in which we live is the phenomenal field that we perceive. He says succinctly "The world is there before any possible analysis of mine."[74]

His succinct response covers a significant concept that even Husserl struggled to fully articulate. He believed that any attempt to limit the perceptual parameters of epistemology commits a fatal problem called the phenomenological reduction.[75] Merleau-Ponty summarized the phenomenological reduction as follows. "Sensationalism [or empiricism] 'reduces' the world by noting that after all we never experience anything but states of ourselves. Transcendental idealism too 'reduces' the world . . . by regarding it as thought or consciousness of the world, and as the mere correlative of our knowledge."[76] The result of empirical limits placed on our sensibility and rational limits placed on the epistemological value of the real world is that:

> we miss once more the basic operation which infuses meaning (*sens*) into the sensible, and which is taken for granted by any logical mediation or any psychological causality. The result is that intellectualist analysis eventually makes nonsense of the perceptual phenomena which it is designed to elucidate[77]

Merleau-Ponty is making the point that knowledge of the real world is neither subjectively empirical nor purely rational. Our mind and our senses work together to perceive and interpret the vast amounts of moral epistemology that is communicated from within the intersubjective relationships that occur between ourselves and other objects situated within an entire phenomenal field. That is how the mind makes sense (*sens*) of the world. Also, that is the way in which we make moral judgements regarding what we perceive in the world around us.

In Merleau-Ponty's mind, "The true *Cogito*" does not derive knowledge of itself and the world from its own thoughts about the world. Rather, "On

---

73. Merleau-Ponty, *Phenomenology of Perception*, xii.
74. Merleau-Ponty, *Phenomenology of Perception*, x.
75. Merleau-Ponty, *Phenomenology of Perception*, x.
76. Merleau-Ponty, *Phenomenology of Perception*, xvii.
77. Merleau-Ponty, *Phenomenology of Perception*, 39.

the contrary it recognizes my thought itself as an inalienable fact, and does away with any kind of idealism in revealing me as 'being-in-the-world.'"[78] He does not deny the importance of our rationality in perceiving that moral knowledge, he simply suggests that our rational mind must be embodied in our phenomenal environment. The "cogitatio . . . is not without place in the phenomenological world. The world, which I distinguish from myself as the totality of things or of processes linked by causal relationships I rediscover 'in me' . . . as a dimension in relationship to which I am constantly situating myself."[79] The reflection of a "Cogito" that truly perceives reality will necessarily "reveal me in a situation" that includes other creatures and the landscape.[80] Merleau-Ponty suggests we must "be-in-the-world" (*être-au-monde*), or "for the world" (*pour le monde*) to perceive our full identity as creatures. Here we see the strong connection to Traherne's concept that we must retire into the natural world to discover our true glory as creatures. For Merleau-Ponty, as it is for Traherne, we can go "to the world" to "know."

We must be in the world in order to perceive the knowledge that the world communicates to us by our senses. If we retreat into the solitude of our minds, we do not fully make "sense" of our place in it. That is what Merleu-Ponty means when he writes that being "drawn away from reflection" causes us to "miss once more the basic operation which infuses meaning (*sens*) into the sensible."[81] As opposed to a "noetic analysis," which does not necessarily include the "basic operation" of our senses, Husserl suggested the full perception of our relationship to the world among which we are situated happens by a process of "noematic reflection."[82] Merleau-Ponty employs contemporary psychology to expand Husserl's theory and begins to describe how we perceive information about the natural world around us.[83] Merleau-Ponty posits that we are constantly inundated with non-reflective experiences from our natural phenomenal field. We constantly perceive knowledge that is communicated by our natural environment and creatures in it. Our body does not wait for a rational judgement before we really begin to "make sense" their presence or communication. The phenomenal reality outside of yourself communicates significant knowledge about the nature of your relationship to that reality. Creatures are not only inherently morally significant, but their presence in our phenomenal field is epistemologically

---

78. Merleau-Ponty, *Phenomenology of Perception*, xiv.
79. Merleau-Ponty, *Phenomenology of Perception*, xiv.
80. Merleau-Ponty, *Phenomenology of Perception*, xiv.
81. Merleau-Ponty, *Phenomenology of Perception*, 39.
82. Merleau-Ponty, *Phenomenology of Perception*, x.
83. Merleau-Ponty, *Phenomenology of Perception*, ix, 198n18.

significant. A human being can perceive her identity as a thinking, judging, active being within that field of significant relationships with other creatures.

By reconnecting sense and sensibility that were being disassociated in the time of Hobbes and Descartes, phenomenologists were trying to overcome the reduction of both beings and knowledge. By acknowledging the epistemological importance of our relationship to other creatures, every being and relationship becomes inherently morally significant. Human beings need to consider the morally significant nature of our natural, biological, sensual, and spatial relationship to other creatures if we are to ever "know" them, and our identity among them. Being-in-the-world is the posture by which we can more fully perceive knowledge about the world and our identity as a creature who is related to it. Because moral formation begins before cognitive exercises, even young children participate in this morally significant "noematic reflection" because it is a social, sensory experience of being-in-their-world.

Merleau-Ponty says that phenomenology is not so much a new philosophy, as much as it describes what we have always known about ourselves, and "Realizing what we have been waiting for."[84] His contribution from our side of the epistemological divide brings Thomas Traherne's warnings of the same divide into sharp focus. Traherne saw the epistemological divide in its conception, and was offering a similar critique from the other side of the epistemological divide. He experienced an education that was beginning to embrace the epistemological bifurcation. Against the reduction of creation as well as our native ability to make moral sense of the perceptions that we receive through our communion-in-creation, he counsels:

> By an Act of the understanding therefore be present now with all the creatures among which you live; and hear them in their beings and operations praising God in an heavenly manner. Some of them vocally, others in their ministry all of them naturally and continually. We infinitely wrong ourselves by laziness and confinement. . . . You are never what you ought till you go out of yourself and walk among them.[85]

Having realized the epistemological significance of Traherne's position from Merleau-Ponty's vantage point, we now return to this critical passage that frames Traherne's theory of "retirednes." Traherne shares the same notion that human beings should be present to the natural creatures among which they live. Being-in-the-world allows human beings to "hear them in their

---

84. See Merleau-Ponty, *Phenomenology of Perception*, viii, 246.
85. Traherne, *Centuries, Poems, and Thanksgivings*, 1:94.

beings and operations praising God." This kind of perception is morally significant. Until we perceive this "naturally and continually" communicated knowledge, we will not fully become living, moral beings who exist between ants and angels. This kind of retirement cannot happen in the "confinement" of our minds, nor in the "laziness" of mere observation of scientific or social utility. Like Merleau-Ponty, Traherne is quite clear that in order to know creatures and God's will for human being-in-creation, you "ought" to "go out of yourself and walk among them."

Natural "Rules" of Perception Begin with Our Social Nature

Traherne affirms that we can not realize our fully human identity if we maintain a sterile scientific or cognitive distance from other creatures. Merleau-Ponty arrived at his similar conclusion based on the psychology of perception. Traherne's prescient defence against the Hobbesian and Cartesian disassociation of the senses is based on his theological affirmation about the nature of human perception. The way in which humans naturally perceive follows from human nature itself. "For Man is made a Sociable Creature, and is never Happy till His Capactities are filled with all their Objects, and his Inclinations have attained their proper Ends"[86] Because we are social beings, our proper ends are attained by being-in-relationship. Our social "capacity" helps us attain our formation as moral human beings. In *Inducements*, Traherne explains that social "capacity." Among the "*Treasuries* of *Humanity*" our natural social capacity is a human's natural "glory," or "power" by which we can perceive this Divine knowledge in our retirement.

> In Retirement man approacheth to his Power. . . . What is most profitable that He may do nor does any thing impose a Law upon his Actions but his Blessedness and Glory. If any one object that God's Glory is the End and Scope of his Actions, and is therfore his Law, the Answer is, that as God and He so the Glory of God and his Blessedness are united. Neither doth the Glory of God require any thing of him, but that which is Supremely conducive to his own.[87]

God's "Glory" is "Supremely conducive to" the glory of the human being. Just as there is a symmetry between our human nature and our natural

---

86. Traherne, *Inducements to Retirednes*, 11–12. I have already demonstrated the way in which Traherne's view of human nature as social is a rebuke of Hobbes. See chapter 2 of this volume.

87. Traherne, *Inducements to Retirednes*, 22.

perception, there is a necessary symmetry between God's will for creation (here Divine "Law") and the nature of our creation. There must be a symmetry or a continuity between God's creative grace and our created nature. As a natural part of creation, human beings have the "capacity" to perceive the way creation naturally communicates God's Glory.

In order to describe that innate, perceptive capacity by which we perceive knowledge of the Creator by being-in-creation, Traherne looks to a human who engaged creation for the first time as a stranger, or as a child. He spends a great deal of poetic and prosaic space delineating the principles of human nature by which Adam first perceived knowledge of creation.

In *Inducements*, Traherne outlines those parameters according to three "Rules" by which Adam knew.[88] The rules are: 1) his principles, 2) his Interest, and 3) his Objects.[89] "Principles" refers to his human nature. These are the principles by which he operates as a creature. By "Interest" Traherne means "the Relation of his Nature to the object on which he thinketh."[90] The "object" is simply the creature that he is associating with. Subsequent chapters will explore the second and third point, Interest and Objects respectively. The remainder of this chapter will focus on the first of these three "Rules" for retirement, Adam's principles.

Adam's "Rule" of Perception: Wonder is the Natural Principle of Human Perception

The last section of *Inducements* explains the "rules" or methods of retirement. He titles this section:

> Heer are Farther Inducements to Retiredness from the Example of holy persons, and the Felicity of living in Communion with them and the possibility by devine Assistance to Enjoy all Glorious Objects as devinly, at least as desirously and sweetly as they did.[91]

Through retirement, we can be among the "Glorious Objects" of creation in the same way as "holy persons." The "rules" by which these holy persons perceived communion are yet available to us.

> What Adam did in Paradice, What Moses in the Wilderness, what Elijah at the Brook Cherith, while he tarried there so long,

---

88. Traherne, *Inducements to Retirednes*, 30.
89. Traherne, *Inducements to Retirednes*, 30.
90. Traherne, *Inducements to Retirednes*, 30.
91. Traherne, *Inducements to Retirednes*, 29.

> few can imagine. Yet are there certain Rules wherby we can discern their most Secret and hidden Thoughts, and have Communion with them in all their Solitudes. When Jesus was in the Wilderness, and John the Divine in Patmos, neither of them was alone.[92]

Those who engage their "capacity" to retire among creation know that they are not alone because they naturally participate in communion among creation. Traherne acknowledges that Adam's "Conscience did intimat and feel a Dietie," which was "the Donor" of that intimation.[93] He is "certain that Adam when his Eys were first Opened was taken with a Surprize, to see a World so New, so Divine and Glorious."[94] Because Adam was new to the world, a "stranger" in Traherne's terminology, Adam must have felt an inspiring sense of novelty as he perceived creation for the first time. In a state of innocence, Adam must have apprehended knowledge before he "swerv[ed] from the Principles of a Righteous Nature." Traherne agrees that the thought of being able to "Disclose Adams first Imagination" seems "*Arrogant*." And indeed it would be if he suggested we could know what it was like to apprehend creation before the fall. He explains this point in a marginal gloss:

> It would appear Arrogant and were indeed soe: if we should pretend a minute, Exact, knowledge of Adams Imaginations: but by our owne Souls we can [feel?] his Sentiments soe fare as we can make True Apprehensions of him and of all those Objects present unto him in such an Instantaneous manner as they were.[95]

Traherne's marginal gloss acknowledges that the "Apprehensions of Men of soe different Conditions as we are now by Corruption from Adam in Innocency"[96] are surely different. However, the natural methods by which we perceive are yet the same. The purity of the apprehension is not as important as the fact that naked sensory perception is a morally significant principle by which human beings perceive knowledge. Our human ability to feel "his Sentiments" and "True Apprehensions of him and of all those Objects present to him in such an Instantaneous manner as they were" is the

---

92. Traherne, *Inducements to Retirednes*, 28.
93. Traherne, *Inducements to Retirednes*, 31.
94. Traherne, *Inducements to Retirednes*, 31.
95. This marginal gloss is referenced in Traherne, *Inducements to Retirednes*, 28n44.
96. This quote is taken from the marginal gloss recored by Jan Ross in Traherne, *Inducements to Retirednes*, 30n46.

same. Our perception created objects is not as Adam did before the fall, but as Adam, Moses, Elijah, Jesus and John all did after the fall.

In *Kingdom*, he made the case that we "feel" these "Sentiments" through our senses as human beings have been blessed to do in our fallen state, unlike the rational Angels or Adam in his first state.[97] He theorized that we are in a better state since the fall for being able to experience joy through our sensory apprehensions. In *Inducements*, he recapitulates that belief that since the fall, we have been given an "Addition of mercies."[98] Our knowledge now is not speculative, or merely rational as the angels, but a whole, unified knowledge of the value of the object.[99] By using our senses, he estimates that we are in a better position after the fall to apprehend the joy of that knowledge that is communicated by created objects. Sensory perception is not a human limitation, but rather an addition of God's mercy that is bequeathed by the nature of our creation. As part of our identity, we can perceive creation's "noematic" influences, transpirations and reflections by engaging our senses as a "stranger," or as a child, would first encounter creation and other creatures. It is a principle of our human nature that the novelty of discovery creates that sense of wonder that Adam had when he first experienced creation, as a "stranger," or a child.

In *Inducements*, Traherne deploys a mixture of Imagination, Amazement, Joy and Reverence to describe our sensory apprehension of creatures. Among this list, he names Wonder as a significant way of apprehending creation's communication.

> when he first waked out of his Dust, and saw so Magnificent a Frame, as that of Nature is, to entertain Him; his first Thought was a Mixture of Amazement, Wonder, Joy and Reverence, to see Him self Exalted by the Dietie to such a Great Dominion in a World so Glorious.[100]

Wonder, as a state independent from our state of righteousness, is an impulse of our living, moral, human nature. By appealing to wonder as a means of perceiving knowledge in retirement, Traherne was asking his readers to go beyond, or possibly behind, a mere cognitive epistemology, and engage in a relational form of embodied knowing. If we are going to truly "know," we must enter into society with the natural order in the way that Adam first did; as a stranger who would see the world for the first time, with true wonder

---

97. For a full discussion of this topic, see chapter 2.
98. Traherne, *Inducements to Retirednes*, 31.
99. Traherne, *Inducements to Retirednes*, 32.
100. Traherne, *Inducements to Retirednes*, 29.

that employed all facets of their perception. This is what it means to become as a child. He does not believe that children are able to perceive the communication of God's grace because they are pure. Children utilize the natural means of instantaneous perception that is built into our human nature. That is, they, like Adam, are full of wonder. Among the Margoliouth sequence, Traherne's poem "Salutation" equates Adam's first wondrous perception of creation after rising from the dust with a child's first experiences after birth. Through the treasury of his senses, the newborn perceives creation for the first time:

<pre>
                    1
             These little Limmes,
       These Eys and Hands which here I find,
       These rosie Cheeks wherwith my Life begins,
             Where have ye been,? Behind
         What Curtain were ye from me hid so long!

                    2
              When silent I,
          So many thousand thousand yeers,
          Beneath the Dust did in a Chaos lie,
              How could I Smiles or Tears,
         Or Lips or Hands or Eys or Ears perceiv?
            Welcom ye Treasures which I now receiv

                    3
             I that so long
          Was Nothing from Eternitie,
      Did little think such Joys as Ear or Tongue,
              To Celebrat or See:
   Such Sounds to hear, such Hands to feel, such Feet,
      Beneath the Skies, on such a Ground to meet . . .

                    5
              From Dust I rise,
          And out of Nothing now awake,
      These Brighter Regions which salute mine Eys,
              A Gift from GOD I take.
    The Earth, the Seas, the Light, the Day, the Skies,
       The Sun and Stars are mine; if those I prize . . .

                    7
              A Stranger here
       Strange Things doth meet, Strange Glories See;
      Strange Treasures lodg'd in this fair World appear,
              Strange all, and new to me . . .
</pre>

Out of the dust of birth, Thomas engages the world as a stranger would. Just as Adam did, he praises the fact that he can perceive this world through his sensibilities. He specifically calls this means of perception "wonder" in his poem entitled "Wonder." Referring to his first childhood engagement with the world, he writes:

> How like an Angel came I down!
> How Bright are all Things here!
> When first among his Works I did appearance
> O how their GLORY me did Crown?
> The World resembled his Eternitie,
> In which my Soul did Walk;
> And evry Thing that I did see,
> Did with me talk.[101]

Traherne is sure that by curiously and physically entering into close society with other creatures, the child is able to sense the Influences of their exhalations, and communications. The natural world actually "talks" to the child. Nature was his tutor through the "noematic" manner in which "The Skies," the "Lovely Air," and even "The Stars did entertain my Sense." In this Adamic, which is to say wondrous, state of sensory engagement, he remembers:

> A Native Health and Innocence
> Within my Bones did grow,
> And while my GOD did all his Glories shew,
> I felt a Vigour in my Sence
> That was all SPIRIT. I within did flow
> With Seas of Life, like Wine;
> I nothing in the World did know,
> But 'twas Divine.

Here we can see that Traherne describes the sense of wonder that resonates in his "Bones." DeNeef proposed a working definition of wonder which closely relates to this use. "Wonder, here, is 'mysterious,' but because it can be felt in the vibrating, resonating, echoing saying of language, it is heard as a harmony, a singing."[102] The influence that created objects have upon one another through transpiration and exhalation is a kind of resonance of light, particles, and moisture that communicate "vital spirits." The perception of

---

101. These are the words from version D in Margoliouth's volume. However, the only difference in this stanza between the two versions is the inversion of "me did" in the fourth line. See volume 2 of Traherne, *Centuries, Poems, and Thanksgivings*.

102. DeNeef, *Traherne in Dialogue*, 55. DeNeef's theory, however, is based on the resonances that originate in the experience of verbal communication. Traherne is sure that imagination comes from the real experiences of communion, not vice versa.

this kind of resonance is what Traherne has in mind when he speaks of the way that the holy ones "feel" the "Sentiments" of creatures. This seems to be a good working definition for Traherne's concept of wonder, and is summarized beautifully in the following quote:

> Therefore hath God created living ones, that by lively motions, and sensible desires, we might be sensible of a Deity. They breathe, they see, they feel, they grow, they flourish, they know, they love. O what a world of evidences! We are lost in abysses, we now are absorpt in wonders, and swallowed up of demonstrations. Beasts, fowls, and fishes teaching and evidencing the glory of their creator. But these by an endless generation might succeed each other from everlasting. Let us therefore survey their order, and see by that whether we cannot discern their governor.[103]

By sensing the "lively motions" we can "be sensible of a Deity." Traherne proposes that we can "discern" the glory of God by surveying creation, retiring into creation in order to perceive this kind of knowledge. We can be "swallowed up" in the "demonstrations" of these "wonders." Traherne suggests this is the consistent method by which he "felt a Vigour in my Sence." When he retired into creation, his "bones" resonated with the "flow" of creation's communication.

In the process of describing the role that wonder plays in developing a spirituality of attentiveness, Esther De Waal briefly considers Traherne's earlier known writings.[104] She describes his concept of wonder as a kind of unifying force that allows us to be "happy with my relationship to myself, to my own inwardness, and also to my own outwardness."[105] Rather than excluding the self as is the case with the gaze of scientific observation or retreating into the internal self as is the case with rationalism, "wonder" is the connection between the inward and the outward. Because of this unity, the concept of "wonder" holds a great deal of possibility for interpreting Traherne's moral theory. Traherne was presciently warning against that bifurcation of knowledge that would eventually displace moral epistemology from the sciences.[106] Based on that fact, I believe De Waal is correct in suggesting that Traherne understood that wonder was not a faculty that

---

103. Traherne, *Centuries, Poems, and Thanksgivings*, 1:70 (emphasis added).

104. de Waal, *Lost in Wonder*. I will explore the notion of attentiveness and its role in perception in chapter 6 of the current study.

105. de Waal, *Lost in Wonder*, 31.

106. Mark Allen McIntosh explores themes similar to this in McIntosh, *Discernment and Truth*.

directed our gaze from bodily perception towards an internalized mental exercise. Wonder is that faculty of human nature which holds together the internal and the external, the sensory and the cognitive, the physical world and the spiritual in a unified moment of perception. This kind of wonder is the concept with which Traherne holds together our outward, sensory process of experiencing the communication of the object's vital spirits, and the inward process of contemplating, or "knowing" the object.

By engaging creation as Adam did, human beings can perceive a moral epistemology which is woven into the real fabric of creation. The perception of this knowledge helps us to achieve the "glory" of our creation. As a critical part of Traherne's moral theory, "Wonder" describes an embodied way of "knowing" which utilizes our natural human principles. Because wonder is a "principle" of perception that is natural to our human nature, it is a "principle" childhood. Traherne summarizes this sentiment in his poem, "Innocence."

> What ere it it, it is a Light
> So Endless unto me
> That I a World of true Delight
> Did then and to this Day do see.
> 5
> That Prospect was the Gate of Heav'n, that Day
> The anchient Light of Eden did convey
> Into my Soul: I was an Adam there,
> A little Adam in a Sphere . . .
> An Antepast of heaven sure!
> I on the Earth did reign.
> Within, without me, all was pure.
> I must becom a Child again.[107]

For Traherne, as with Merleau-Ponty, moral epistemology has a social nature that can be discerned from "without." Traherne believes that we are, by nature, social beings, and we are naturally equipped to perceive creation's natural communication of this kind of knowledge. A child's wondrous ability to perceive the kind of moral epistemology that circulates through creation is the reason that he believes the child is a philosopher *par excellence*. To become a child again is to embrace the glory of being fully human. Now we can more fully understand the reason that he believes Christ's word about becoming a little child and retiring among God's works:

> is deeper than is generally believed. It is not only in a careless reliance upon Divine Providence, that we are to become little

---

107. Traherne, *Centuries, Poems, and Thanksgivings*, 2:18.

children, or in the feebleness and shortness of our anger and simplicity of our passions, but in the peace and purity of all our soul. . . . So these things would appear to us only which do to children when they are first born. . . . God in His works, Glory in the light, Love in our parents, men, ourselves, and the face of Heaven: Every man naturally seeing those things, to the enjoyment of which he is naturally born.[108]

Wonder as Perception

Many child psychologists and attachment theorists have been recently interested in wonder as an innate aspect of human perception. Colwyn Trevarthen has studied the extent to which children have the natural ability to perceive communication of other beings, and the extent to which their perception is psychologically and morally proformative. Trevarthen asks:

> How do human beings know each other? For an empiricist, this is a question about how we take up, remember, and make sense of experience—how we get physical (nonmental) information about what other persons are and what they do. In order to answer this question, however, we must also consider the processes that make a person want to know other persons. What motivates communication? What are the active communication-seeking functions that give each one of us personal qualities that others seek to perceive? We have to entertain the idea that such other-seeking and other- satisfying properties of the mind could be innate, anticipating experience of others and promoting further communication with them.[109]

He identifies the epistemological question that lies at the heart of empiricism, rationalism, and more recently phenomenology. How do we get physical (nonmental) information about other beings and what they do? This is the kind of noematic communication with nature that Traherne is trying to comprehend in his moral theory. But Trevarthen, like many contemporary psychologists understand that this is not a simple question of empiricism versus rationalism. He knows that it is also a question of motivation. Resembling Traherne's anthropological rationale that our perception of "knowledge" about other creatures is a product of our social nature, Trevarthen suggests that empiricists and rationalists alike must consider that

---

108. Traherne, *Centuries, Poems, and Thanksgivings*, 1:113.
109. Trevarthen, "Self Born in Intersubjectivity," 121.

the "other-seeking," "other-satisfying" ability to experience communication with other beings is an innate part of our human nature.

In order to understand this innately social orientation, Trevarthen has studied the "perceptual equivalences" and the "preferential orientations" of newborn babies. "Perceptual equivalences" refers to the cognitive symmetry that is generated by different physical stimuli. For example, we can read the letter "a," or we can also feel the shape of the letter "a" in the sand. Both stimuli cause us to perceive an "a."[110] "Preferential orientations" refers to the question of motivation. For instance, given the option to look at a person with an angry face or a person with a happy face, the infant will generally orient their gaze and attention towards the happy person, thereby showing an orientation towards perceiving certain types of phenomenon.[111] By studying these basic perceptual phenomena, Trevarthen has demonstrated that in the "proto-conversation" through which babies engage their surroundings, there is an innate motivation to respond to physical interactions with other beings and objects. Psychologists have long been aware that infants of all species engage in proto-conversations. But, Trevarthen's research shows that human babies engage in a kind of conversation that exceeds that of "animalistic" interactions, which is to say, proto-conversations go beyond acquiring basic bodily needs.[112] Against other well known behavioralist and cognitivist theories, such as that of Kenneth Kaye,[113] Trevarthen demonstrates that there is an innate quality to the human baby's ability to engage in these complex interactions.

> In short, there is an anatomical-physiological basis in the brain for the endogenous coordination that holds together all of a subject's behaviors and perceptions at any given moment. . . . The basic integrity and form of motives is created in the developing central nervous system before it becomes the receiver of input

---

110. Trevarthen, "Self Born in Intersubjectivity," 134.

111. Trevarthen, "Self Born in Intersubjectivity," 134.

112. Of course, the work of anthropologists such as Frans de Waal and others demonstrates that other species demonstrate that this is not a species specific argument. Other animals engage in proto-conversations that go beyond their "animalistic" needs. See de Waal, *Good Natured*.

113. Kaye, *Mental and Social Life*. Psychologist Kenneth Kaye has documented and observed this maternal/infant matrix through analysis of nursing. He describes the act of nursing as communication. Kaye observes how the human act of nursing is actually an intricate "conversation" in which children first build their sense of identification with the other. Kaye's theory differs from Trevarthen's in that Kaye's is built on a behavioralist model. That is, behaviors must be conditioned, socially or cognitively. This leaves a question regarding the innate nature of these proto-conversations, and exactly what is the root cause of these behaviors.

from the body and outside environment. It does not have to be constructed in the infant after birth by "mutual assimilation" or conditioning of reflex systems generated separately, as Piaget believed—though such processes of accretion and selection play an essential part in further differentiation and development.[114]

Babies seem innately able to perceive significant knowledge of their interaction with other beings, and respond accordingly. However, the significant point to note here is that against the ethologist, or behavioralist notions of perception, Trevarthen asserts that this innate aspect of our human nature does not require "mutual assimilation." And against the cognitivists, who are here represented by Piaget, this mode of perception does not require cognitive conditioning.

The theory to which Trevarthen refers is Piaget's concept of "centering." Piaget believes a young child is "centered" in their environment from birth, and she cannot distinguish between herself and nature around her. This is the "figurative" stage of thought in which Piaget believes the child only responds to physical perceptions that personally affect her. Piaget believes that the child does not yet have the ability to make mental or moral judgements. A child cannot make allocentric moral judgements while they are in this "egocentric" stage. They must cognitively mature before they can perceive their moral relationship to others. Piaget suggests that a child must first "decenter" themselves, or differentiate themselves as an individual from their environment before they can make moral judgements.[115] In this cognitivist mode, a child must achieve a state of cognitive distance from their environment before they can truly know, or make a moral decision.[116] The radical assumption of this kind of constructivism is that a child's moral development is dis-continuous with the child's nature. Children must overcome their nature and embodied location in order to make cognitive moral judgements.

Trevarthen agrees with Piaget's point that cognitive development certainly assists in the child's ability to make moral judgements as they mature,

---

114. Trevarthen, "Self Born in Intersubjectivity," 125.

115. Jean Piaget writes: "Signs begin by being part of things or by being suggested by the presence of things in the manner of simple conditioned reflexes. Later, they end by becoming detached from things and disengaged from them by the exercise of intelligence which uses them as adaptable and infinitely plastic tools" (Piaget, *Child's Conception of the World*, 161).

116. For Piaget, this decentering does not occur through "direct intuition but from an intellectual construction," which causes a "dissociation of the contents from primitive consciousness" (Piaget, *Child's Conception of the World*, 129). This "primitive consciousness" is not, for Piaget, the same as moral awareness of the self.

and that high levels of moral reasoning can certainly benefit from cognitive distance. But he opposes the major lacuna underlying the assumption that a "figurative," or "pre-conventional" child is not already engaged in significant moral reasoning based on the way their perception of their environment affects their behavior. Against the notion that children must first be cognitively mature to make sense of empirical interactions, Trevarthen argues that:

> We are adapted, in our bodies and how we move, to make use of the properties of the environment as *affordances* for action in the near future. And, since we must exchange matter with the environment to stay alive, we appreciate the beneficial or noxious properties of objects or substances that may be taken in, or that are to be rejected. We feel and care about what is going to happen when we act, with emotional values that, as Jaak Panksepp explains, are not subservient to reason, or language.[117]

Trevarthen argues that current research suggests the opposite causality, and that moral reasoning is related to a child's nature and embodied location. In a child who does not present a pathological condition that prevents this fundamental activity, the anatomical-physiological parameters for holding together perception and moral behavior are naturally in place from birth. A child's ability to learn via our body's embeddedness within the environment is a natural "affordance."[118] Based on his study of perceptual equivalences, Trevarthen suggests "It is probable that cognitive dynamics and the chronometrics of awareness and thinking in active behavioral engagement with the environment are coincident with motive dynamics—that is, behaving and perceiving are generated in the same core motivating system of the brain."[119] Of course, the quality of the behavioral response evolves over time with differentiation and interaction with other beings in the environment. But his claim that "an anatomical-physiological basis" for perception is intact "before it becomes the receiver of input from the body and outside environment" is significant for our point. We naturally "feel and care about" the exchange of matter between beings, and appreciate our natural commerce with the environment.

Trevarthen goes on to suggest that this preferential capacity to appreciate these natural affordances is the reason that children perceive the

---

117. Trevarthen, "Innate Moral Feelings."

118. The relationship between peception, motor development, and the Perception-Action loop that is based on these affordances is described in Damon et al., *Handbook of Child Psychology*, 163.

119. Trevarthen, "Self Born in Intersubjectivity," 156.

various layers of communication that contribute to their accumulation of knowledge about the other beings that they encounter. He writes:

> Everyday conversational discourse is not held together by cognitively tidy grammatical rules or abstract theoretical explanations but by empathic cooperation of an immediately persuasive, "phatic" kind. Interpersonal relationships in the family and in society are certainly supported on this level of direct, intuitive, and emotional communication. Given this universal immediacy of human interpersonal understanding in communication, why should we be surprised that a young infant can experience others and their psychological activities with a well-formed readiness that requires little practice to be functional? We need not suppose that awareness of the human self in relation to the human other is constructed by reason from accumulating social experience, or built from verbally encoded concepts or theories about other persons' minds, personalities, intentions, consciousness, or beliefs.[120]

Trevarthen claims that healthy infants are capable of perceiving knowledge of other beings in their environment because a large part of communication has a "phatic" nature.[121] He cites his own studies about the communication that is transmitted through music. He describes the "intersubjective" communication of "resonant tones" that are "seeking to engage others in activity of the body and mind" and "invite the spirit of moving and breathing in body and limbs."[122] Based on the theory of Intrinsic Motive Pulse, or IMP, which has been observed in children with sensory handicaps, he attributes the communicative efficacy of music to resonances, as opposed to sight.[123] In one study, a 5 month old girl who was born blind, demonstrated an "innate sympathy" that occurred between the body of mother and daughter which demonstrated a "shared feeling about the moving that is independent . . . of how the movement is sensed."[124] These kinds of "resonances" are sensory based, and can be perceived by a direct, intuitive curiosity which all children have. "It seems these impulses of a social self with potentiality for

---

120. Trevarthen, "Self Born in Intersubjectivity," 159.

121. Trevarthen suggests that even musical interactions have the ability to transmit knowledge that leads to the fomation of sympathy in young children. See Fergusson and Dower, *Critical Perspectives*, 77–118.

122. Trevarthen, *Free Will*, 9

123. Thomas Traherne's notion of sensory handicap was the subject of Mintz, "Strange Bodies." However, by her reading, being handicapped protects the human from perceiving negative social communication.

124. Trevarthen, *Free Will*, 10

a conscience are alive early in infancy, far earlier than have been assumed by a dominant social-learning theory."[125] For this reason we should not be surprised to know that infants are ready to "experience" others before they cognitively construct categories of verbal, social conventions such as Piaget suggested.

Contrary to Piaget's causality, Trevarthen observes "the efficiency of language to transmit information about objects, intentions and judgements depends on a preceding and underlying 'mimetic' capacity for direct sympathy with states of awareness, appraisal and purpose in other individuals."[126] This underlying capacity to seek out "direct sympathy" with other individuals is a state of moral awareness that is innate in human children. This capacity allows children to co-perceive their own identity as they perceive their relationship to others. Children have the capacity to perceive their being-in-the-world in morally significant ways that respect their cognitive stage, but do not depend on developing advanced cognitive functioning.[127] This native capacity is the "capacitie" that Traherne calls "the beginning of Gifts, the first thing which God bestows to every infant, by the very right of his nativity."[128]

Wonder as the Basis of Co-Perceiving Our Moral Identity

Trevarthen's theory of the way we perceive our selves within the time and space of our environment is conceptually similar to Husserl's "noematic reflection." Our natural environment has an influence upon our ability to perceive knowledge of ourself as being-in-the-world through a "phatic" kind of communication that comes from other beings in the natural environment. However, Trevarthen mostly writes about the infant's relationship to other human beings, while Traherne mostly writes about a child's relationship to other creatures. For our purpose the question remains, can children demonstrate this kind of perception in relationship to non-human creatures? Can a child create a meaningful communion from which they are able to perceive this same kind of resonant "knowledge" in relationship to the non-human natural world, as Traherne suggests? Does being-in-the-world as

---

125. Trevarthen, *Free Will*, 11

126. Trevarthen, *Free Will*, 2.

127. Trevarthen confirms, "The rich variety of responses and initiatives observed in a detailed neonatal assessment proves this variability of potential in human nature at birth" (Trevarthen, *Free Will*, 11).

128. Traherne, *Centuries, Poems, and Thanksgivings*, 1:57.

Merleau-Ponty suggests, or retiring into creation as Traherne suggests, help us perceive significant moral knowledge of our identity in relationship to creation?

Psychologist J. J. Gibson wrote "To perceive the world is to coperceive oneself."[129] He suggests that a direct relationship exists between perception of our place in the world and moral epistemology. Reflecting on Gibson's theory of the significance of place, Marjorie Grene expanded Gibson's comment. She writes:

> Accepting [Gibson's] maxim, I want also to reverse it: To perceive oneself is, except in very peculiar circumstances, to coperceive the world. As J.J. Gibson put it some pages earlier than the statement just cited, "We were created by the world we live in."[130] Thus, to be aware of ourselves, I would say, is to be aware not only of a product of that world but also of aspects of the world that bear on its production. Self-knowledge is fundamentally and inalienably ecological, and so is the object of such knowledge.[131]

Grene believes that while Gibson is correct, the converse is equally true. Perception is not only about knowing ourselves, but perceiving knowledge about the world in which and by which we perceive. The knowledge that helps us comprehend who and what we are can be perceived from the world in which we, as a creature are located. That knowledge is "fundamentally and inalienably ecological," as is "the object of such knowledge." Place-based philosophies across many disciplines recognize that the physical environment is a crucial aspect of perception.[132] Moral knowledge of the self can not be, as Piaget conceptualized, separated from our perception of our environment. This epistemological notion is confirmed by research in embodied cognition or embodied perception.

Neuroscientist Michael Gazzaniga has researched the relationship between the visual field and the hemispheres of the brain which control various thought processes.[133] His studies confirm images that are perceived in the right visual field are processed in the left hemisphere of the brain,

---

129. Gibson, *Ecological Approach*, 149.

130. Gibson, *Ecological Approach*, 130.

131. Grene, "Primacy of the Ecological Self," 112.

132. For theological, sociological, pedagogical, and economic examples, consider Inge, *Christian Theology of Place*; Harrison, "Why Are We Here?"; Brown, *God and Enchantment of Place*; Gruenewald and Smith, *Place-based Education*; Theobald, *Teaching the Commons*.

133. His many studies and articles were compiled in Gazzaniga, *Bisected Brain*.

and vice versa. Gazzaniga has mapped pathways between stimuli in the field of perception, the activity of our nervous system, and the expression of thought. The "maps" demonstrate that the spatio/physical, even geometric, relationship between the environment and the nervous system constitutes a human/environmental matrix of perception and consciousness.[134] Gazzaniga demonstrates that in general our physical location within our environment influences our perceptual consciousness and cognition.

Psychologists Newcombe and Huttenlocher have been more precise about the extent to which spatial cognition through sight, touch and sound impact a young child's ability to make moral decisions. Piaget previously thought this mode of cognition was not possible for infants because they are in the stage of egocentric "figurativism." But new research suggests that graduated stages of spatial perception (such as being able to sit up and twist in order to see other parts of the environment, and subsequently being able to crawl towards objects within the space) elicit increasingly allocentric behaviors. As Trevarthen suggests there is a relationship between our ability to physically interact with objects in our spatial environment and our behavior. Based on this research, Newcombe and Huttenlocher suggest that there is a far more subtle and incremental relationship between the child's ability to physically perceive their environment and the development of cognitive moral responses, such as empathy, than Piaget or Kohlberg may have observed.[135] Therefore, children may not need a cognitive disassociation from their environment in order to commence moral reasoning as the cognitivists suggest. On the contrary, these studies show that children may need to be more rooted in their environment to nurture their perceptual wonder.

In his study, "Childhood Artistic Creation, and the Educated Sense of Place," Kenneth Robert Olwig agrees that a crucial component of developing an allocentric, moral sense in children is increasing their "sense of place." Against Piaget's suggestion that children cannot make moral judgements, or "philosophize" until they achieve a certain mature "decentering" from their physical environment, Olwig suggests that a child's ability to make moral judgements about their place within a physical environment is to engage in what Terence Turner calls "recentering." The formation of a young child's interdependent, allocentric, social and moral identity can and should be done in continuation with their natural, embodied ecological location. By engaging children in various environmental projects, Michael Littledyke demonstrated that a large majority of children across all age groups showed

---

134. While Gazzaniga's experiments were originally compiled in *Bisected Brain*, the experiments were expanded into a look into this relationship between sensory perception and consciousness in Gazzaniga, *Social Brain*.

135. Damon et al., *Handbook of Child Psychology*, 744.

a proportional increase in "emotive concern for caring towards aspects of their perceived environment" when they have direct access to the environment.[136] One young child reported:

> It feels like, where have all our animals gone? I always think about the animals, because I go bird watching, I have got a pair of binoculars, and every time I see a bird I think fumes go away. I am never ever going to buy something like that [a car].[137]

The child suggests direct observation of the birds is a key factor in developing empathy that leads to their belief about the relative moral influence of cars on their environment. Along with Newcombe and Huttenlocher, Littledyke concludes that the child's physiological maturation contributes to a child's empathy as much as cognitive development because it allows them to access their physical environment and widen their experience of natural phenomena.[138]

Paul Harris agrees that increasing a child's access to nature can be a source of developing moral "beliefs" such as empathy. Piaget and Kohlberg famously proposed that "beliefs" and false beliefs are informed by language and mature cognitive development when a child is able to comprehend the "other" rather than the self.[139] But Harris argues that children as young as three are capable of distinguishing between beliefs and false beliefs if they have physical access to the scenario. For instance, a young child sees a dog owner leave his dog in one place, and then the dog is moved to another place. Three year old children generally predict that the owner will return to the place in which he left his dog in order to retrieve the pet. This means that having experienced the scene, the child will take into account the perspective of the other individual when making a judgement about the other person's reaction. Based on such "unexpected displacement" experiments, Harris concludes children between the age of three and five do exercise the relationship between sensory perception, desires and belief and false-belief to make allocentric judgments.[140] Furthermore, Harris demonstrates that children between the ages of three and four know that access to various types of sensory perception is a key to obtaining consequential knowledge. In experiments where a correct outcome is dependent upon sensory perception, such as properly distinguishing between a rock and a painted

---

136. Littledyke, "Primary Children's Views on Science," 224.
137. Littledyke, "Primary Children's Views on Science," 244.
138. Littledyke, "Primary Children's Views on Science," 227.
139. Kohlberg, *Psychology of Moral Development; Philosophy of Moral Development*.
140. Damon et al., *Handbook of Child Psychology*, 825.

sponge, children will manipulate their environment in order to gain direct, sensory access to the object. This seems to be a rather obvious finding, but Harris recognizes that children naturally know that "perceptual access is a key to accurate knowledge."[141] They will seek to manipulate, or play with, their environment in order to develop their beliefs about the environment.

Many case studies have shown that increasing a child's direct physical perception of their natural environment positively affects a child's ability to articulate empathy, beauty, peaceableness and happiness through discursive interviews, art and poetry. Susan Engel illustrates the way children symbolize perceived physiognomic characteristics of the environment.[142] Children universally organize their experience of themselves in relationship to their environment into value laden information, and spontaneously reveal that meaning in art and poetry.[143] Engel acknowledges that differences between "domains of experience" render different outcomes. For instance, looking at the clouds to scientifically determine the weather develops a different "symbolic process" than describing the mood that clouds evoke. But regardless of the reason for engaging the environment, Engel concludes that a child's physical relationship to the world has clear epistemological ramifications. The expressive qualities that are communicated by even the inanimate environment "make children feel closer to, and more situated in their environment, it can expand and deepen the aspects of the environment they know about . . . and it stretches children's symbolic capacities."[144] An experiment by Janet Loeboch and Jason Gilliland demonstrated children's capacity to render their experience in morally significant symbols. They utilized a "child-led protocol" which allowed children to record their own perceptions of their local environment with cameras, and narrate their pictures without the direction of adult interpretation. Their results showed a high degree of correlation between children's sense of fear and insecurity in areas of their neighbourhood with high levels of traffic or noise, neglected, derelict or overgrown properties, as well as play-parks with rubbish or graffiti. On the other hand, high incidences of community pride, safety, beauty and belonging were associated with natural and public spaces that contain shade trees, flowers, well maintained plants and green places.[145] As Susan Engel concludes, when children engage with the physical world, they are capable

141. Damon et al., *Handbook of Child Psychology*, 826.

142. This notion of the physiognomic qualities of inanimate, natural objects follows Werner's thesis, which is presented in Werner and Franklin, *Comparative Psychology of Mental Development*.

143. Engel, *Children's Environments*, 44–45.

144. Engel, *Children's Environments*, 45

145. Loebach and Gilliland, "Child-Led Tours," 66–67, 77–78.

of deriving meaning out of their sensation of the physical characteristics of their environment.[146] A child's natural, curious wonder is part of an innate, morally significant pathway towards developing a moral framework.[147]

These case studies demonstrate that wonder is a kind of manipulation driven by curiosity. Children acquire moral knowledge through play.[148] Wonder is at the centre of the way in which a young child plays in their environment and learns about their environment. Additionally, playing in their natural environment is the way a child learns about their being-in-that environment. As shown in the child-led experience of their neighbourhood, the wonder of free play is a method by which a child can form the necessary relationships to experience matrices of care, and interpret their moral import.[149] Of course, what we now consider "free play" was simply childhood in Traherne's day. He remembers that some of his greatest moments of communion came during times of solitary play in nature and exploration of creation. He cites multiple examples of this kind of play based perception.[150] One in particular is described in his poem, "Shadows in the Water." He writes:

> In unexperienc'd Infancy
> Many a sweet Mistake doth ly:
> Mistake tho false, intending tru;
> A *Seeming* somwhat more than *View'*
> That doth instruct the Mind
> In Things that ly behind,
> And many Secrets to show
> Which afterwards we com to know.

---

146. Engel and Franklin, "Aesthetics," 3.

147. The concept that children can perceive a kind of moral epistemology from their interaction with nature is part of the *Tblisi Declaration* (1977) approach to environmental education. This notion forms the basis for the moral, aesthetic and ethical component of British environmental education curricular guidelines, which includes components of learning in and from the environment, not only learning about the environment. The Welsh curriculum summarizes the "spiritual and moral" significance of environmental education for developing "feeling and convictions about the significance of human life and the world as a whole, a sense of fairness and justice," and "understanding of: moral and ethical issues" and "codes of human behavior." Details of these curricula can be found in Palmer and Neal, *Handbook of Environmental Education*, 224.

148. This connection is also suggested by Northcott, "Place of Our Own?," 144. Northcott cites the direct correlation between the urban environment and the child's play in the urban-built environment, particularly in high poverty areas of Britain, and the moral significance of that experience.

149. Zhang, "Of Mothers and Teachers," 515; Naess, "Maturity, Adulthood, Boxing, and Play"; James et al., "From Play in Nature."

150. Several of these will be explored in subsequent chapters.

Traherne is clear about two things. First, he believes that there is a difference between what a child can know and that which an adult, "afterwards we com to know." This is consistent with the constructivist notion of moral development. However, he is also clear that in "unexperienc'd Infancy," there is a kind of knowledge that clearly is a "Seeming," more than just a "View." A child doesn't just physically see nature, those "naked" perceptual interactions are instructive. This poem recounts one such interaction with a puddle of water. As a young child of around the age of four, he was playing by the water's edge.

> Thus did I by the Water's brink
> Another World beneath me think...
> As by som Puddle I did play
> Another World within it lay.

Play led him to perceive the world from another point of view, that of a child. His perception in that period of play caused him to see his own world from another perspective. Through play, he "saw" the world for the first time from another perspective. This new mode of perception taught him something about his relationship to those "Companions" that inhabited his play. This first time, new perception of other beings is the product of Wonder:

> O ye that stand upon the Brink,
> Whom I so near me, through the Chink,
> With Wonder see: What Faces there,
> Whose Feet, whose Bodies, do ye wear?
>   I my Companions see
>   In You, another Me.

His allocentric perception of our "second Selvs" caused a discernment about the significance of those other people, animals, and tracts of land which extended below him in the puddle, who became his instructive "play-mates."

> Of all the Play-mates which I knew
> That here I do the Image view
> In other Selvs; what can it mean?

Through this "Looking-Glass" he learned to look at creatures in another way whereby he came to know the "Virtues" of "Life, Joy, Lov, Peace."[151] Through the act of wondrous play, he exercised the abiding, native "sense"

---

151. This is later expounded in the poem "Sight" (Traherne, *Centuries, Poems, and Thanksgivings*, 2:134).

that helped the child explore "The very Ground and Caus of Sacred Laws" that "God and Nature do include."[152]

Traherne reveals a two fold benefit of "play." First, the child's natural desire to manipulate the environment, or play, helps the child form a sense of identity from a different perspective, namely in relationship to other creatures.[153] Second, moments of wonder assist the child's desire to "know" the purpose of those other beings that they have perceived in relationship to themselves. Playing is the expression of the child's natural desire to gather moral knowledge of their identity in relationship to the other, which is the fundamental task for moral philosophy. This is the reason that the wondering child, for Traherne, the philosopher *par excellence*. In his book entitled *Wonder* Robert Fuller recalls that Socrates is attributed with the quote, "Wonder is the feeling of the Philosopher, and Philosophy begins with Wonder."[154] Merleau-Ponty agrees that "the first philosophical act would appear to be to return to the world of actual experience which is prior to the objective world, since it is in it that we shall be able to grasp the theoretical basis no less than the limits of that objective world, restore things to their concrete physiognomy, to organisms their individual ways of dealing with the world."[155] Children have natural and complex ways of "dealing with the world," that include the ability to utilize their senses to perceive the physiognomic significance of objects in their environment, and conceive of their moral significance. Far from being reserved for mature cognitive operations, children have "ways" of grasping the physical and theoretical moral limits of other beings through play. Gareth Matthew's ground breaking studies on the *Philosophy of Childhood* makes the connection between play and moral enquiry by suggesting "what philosophers do (in rather disciplined and sustained ways) is much closer than usually appreciated to what at least some children rather naturally do (albeit fitfully, and without

---

152. Traherne, *Centuries, Poems, and Thanksgivings*, 2:134.

153. Non-verbal communication is also a principle of childhood in the philosophy of the father of the radical ecologist movement known as "deep ecology." Arne Naess often utilizes notions of exploration and play as ways to enter into a significant relationship with nature. Naess believes that by entering into a physical nexus with creation a child's moral identity is necessarily influenced. Naess knows that "the young child's world is that which is close and easily apprehendable around him." Naess urges us to encourage our children to play, explore and climb. Naess knows that having an embodied experience of creation will lead us to form our moral identity in relationship to our knowledge of that creature. He suggests that by climbing a mountain, we may learn to "think like a mountain." See Naess, *Ecology, Community, and Lifestyle*, 2.

154. Fuller, *Wonder*, 1.

155. Merleau-Ponty, *Phenomenology of Perception*, 66.

the benefit of sophisticated techniques)."[156] Techniques of perceiving and processing moral knowledge are more complex and naturally related than many cognitivists or behavioralists generally allow.

The Moral Significance of the Ecological Self

Questions regarding the relationship between the empirical, cognitive and spiritual aspects of a human's physical perception and moral processing of concepts such as empathy, beauty, peaceableness, or happiness have been posed in various forms since ancient Greece, for instance in Aristotle's *De Anima*. But many psychologists and philosophers perpetuate the bifurcation between empiricism and rationalism in the form of "nativist" and "behavioralism" theories.[157] Our native ability to perceive is related to a brutish, evolutionary response to the presence of others, while rational cognition is part of a higher moral process. However, Newcombe and Huttenlocher agree that recent studies have begun to blur the lines between perception and cognition.[158] Coupled with their own research into the spatial cognition of infants and children, Newcombe and Huttenlocher suggest that the "debate [between nativism and behavioralism] should be reconceptualized as the search to understand the starting points for cognitive development, the nature and timing of crucial environmental input, and the precise specification of how children use environmental input at specific points in their development from their initial starting points."[159] There is much at stake than an argument between nativism and behavioralism. But one fundamental question is, do our native perceptions serve as more than an evolutionarily beneficial system of agency detection? Do they contribute to our moral consciousness?

Our native ability to perceive other beings in our spatial environment is an evolutionarily advantage. Agency detection allows us to determine which creatures are friends, foes, or potential prey.[160] Obviously the animal

---

156. Matthews, *Philosophy and Children's Literature*, 7–16. The extent of his work on the philosophy of childhood can be found in Matthews, *Philosophy of Childhood*; *Dialogues with Children*.

157. A good analysis of the differences between nativism and behavioralism can be found in Edwards, *Discourse and Cognition*.

158. Their analysis of the role that our innate spatial cognition plays in the development of consciousness is presented in Damon et al., *Handbook of Child Psychology*, 734–76.

159. Damon et al., *Handbook of Child Psychology*, 767.

160. The moral and social implications of the human being's agency detection is the subject of King, *Being With Animals*. The implications that this aspect of our human

that can best make that judgement lives the longest or healthiest. But the studies above suggest a child's natural means of agency detection serve for more than a simple trigger for a fight or flight response.[161] Our innate ability to perceive creatures in our spatial and natural environment has moral and psychological import. Grene recognizes this point as a significant aspect of Gibson's ecological theory of the self. She writes:

> if who we are is where we are, where we are includes not only being in a world of inanimate sights and sounds but being with our conspecifics in a shared (in our case) human environment. J. J. Gibson remarks at the very start of Ecological Approach: "The surroundings of any animal include other animals as well as the plants and the nonliving things. The former are just as much parts of its environment as the inanimate parts. For any animal needs to distinguish not only the substances and objects of its material environment but also the other animals and the differences between them. It cannot afford to confuse prey with predator, own-species with another species, or male with female"[162] Such matters are dealt with, presumably, in the study of what Neisser has called the "interpersonal self." But, again, I want to ask: Is this another, other than ecological, self? Surely not. Other persons are parts of each person's environment; being with others is one aspect of being in a world.[163]

---

nature has upon our ability to associate with the natural environment, specifically with animals, is the subject of King, *Evolving God*. This concept of the social, moral value of "agency detection" is called "projicience" by the work of neurophysiologist Charles Sherrington in Sherrington, *Integrative Action*.

161. Historically, consciousness has normally belonged to categories reserved for higher cognitive functioning, which is to say, the operations of our human pre-frontal cortex as opposed to the animalistic parts of our brains. Darcia Narváez has built her moral theory on the fact that the prefrontal cortex is the location for higher moral cognition, which moves us beyond basal motives towards security and the concomitant fight/flight response to objects in our environment. Thoughts of morality such as grace as opposed to revenge, are signs of activity in our highly evolved pre-frontal cortex. Barring pathological conditions which block either the brain from communicate between lobes (example) or conditions which pervert sensory processing (such as various conditions on the autism scale), Narváez's psychological research suggests that that children are capable of utilizing this advanced 'moral' part of their brain before they necessarily reach any formal or post-conventional stages of cognitive reasoning. See Narváez, "Triune Ethics."

162. Gibson, *Ecological Approach*, 7.

163. Grene, "Primacy of the Ecological Self," 133. Two other resources are included in this quote which are cited in the current work. See Gibson, *Ecological Approach*; Neisser, *Perceived Self*.

By extending Gibson's theory, Grene concludes that the living and non-living members of our shared environment have epistemological import, and that this sensory knowledge of what others have called our "ecological self" (which is normally a reference to our biological, animal self) are contiguously inseparable from knowledge of our "interpersonal" self, or our moral self.[164] This simple continuity between our sensory perception and what we call "knowledge" is a fundamental aspect of discerning what we truly are, which she calls a "being in a world." We can now see the connection to the epistemological theory suggested early in this chapter. Moral "knowledge" of ourself is continuous with our native sensory perception, which is fundamentally dependent upon our being located within an environment among other communicating and perceiving beings. There is a direct link between ecological, sensory perception and epistemology. This connection is already established at some level in children. Grene summarizes this point:

> Awareness of persisting structure describes equally the child's recognition of a kitten and the physicist's recognition of a muon or a pion; the extracting and abstracting of invariants are equally characteristic of both cases. Yet if knowledge is in fact continuous with perception, why do we persist in making a distinction of kind between "perception" and "thought"? "Our reasons for supposing that seeing something is quite unlike knowing something," Gibson explains, "come from the old doctrine that seeing is having temporary sensations one after another at the passing moment of present time, whereas knowing is having permanent concepts stored in memory." Once we have shed this albatross we can acknowledge that, again in Gibson's words, "knowing is an extension of perceiving."[165] No one, so far as I know, has yet articulated adequately the philosophical implications of that acknowledgment. To do so would be to present a fully elaborated ecological epistemology. Perhaps Merleau-Ponty on the Continent and Polanyi in Britain came as close to such a view as any one could whose work antedated Gibson's.[166]

Gibson thought the separation between perception and knowledge was due to "the old doctrine" which was the bifurcated dualism between empiricism and rationalism. Grene states that "once we have shed this albatross" we can acknowledge that "knowing is an extension of perceiving." Our moral identity is somehow continuous with our nature. Grene acknowledges that

---

164. This is a reference to Neisser's work, in which Trevarthen's chapter (above) is included. See Neisser, *Perceived Self*.

165. Gibson, *Ecological Approach*, 258.

166. Grene, "Primacy of the Ecological Self," 258.

perhaps Merleau-Ponty came close to realizing the full potential of such an "ecological epistemology."

Before Gibson, Merleau-Ponty suggested there is no hard philosophical or empirical separation between perception and knowledge of the thing perceived. He says this in the strongest possible terms when he writes, "every perception is a communication or a communion . . . the complete expression outside ourselves of our perceptual powers and a coition, so to speak, of our body with things."[167] The whole phenomenal field, all of the creatures, living and non-living which actually exist in our shared environment contribute to the "flux" or flow of information that is communicated to our senses.[168] He believed that the whole body was a system of "perceptual powers" and that "what I call experience of the thing or of reality—not merely of a reality-for-sight or for-touch, but of an absolute reality—is my full co-existence with the phenomenon."[169] If we are to know an object, we must engage all of our senses in the task of perception. Also "a thing would not have this colour had it not also this shape, these tactile properties, this resonance, this odour, and that the thing is the absolute fullness which my undivided existence projects before itself."[170]

Much like Trevarthen's understanding of the resonant basis of infant proto-conversations, the "resonance" that is caused in our sensory perception is a vehicle for the transfer of knowledge. For Merleau-Ponty, "The passing of sensory givens before our eyes or under our hands is, as it were, a language which teaches itself, and in which the meaning is secreted by the very structure of the signs, and this is why it can literally be said that our senses question things and that things reply to them."[171] The perception of sensory resonance is "literally" a non-linguistic form of communication with creation which is achieved precisely because we are in a close relationship with the thing. Physically standing before an object is an integral step to perceiving the object's communication, so that "knowledge of the object can 'think itself in' the subject."[172] Being-in-the-world is necessary because "The relations between things or aspects of things having always our body as their vehicle, the whole of nature is the setting of our own life, or our

---

167. Merleau-Ponty, *Phenomenology of Perception*, 373.

168. Merleau-Ponty, *Phenomenology of Perception*. "The Phenomenal Field" is the title of chapter 4.

169. Merleau-Ponty, *Phenomenology of Perception*, 372.

170. Merleau-Ponty, *Phenomenology of Perception*, 372.

171. Merleau-Ponty, *Phenomenology of Perception*, 372.

172. Merleau-Ponty, *Phenomenology of Perception*, 249 (emphasis added).

interlocutor in [this] sort of dialogue."[173] Nature is the setting for this mode of epistemology because "the thing is correlative to my body and, in more general terms, to my existence."[174]

This kind of communion which happens in space and time, allows the subject to perceive the object in the same mode that the subject perceives herself. The "wonder" of this mode of dual processing gives "meaning (*sens*) to the sensible."[175] Merleau-Ponty was trying to "shed this albatross" that divided sense and sensibility, or perception and knowledge. He acknowledges "The fact that this may not have been realized earlier is explained by the fact that any coming to awareness of the perceptual world was hampered by the prejudices arising from objective thinking."[176] Like many of the current psychologists who are mentioned above, he recognized that humans beings have the "natural powers" to "wonder in the face of the world."[177] And so he proposed a phatic, noematic method of reflection that "does not withdraw from the world towards the unity of consciousness as the world's basis" but rather "steps back to watch the forms of transcendence fly up like sparks."[178] Thomas Traherne also wrote of "Sparks" of knowledge which fly up from the perception of our natural environment. He wrote:

> The Generous principles of Nature, are Seeds and Sparks as it were of Eternal Goodness. And the contemplation of this goodness is the fuel and food of faith. It is not A transeunt Glance, but a fixed Ey, and a Steady intuition (that leavs a Sence behind it) that Enables the Soul to believ its Greatness, when it appeareth in its Effects.... Before the fire be Kindled, that will giv us Light, we must stay upon the object, and the Application must be continued some time, that it might pierce and Enter; otherwise, the concession will be very feeble, and the Impression that is left will never enflame us, but fleet away.[179]

Traherne highlights various scenes in nature by which goodness can be discerned from the social activity of hens, pelicans, tigers and other animals. He then suggests if we stand in the environs of such scenes and contemplate creation, that "Eternal Goodness" emanates like "sparks" from the "generous principles of nature." Standing in the presence of the object for some

---

173. Merleau-Ponty, *Phenomenology of Perception*, 372.
174. Merleau-Ponty, *Phenomenology of Perception*, 373.
175. Merleau-Ponty, *Phenomenology of Perception*, 39.
176. Merleau-Ponty, *Phenomenology of Perception*, 373.
177. Merleau-Ponty, *Phenomenology of Perception*, xv.
178. Merleau-Ponty, *Phenomenology of Perception*, xv.
179. Traherne, *Kingdom*, 292.

time and applying our intuition to the scene in a manner that "leavs a Sence behind it" is the "fuel and food" for the "soul" to "believe" and have "faith." He even counsels that we must continue to stand in the object's presence for some time so that the impression can "pierce and Enter" us, otherwise the moral impression will not last. The longer we maintain our place in the flux of creation's communication, the more significant the moral impact. Centuries before Merleau-Ponty wrote of our need to stand in the flux in order to perceive so that we can know, Traherne wrote of our need to stand in the midst of the "Circulation" in order to perceive so that we can know. In his poem entitled "Circulation," he writes:

> As fair Ideas from the Skie,
> Or Images of Things,
> Unto a Spotless Mirror flie,
> On unperceived Wings;
> And lodging there affect the Sence,
> As if at first they came from then;
> While being there, they richly Beautifie
> The Place they fill, and yet communicate
> Themselvs, reflecting to the Seers Eye,
> Just such is our Estate.
> No Glory in our selvs possess,
> But what derived from without we gain,
> From all the Mysteries of Blessedness.[180]

This poem shows that knowledge of virtues such as beauty must be informed by a "Sence." The reason is the "glory" of our knowledge is not self possessed. Knowledge of these things comes from objects that exist outside of our minds. This is why he praises "the five senses, whose office it is to represent all sensible Objects, and effects to the common power of Perceiving, as the office of that is to represent them to the Understanding."[181] But also he writes how the "Circulation," or flux, of sensory communication helps us to know ourself and our own existence.

> All things to Circulations owe
> Themselvs; by which alone
> They do exist: They cannot shew
> A Sigh, a Word, a Groan,
> A Colour, or a Glimps of Light,
> The Sparcle of a Precious Stone,
> A virtue, or a Smell; a lovly Sight,

---

180. Traherne, *Centuries, Poems, and Thanksgivings*, 2:152.
181. Traherne, *Kingdom*, 487.

> A Fruit, a Beam, an Influence, a Tear;
> But they anothers Livery must Wear:
> And borrow Matter first,
> Before they can communicat.
> Whatever's empty is accurst:
> And this doeth shew that we must some Estate
> Possess, or never can communicate.[182]

Again, he affirms our social nature and the fact that we cannot exist alone.[183] We owe our biological existence to our participation in this "Circulation" of matter. Also by our perception of this communion or "communication" of matter we perceive what we are. Like Gibson and Merleau-Ponty, Traherne confirms that when we perceive this "Circulation" we "know" the object, and when we perceive this resonant flux, we coperceive our self.

Retiring into a close relationship to creation engaged us in the kind of non-verbal communication that prepares us to realize the full "glory" of our created nature. By virtue of coming to this world as a stranger, "Wonder" allows this child to behold the "innumerable Depths of Love and Goodness, and Wisdom and Treasure" that creation communicates. Traherne knew significant non-verbal influences of the entire phenomenal field were perceived by children who approached nature with an innate perceptual wonder. Through manipulation of the environment, which is an innate mode of perception for a child, play and exploration have the potential to place children into highly communicative, relational matrices with all manner of creatures.

Colwyn Trevarthen writes that such a nuanced concept of the child's innate perception "accepts that there is a nature of human feelings which is spiritual in the widest sense, and present in young children as part of their 'relational consciousness.'"[184] Even more directly, Rebecca Nye sees "relational consciousness" as the basis of "children's spirituality."[185] When a child arrives as a stranger into a new relationship with another being-in-the-world, their wonder guided interaction is an act of coperception. It is,

---

182. Traherne, *Centuries, Poems, and Thanksgivings*, 2:153.

183. He writes in the stanza that follows: "A Spunge drinks in that Water, which/ Is afterwards exprest./ A Liberal hand must first be rich:/ Who blesseth must be Blest./ A Thirsty Earth drinks in the Rain,/ The Trees such Moysture at their Roots,/ Before the one can Lavish Herbs again,/ Before the other can afford us its Fruits./ No Tenant can rais Corn, or pay his Rent,/ Nor can even hav a Lord,/ That has no Land. No Spring can vent,/ No vessel any Wine afford/ Wherin no Liquor's put. No empty Purs,/ Can Pounds or Talents of it self disburs" (Traherne, *Centuries, Poems, and Thanksgivings*, 2:153).

184. Trevarthen, "Innate Moral Feelings," 13. Here, Trevarthen is referring to a phrase by Hay and Nye.

185. Richards and Privett, *Through the Eyes*, 68.

as Traherne believes, a kind of communion fit for a child's perception of the world.

The implications of the child's innate wonder leads Trevarthen to ultimately question, like Gibson and Merleau-Ponty, all the social theories that follow the constructivist cognitivism of Darwin, Freud and Piaget. He writes:

> The findings qualify the highly influential theories of Freud and Piaget, invalidating their basic assumptions concerning how we discover we have a self, how we begin to rationalise about one another as "objects" of interest, peculiarly animate "things" that affect our selves, and how children acquire knowledge and skills by learning socially contrived rules for their own interest. This new, or reanimated, theory of human nature is, I believe, comparable in its significance with the revolutionary theory of human nature and its evolution enunciated by Charles Darwin in the nineteenth century, of which it is a continuation or extension. It is incompatible with the theory of evolution as a competitive "commercial" process between self-serving genetic forces in development of individuals.[186]

In his poem "The Review," Traherne offers a similar evaluation of the epistemological limitations cognitivist theories as Trevarthen does in the quote above. He reflects on the time he passed from childhood to "adulthood." It was the period in which his identity shifted from being based on a relationship to natural creatures to being based in the world of mental cognition. And he questions:

> Did I grow, or did I stay?
> Did I prosper or decay?
> When I so
> From *Things* to *Thoughts* did go?
> Did I flourish or diminish,
> When I so in *Thoughts* did finish
> What I had in *Things* begun?
> When from God's Works to think upon
> The Thoughts of Men my Soul did com?[187]

In the end, he concludes that this move towards an identity based in cognitive "Thoughts" did decenter him from his true identity. He knows that re-centering himself in relationship to natural "things" of God will help restore his true, natural identity. The formation of his moral identity is continuous

---

186. Trevarthen, "Innate Moral Feelings," 394
187. Traherne, *Centuries, Poems, and Thanksgivings*, 2:151.

with his ecological location. Recentering will bring his life into a complete "circle" as he becomes a child again, and finds his real identity as a being-in-relationship to the "things" of creation.

> My Child-hood is a Sphere
> Wherin ten thousand hev'nly Joys appear:
> Those *Thoughts* it doth include,
> And those Affections, which review'd,
> Again present to me
> in better sort the *Things* which I did see.
> Imaginations *Reall* are,
> Unto my Mind again repair:
> Which makes my Life a Circle of Delights;
> A hidden Sphere of obvious Benefits:
> An Earnest that the Actions of the Just
> Shall still revive, and flourish in the Dust.[188]

Traherne believed that the child had an innate ability to perceive the communication that permeated the entire phenomenal field of creation. I have shown that his thesis is based not on a naïve nativist view of children as soteriologically pure. Rather, this view is based on the belief that human beings enter the world with an innate principle to "wonder" that equips the human child to perceive the kind of "influences" and "reflections" of goodness that creation naturally communicates. A social nature, a curious desire to wonder, and the ability to process non-verbal, sensory perceptions into knowledge are all "natural" qualities that Adam and each new "stranger" to creation possess. He believes that this "principle" can be used to cultivate the child's sense of moral identity as a being-in-creation. He believes that the cognitivist, rationalist concept of human cognition, which sends us into our minds to confirm our identity, decenters us from our true identity which is as a being who can utilize our senses to "know." At that point, as Chrystostom suggests, the "bondage of opinion and customs . . . enthrals and binds us,"[189] leading us farther away from our natural means of "knowing" our identity. While Piaget believed this decentering was necessary for cognitive development, Traherne equated it to the death of part of the child's human principle. He wrote:

> But I,
> I knew not why, Did learn among them too . . .
> Upon som useless gaudy Book,

188. This excerpt comes from the second part of this poem (Traherne, *Centuries, Poems, and Thanksgivings*, 2:152).
189. Traherne, *Centuries, Poems, and Thanksgivings*, 115.

> When what I knew of God was fled,
> The Child being taught to look,
> His Soul was quickly murthered.[190]

By pursuing the linguistic, cognitive view of human being and knowledge which he calls the "Non-Intellegence of Human Words,"[191] we become "More fools at Twenty than Ten,"[192] And after we have become decentered, part of our path back to "become a little child" as Christ calls, leads us to recenter ourselves by retiring into creation. When we re-center, or "Return" to this manner of knowing God, Traherne claims "To Infancy, O Lord, again I com, That I my Manhood may improv: My early Tutor is the Womb; I still my Cradle lov."[193]

Conclusion: Perceiving Nature as Grace

Of course, Traherne did not possess an understanding of the embodied realities of dual processing, or even a sophisticated psychological theory to demonstrate his understanding of perception and cognition. Traherne argued his philosophical point based on experience and a theological perspective on the cooperative continuity between God's grace and the nature of human being.

In the treatise, *Seeds of Eternity or Nature of the Soul*, Traherne acknowledges that all "Science in Philosophy" seeks the knowledge of two things—the self and God.[194] He fundamentally believed that science and philosophy, that is nature and grace, cooperate in the search for knowledge. He presents a basic notion of the tripartite human soul, desires, rationality, and spirit, which is at home within the Hooker inspired *via media* of his beloved Anglican Church.[195] After outlining Aristotle's notion of the soul,[196] he affirms with him and the other "Heathen Authors," such as Aristotle,

---

190. Excerpt from the poem "The Apostacy" (Traherne, *Centuries, Poems, and Thanksgivings*, 2:97).

191. Excerpt from the poem "Dumnesse" (Traherne, *Centuries, Poems, and Thanksgivings*, 2:40).

192. Excerpt from the poem "The Apostacy" (Traherne, *Centuries, Poems, and Thanksgivings*, 2:95).

193. Excerpt from the poem "Return" (Traherne, *Centuries, Poems, and Thanksgivings*, 2:87).

194. Traherne, *Seeds of Eternity*, 238.

195. Allchin has explored the thesis that this concept of participation has largely been lost in Anglican theology. Traherne is an example that it was present and in operation. See Allchin, *Participation in God*.

196. Traherne, *Seeds of Eternity*, 239.

Plato, Plotinus, Proclus, Trismegistus, Theophrastus, along with the teachers of the Church, Augustine, Gregory of Nyssa, Macrina, Justin Martyr, Denise, Jerome, and Tertullian, that reason held within the soul is that which "makes us to know our selvs."[197] However, along with his praise of reason he acknowledges that their exists a tendency to view the body as merely "the Case of the Soul." He is keen to "repell that opinion as a vulgar Error, that maketh it the impediment and prison of the mind, and looking on it as a glorious Instrument and Companion of the soul, utter things more advantagious concerning it."[198] He stated in *Kingdom* that "Our Bodies are not as Som Imagine them, Enemies to be used, with all kinds of Rigor; They are Vessels worthy of the Treasures they inclose; and you must believ they are very Dear to the Power, which Created them."[199] The body is a partner in the task of coperceiving ourselves and other creatures, precisely because of its natural ability to feel wonder about that power of the Creator. Rather than dividing phenomenon from thought and spirit, his innate desire for wonder is the proof that nature and grace ultimately cooperate in seeking knowledge.[200]

> Humanity, which is the Handmaid of true Divinity, is a noble Part of Learning, opening the best and rarest Cabinet in nature to us, that of our Selvs: Which it doeth either by discovering the Excellencies of our Bodies, or the faculties of our souls together with the Graces and vices of either. . . . [The Soul] is admirable, because it unfoldeth Wonders that are incredible; but more because it doth it in a maner so plain and easy, for its Objects are within us; it is therfore the most certain of all Sciences, because we feel the Things it declares, and by my Experience, prove all it revealeth. It is Sublime because by it we are allied to heaven, in it all the Glories of the Celestial Kingdom are apparent and by it are made near and familiar.[201]

---

197. These quotations are taken from a paragraph in Traherne, *Seeds of Eternity*, 238–39.

198. Traherne, *Seeds of Eternity*, 241.

199. Traherne, *Kingdom*, 488.

200. Traherne writes: "Whether then this World were made by Chance, or not at all, or in Love or Hatred, for the Happiness of the misery of Creatures, or remissly and negligently without any certain End, the nature of man must of necessity enquire bec. it feels it self most eminently concerned in the Original and End of that Creation. And this interior facultie engages all the Passions and Affections of the Soul" (Traherne, *Seeds of Eternity*, 244).

201. Traherne, *Seeds of Eternity*, 233.

This cooperation between grace and nature is the way to discover the "science" that all philosophies seek concerning our selves, and God, and it is part of our nature. This curious principle of our human nature to seek knowledge through a sensory, social communion with our environment is not only theologically and philosophically significant, but it is demonstrated as an active principle of developmental psychology. Colwyn Trevarthen has written:

> The theory of an essential cooperative and creative nature of human motivation in infancy has a firm empirical foundation, and it accords well with certain ancient traditions of the humanities, as well as with the latest discoveries in brain science.... It shows we are born to make our intentions work to formulate "narratives" of agency in engagement with the "lived experience" of a conceptual world that is both absorbingly private and passionately social.[202]

David Carr has stated that every philosopher, and for that matter theologian or scientist, who seeks "to know" bases their moral theory on some notion of human "being."[203] If we want to test the validity or limits of any moral theory, we must understand the principles of human nature upon which that theory is built. This chapter has outlined Traherne's "Principles" of human nature. He underwrites his moral theory with an unflinching notion that human nature is fundamentally social, that our social nature is symmetrical to the creative will of God's grace, and that as a social being-in-creation, we must go out of ourselves in order to perceive knowledge of our self and God. Along with other psychologists, Trevarthen has suggested that this kind of cooperative, relational notion of human nature has significant epistemological import, as nurturing this innate relational mode of perception forms the foundation for an empathetic, moral state of awareness.

I began this chapter with the claim that the child is Traherne's philosopher *par excellence*. The "Principle" of our innate wonder, which stems from our social nature and leads us to engage the world as an "Adamic" stranger, makes the child particularly suited to perceive the knowledge of God's goodness that is communicated through creation's relational nature. So, what does Traherne say about the creatures that are the other being in this morally significant relationship? In the next chapter, I will consider the "Objects," which are the second aspect of Traherne's theory of retirement.

---

202. Trevarthen, "Innate Moral Feelings," 9.
203. Carr, *Educating the Virtues*, 18.

4

Retirednes

The Role That Created Objects Play in the Formation of a Child's Inter-Subjective Moral Identity

Introduction

IN CHAPTER 3, I explored one of three aspects of Traherne's moral theory that are revealed in *Inducements to Retirednes*. Through the "principle" of wonder, children can perceive significant aspects of moral epistemology in communion with creation. The following chapter will address the second aspect of Traherne's theory concerning the Objects which we perceive in creation.

In the last chapter, I suggested that empirical moral theories and cognitivist, rational moral theories reduce the moral significance of creatures and the phenomenal environment. I then demonstrated that Traherne's moral theory respects the intrinsic moral value of creatures by suggesting our moral formation is dependent upon going outside of ourselves and participating in the communicative flux of Divine love that circulates among creation. When we place ourselves among that flux, creatures communicate God's goodness in ways that we can perceive. I suggested that in this way, centering ourselves among our fellow creatures contributes to the formation of an allocentric moral identity. In this chapter, I will strengthen that claim by demonstrating the intrinsic moral significance that Traherne maintains for each creature, or created "Object." Each creature in its proper ecological place communicates the Love of Divine creativity, and becomes a theatre for the formation of a caring, inter-subjective identity.

Adam's Objects

In *Inducements*, Traherne conducts a thought experiment. There are three men considering a purse of Gold.[1] The first man only wants to know if the coins profit him. According to his selfish principles, this brute only covets the coin as an object for his own gain. As a caricature of empiricism, everything this man wants to know about the object can be measured by the satisfaction of his appetites. Traherne explains that this man is an animalistic, "dead weight" because he only responds to sensory input, and does not have the moral capacity to wonder about the nature of the creator that gives the coin value. The third man is a celestial being. This being has a relationship with God that is purely rational in the manner of angels described earlier in *Kingdom*. The defining principle of a rational being is to possess a rational knowledge about the Creator who gave the coin its value. Because a rational being does not need the object to know God as the value of the object, the object is condemned as "Remote and useless Babel."[2] However, the second man, is a human being. He is in "the middle between Earth and Heaven."[3] Because this man wonders about the true value of the coin and also how it can serve the virtues of justice, generosity and care of his neighbour, he holds on to the coin and "desires the right Owner should possess it." Having perceived the right use for the coin, he "confides in Vertue, and resolvs into Patience and Contentment without it."[4] The Principles of our human nature lead us to wonder about the whole intrinsic value of an object, as a creature and a creation. Our wonder leads us to seek knowledge "above" simple empiricism, and yet values the actual object "outside" of mere rationalism.

Once again, Merleau-Ponty helps interpret Traherne's thoughts regarding the moral significance of the object. Merleau-Ponty observed that empiricism's tendency to "return to the 'immediate data of consciousness' became therefore a hopeless enterprise since the philosophical scrutiny was trying to be what it could not, in principle, see."[5] Like the first man in Traherne's thought experiment, the empiricist is so concerned about the "immediate data of consciousness" that he fails to actually "see" the moral significance of the object he beholds. And the third being does not need to "see" the object at all to form a rational concept. When we turn our

---

1. See Traherne, *Inducements to Retirednes*, 30.
2. Traherne, *Inducements to Retirednes*, 31.
3. Traherne, *Inducements to Retirednes*, 30.
4. Traherne, *Inducements to Retirednes*, 30.
5. Merleau-Ponty, *Phenomenology of Perception*, 66.

perception to the phenomenal field in which we behold its nature, Merleau-Ponty suggests the object can be:

> understood through a sort of act of appropriation which we all experience when we say that we have "found" the rabbit in the foliage of a puzzle, or that we have "caught" a slight gesture. Once the prejudice of sensation has been banished a face, a signature, a form of behavior cease to be mere "visual data" whose psychological meaning is to be sought in our inner experience, and the mental life of others becomes an immediate object, a whole charged with immanent meaning.[6]

Merleau-Ponty equally abandons "the prejudice" of rationalism when he writes that our perception of objects is also not simple rational intuition "of a reality of which we are ignorant and leading to which there is no methodical bridge—it is the making explicit of the prescientific life of consciousness which alone endows scientific operations with meaning and to which these latter always refer back."[7] While the natural object in our phenomenal field does not simply donate sense data, the object is not dispensable for our full perception. The "methodical bridge" between the two is the beholding of the actual object. This epistemologically unified method of knowing, or "seeing," is Traherne's goal. By definition, the method of the third, moral man in his thought experiment comes to "know" moral epistemology through such a unified perceptual method. Only the moral being ever "sees" the real, natural, intrinsic moral significance of the object, which exists prior to the being's perception of that object.

In order to "know" that object, we have to embrace it. We cannot despise its being as somehow separate from our knowledge of the object. In order to grasp the inherent value of each creature, the human must form a morally significant relationship by beholding creatures as common objects of love.[8] In both senses of the word "common," these common objects are to be found in creation. Traherne assumes if it most certainly is God's will to reveal "goodness" in creation, surely God would reveal goodness through

---

6. Merleau-Ponty, *Phenomenology of Perception*, 67.
7. Merleau-Ponty, *Phenomenology of Perception*, 68.
8. Traherne offers great insight into this notion of beholding a common object of love in the second century of his meditations. He discusses beholding a beautiful woman, which is a very sexually charged experience. Perhaps because it is frought with the possibility of sexual missteps in terms of suggesting a woman as a "common object of love," the way in which Traherne is able to direct our thoughts in a way that both values the beauty of the person, and honours them as a creation of God is the reason that the example powerfully expresses his point. See Traherne, *Centuries, Poems, and Thanksgivings*, 1:90.

the most commonly created objects. According to Traherne, those objects should hold a common value among us.

> For thus, I thought within myself: God being, as we generally believe, infinite in goodness, it is most consonant and agreeable with His nature, that the best things should be most common. For nothing is more natural to infinite goodness, than to make the best things most frequent; and only things worthless scarce. Then I began to enquire what things were most common " Air, Light, Heaven and Earth, Water, the Sun, Trees, Men and Women, Cities, Temples &c. These I found common and obvious to all " Rubies, Pearls, Diamonds, Gold and Silver; these I found scarce, and to the most denied. Then began I to consider and compare the value of them which I measured by their serviceableness, and by the excellencies which would be found in them, should they be taken away. And in conclusion, I saw clearly, that there was a real valuableness in all the common things; in the scarce, a feigned.[9]

Here we see the same notion of "valueableness" that was expressed in the case of the three human beings in Traherne's thought experiment. "Valueableness" goes beyond the inherent value of the creature, and includes the value it has for coperceiving the identity of other creatures in its context. Common objects are valuable because they communicate a unified knowledge about the Divine source of their goodness in relationship to their physical, actual goodness for the benefit of life around them, which is the mutual purpose and end of creatures.

> The Unitie of [the Value and Dignitie of the Object] we may discern by considering the Nature of either. A Thing may bear ten thousand times its value by reason of its Relation, as the Turf and Twig in the Conveyance of an Estate, the Wax and Paper in a Bond . . . the Bread and Wine in the Holy Sacrament . . . between Persons Infinitly near; and Dear to Each other. This Relation can never be known, without Knowledge of the Object, nor valued without a real esteem of the Object.[10]

To alienate knowledge of an object from the way it functions in its natural context turns God's creatures into "meer objects of Speculation, they are Air."[11] Beholding the creature in its natural context helps us know its inherent value, and the way it contributes to the Divine end for its life. If we

---

9. Traherne, *Centuries, Poems, and Thanksgivings*, 1:131.
10. Traherne, *Kingdom of God*, 475.
11. Traherne, *Inducements to Retirednes*, 33.

strive to "know" the goodness of the creature by its natural context, we can perceive both the Divine goodness that created it and the good purpose that it serves in its natural, phenomenological context.

> He that Knows them not shall spurn them under feet, and wonder to what purpose they are suffered to be, or abide in Gods Kingdom. Nor indeed can he think the Kingdom to be Gods, while useless Things are in it. It is therfore necessary to look upon all Things as Valuable Treasure: Nor can I be holy, nor apprehend the Works of God with Reverence unless I so esteem them.[12]

To esteem an object is to see it in its right and useful place. Ultimately, the principle of wonder leads us to desire to know the full value of objects. When we wonder about the full value of an object, it becomes a fountain of love and care. The method of entering into a relationship with various "objects" of creation creates an inter-subjective relationship which becomes:

> the theatre of your Love. It sustains you and all objects that you may continue to love them. Without which it were better for you to have no being. Life without objects is sensible emptiness, and that is a greater misery than Death or Nothing. Objects without Love are the delusion of life.[13]

The "object," or the creature on the other side of the relational "theatre," is an object of love.[14] Love is the attribute of the relationship that helps us not be deluded into merely studying the object. But neither can we simply cogitate on love, for life without these natural objects is "Death or Nothing." To esteem full "knowledge," it is necessary to create a morally significant theatre between the human and the created object.

---

12. Traherne, *Inducements to Retirednes*, 33.
13. Traherne, *Centuries, Poems, and Thanksgivings*, 1:88.
14. It is interesting here that without referring to Augustine, Traherne seems to follow Augustine's formula for moral epistemology that "we know only as we love." Through this Augustinian concept, Oliver O'Donovan demonstrates that theoretical and practical knowledge can be united in the act of loving. For Augustine, as well as O'Donovan, love is the unified moral epistemology that might lead communities of deliberative action to form around common objects of love. See O'Donovan, *Common Objects of Love*.

The Theatre of Inter-Subjectivity

Traherne believes the theatre between a human being and another creature forms a significant part of our moral identity. Because we are made to love,[15] and we are by nature principally social beings, "it is our Duty like God to be united to them creature."[16] Uniting with creatures in a theatre of love is the method of realizing the end of our moral identity. He writes:

> By love our Souls are married and solder'd to the all. We must love them infinitely, but in God, and for God: and God in them: namely all His excellencies manifested in them. When we dote upon the perfections and beauties of some one creature, we do not love that too much, but other things too little. Never was anything in this world loved too much but many things have been loved in a false way: and all in too short a measure.[17]

When the human being-in-creation is "married" to God's beloved creatures in creation we come to the knowledge of the true end, which is love in God and for God. The spatial "theatre" of love that is created between two creatures is the stage for forming of a moral identity of mutuality.

Psychologist Colwyn Trevarthen wrote about the formative nexus between beings as the "theatre of inter-subjectivity." Trevarthen delivered a lecture which aimed to "describe how we interpret the primary psycho-biology of love, hate, pride and shame in relationships, as well as the emotions of individual will and well-being."[18] He suggested that his research is "interested in developing a natural moral philosophy from knowledge of the abilities of infants to enter into intimate, affectionate and creative relationships with their parents." Through various assessments of neo-natal sensitivities which were broadly described in chapter 3, Trevarthen draws significant conclusions about the "biology of intentions and emotions." He suggests that we are capable of a "sympathetic transfer of intentions, interests, and affect appraisals between brains, by detection of these from the purposes and emotions made explicit in other individual's movements."[19] Trevarthen writes that "motives, intentions and feelings of the Self are

---

15. In chapter 2, we explored the beginning of the previous quote that reads, "You are as prone to love, as the sun is to shine: it being the most delightful and natural employment of the Soul of Man: without which you are dark and miserable" (Traherne, *Centuries, Poems, and Thanksgivings*, 1:88).

16. Traherne, *Centuries, Poems, and Thanksgivings*, 1:88.

17. Traherne, *Centuries, Poems, and Thanksgivings*, 1:88.

18. Trevarthen, "Innate Moral Feelings," 1.

19. Trevarthen, "Innate Moral Feelings," 3.

generated and mediated in movement," and that "movements of bodies and their parts become 'advertising' signals, employing 'biosemiosis.'"[20] I do not have the space in this study to explore the theory of "semiosis," but it is significant to note that the physical relationships between creatures in time and space are the "theatres of social engagement [which] communicate in a 'semiosphere.'"[21] Trevarthen suggests that each being, and the space between beings is morally significant in terms of the actual time and space that it takes to engage in a "sympathetic transfer" of knowledge that can impact the perceiver's moral movements. When the human being enters into this "biosemiotic" theatre, they begin to "act and think together for collective benefit."[22] Like Traherne's concept of the importance of perceiving an object in their context as a theatre of love,[23] Trevarthen is suggesting that the theatre created between "objects" is the locus of moral formation. Trevarthen's theory of the child's innate inter-subjectivity is based on his observation of infants in this "theatre." Trevarthen concludes:

> Infants have the ability for communication in them, and this grows from within as well as by entering into dialogues with others. The way a young infant behaves when face to face with the right kind of available person supports a theory of innate inter-subjectivity, a theory that I proposed on the evidence of descriptions of mother-infant interactions.[24]

Trevarthen has come to the conclusion that the motive, or "phatic" perception of other beings, and the development of harmonized awareness of creatures who communicate within the environment are directly related.[25] By effectively entering into this harmonized awareness, an inter-subjective moral identity can be developed.

> It is probable that cognitive dynamics and the chronometrics of awareness and thinking in active behavioral engagement with

---

20. Trevarthen, "Innate Moral Feelings," 3
21. Trevarthen, "Innate Moral Feelings," 3
22. Trevarthen, "Innate Moral Feelings," 3
23. From chapter 3, recall Traherne's quote: "Before the fire be Kindled, that will giv us Light, we must stay upon the object, and the Application must be continued some time, that it might pierce and Enter; otherwise, the concession will be very feeble, and the Impression that is left will never enflame us, but fleet away" (Traherne, *Kingdom*, 292).
24. Trevarthen, "Self Born in Intersubjectivity," 159.
25. Trevarthen discusses the way in which "phatic" resonances such as music and singin between mother and infant contribute to the development of sympathy in Trevarthen, "Proof of Sympathy," 77–118.

the environment are coincident with motive dynamics—that is, behaving and perceiving are generated in the same core motivating system of the brain. If motive dynamics fixed by innate autopoetic rules can be coupled efficiently between subjects, this would, under optimal conditions of inter-subjectivity, result in near complete confluence or harmonization of their internal thinking, learning, and remembering.[26]

Placing a child in the same physical theatre with another significant being is part of the method of developing an empathetic or ethical perception of the world. He writes that when the "social Self" enters this theatre with "Others," the moral significance of the phenomenal field helps you develop "different creativities, cooperations and 'misunderstandings'" that are necessary "to cooperate intelligently in play or work."[27] The young child can develop morally significant allocentric attributes within these inter-subjective "theatres."

The Role of the Inter-Subjective "Theatre" in the Formation of a Child's Moral Identity

We know that when children are allowed to explore, play, and follow where their wonder leads, the non-verbal communication that occurs between themselves and the object they are exploring becomes a major factor in the formation of a child's identity.[28] This psychological theory about the moral import of inter-subjectivity supports the theological corollary in the discipline of moral philosophy. Several moral theologians and philosophers have recently written on the role of inter-subjectivity between humans and natural creatures, as well as the moral significance of inter-subjectivity in the life of children. The relationship between embodiment, the senses, and moral formation has been a critical focus for feminist theologians, and eco-philosophers. Recently, feminist theologians such as Christina Traina have critiqued western theological anthropology based on the fact that it gives cognitive epistemological theories of the rational and linguistic kind primacy of place at the expense of knowledge that is communicated through

---

26. Trevarthen, "Self Born in Intersubjectivity," 156.

27. Trevarthen, "Innate Moral Feelings," 3. Trevarthen also cites previous work done by Buber, MacMurray, Midgley, Reddy, and Braten on the subject of inter-subjectivity.

28. I demonstrated this connection in chapter 3, citing the work of Gareth Matthews on the role of play and the development of a "philosophy" of childhood (Matthews, *Philosophy of Childhood*). This notion is also a part of Carol Gilligan's groundbreaking work, *In a Different Voice*, the significance of which will be explored in the final chapter.

inter-subjective relational theatres.[29] Eco-feminist philosophers put relationships in a prime place in the formation of our identity as well as the transmitting, or communication of moral knowledge.[30]

In his late work, *Dependent Rational Animals*, Alasdair MacIntyre explores this issue through a rather unique philosophical approach. He asks whether animals without language have beliefs. If so, then linguistic cognitive approaches are surely not the only source for moral formation. Based on an affirmative answer, he agrees the virtues can be communicated through an embodied relational method that constitutes an inter-subjective basis for forming the virtues. MacIntyre realizes that:

> in order to flourish, we need both those virtues that enable us to function as independent and accountable practical reasoners and those virtues that enable us to acknowledge the nature and extent of our dependence on others. Both the acquisition and the exercise of those virtues are possible only insofar as we participate in social relationships of giving and receiving, social relationships governed by and partially defined by the norms of the natural law.[31]

Through moral philosophy, MacIntyre arrives at a similar conclusion to Trevarthen. The relational nexus is a significant factor in the development of a class of virtues which he calls the "virtues of acknowledged dependence."[32] Among "those virtues" of dependency, he focuses on the virtue of *misericordia*, or empathy. He suggests rational beings derive humility, empathy, love and "just generosity"[33] by being aware of its dependence upon other beings.

---

29. Christina Traina has suggested that "there is growing contemporary awareness of the phenomenological interdependence of descriptive and evaluative knowledge—of scientific (or factual) and moral characterizations. These sorts of knowledge and their languages are interdependent because scientific and moral knowledge arise simultaneously. 'Empirical' description is in fact always already imbued with moral meaning. This epistemological development has given new credence to the idea that our descriptions of human nature are important sources of information. about what human beings should do and become" (Traina, *Feminist Ethics and Natural Law*, 14). The same theme can be found in Chittister, *Heart of Flesh*. For a fine exploration of this topic as it is treated by feminist theology, I recommend MacKinnon and McIntyre, *Readings in Ecology and Feminist Theology*.

30. For an example of the way in which this critique is carried out from the perspective of eco-feminism, I suggest Plumwood, "Nature, Self, and Gender," 3–27; Shiva, *Violence of the Green Revolution*.

31. MacIntyre, *Dependent Rational Animals*, 155–56.

32. This is also the title of chapter 10 in MacIntyre, *Dependent Rational Animals*.

33. MacIntyre bases his notion of mercy—or empathy—on Aquinas's conception of misericordia. See MacIntyre, *Dependent Rational Animals*, 126.

The method of identification involves ever extending "one's communal relationships so as to include those others within those relationships." After extending the limits of the individual's moral identity to include those that were previously outside their perceived field of dependency, the individual feels "required from now on to care about them and to be concerned about their good just as we care about others already within our community."[34] Identification through non-verbal means help us broaden our rational, moral identity and extend relationships of care. Traherne actually echoes MacIntyre's position on the way "objects" in the "theatre of love" help develop virtues of dependence.

In the final draft of his *Ethicks*, Traherne added Meekness and Humility into his category of less principle virtues.[35] He writes that meekness is super-natural in the sense that it is not a natural human inclination to be meek. However it is not super-natural, in the sense that it would be a charism of the Holy Spirit. Rather meekness is a virtue that can be derived by observing the beauty and serviceableness of biodiversity of creation's Objects. He writes:

> WERE I for my life to interpret that Text of our Saviour, The Meek shall inherit the Earth, I should in the first place say, that every Knowing man may enjoy the beauty and glory of the whole World, and by sweet Contemplations delight in all the abundance of Treasures and pleasant Varieties that are here upon Earth, especially since by the Ordinance of Nature all men are to be his peculiar Treasures. This he might do, I say, did all men love him, and fill the World with Glory and Vertue.[36]

Contemplating the "Treasures" and "Varieties [of creatures] that are here upon Earth" prepares us for the virtue of meekness. The subsequent section on the virtue of humility is the same. Retiring into creation allows us to be "sensible of our Smallness and Subjection" as well as the "high and mighty sence of Benefits," "serviceableness" or "interests" that we receive from creation. Creation's benefits are "the true fountain of it, the goodness and the love of [God]."[37] He believes that contemplating our dependence on diverse

---

34. MacIntyre, *Dependent Rational Animals*, 126.

35. Traherne, *Christian Ethicks*, xxxv. In earlier editions, this placement was different, showing that this positioning was intentional and well thought out. One of Traherne's innovations on the ethical theories of his day was to expand and mingle categories of cardinal and theological virtues. For instance, justice is interpreted as a theological virtue, and Repentance is added to the list of theological virtues.

36. Traherne, *Christian Ethicks*, xxxv.

37. Traherne, *Christian Ethicks*, xxxv.

objects in creation prepares us to apprehend the virtue of humility. Their "serviceableness":

> appeareth to the eye of Knowledge, their Goodness is apprehended by the life of Love, the perfection of their serviceableness to the most perfect End is discerned by Wisdom, the benefit which all Spectators receive is the delight of Goodness, the incomprehensible depth and mysterious intricacy of their frame and nature is the peculiar Object of our wonder and Curiosity; they help our Faith as they shew a Deity and the truth of all Religion and Blessedness.[38]

When we perceive the "serviceableness" or benefits of diverse and often small objects in our environment, we receive the delight of knowing our dependence upon those creatures and our moral identity extends to them out of gratitude.[39] Identifying with the microscopic parts of our environment can "teach us Humilitie and Admonish us of that unitie; and Reciprocal officiousness, that ought to between us."[40] In turn, meekness and humility become part of Christian virtues that lead to happiness and holiness.[41]

Norwegian Philosopher Arne Naess employs a very similar understanding of moral identification. As a child, Naess identified with the small and often overlooked or humble creatures in his local ecosystem. Coming face to face with the knowledge that he was somehow dependent upon little ones formed a sense of humility. He describes that even as a four year old, he marvelled at "the overwhelming diversity and richness of life" and "the tiny beautiful forms which 'nobody' cared for, or were even unable to see" yet were a part of his identification. He writes:

> These reflections instilled within me the idea of modesty—modesty in man's relationships with mountains in particularly and the natural world in general. As I see it, modesty is of little value if it is not a natural consequence of much deeper feelings, a consequence of a way of understanding ourselves as part of nature in a wide sense of the term. This way is such that the smaller we come to feel ourselves compared to the mountain, the nearer we come to participating in its greatness.[42]

---

38. Traherne, *Christian Ethicks*, xxxv.

39. The role of gratitude plays a central role in Wirzba, *Paradise of God*. Wirzba briefly explores the earlier writings of Traherne.

40. Traherne, *Kingdom of God*, 382.

41. To borrow a phrase from the title of Traherne and Inge, *Happiness and Holiness*.

42. Naess, *Ecology, Community, and Lifestyle*, 3.

Here, as in many of his personal reflections, Naess is writing about the actual experience of climbing a mountain as a child. He knows that "the young child's world is that which is close and easily apprehendable around him."[43] He encourages our children to play, explore and climb, because they can have an embodied experience of creation that leads them to form a moral identity in the knowledge of their dependent relationship to that creature.[44] By identifying with this dependent relationship between a child and the ecological diversity of life that is a mountain, Naess extended his moral identity, and began to learn the wisdom of humility and care. He suggests that by climbing a mountain, we may learn to "Think like a mountain." Interestingly, Naess is suggesting a similar conclusion to Trevarthen, that the "cognitive dynamics and the chronometrics of awareness and thinking in active behavioral engagement with the environment are coincident with motive dynamics." In other words, by physically engaging with an object, we begin to behave according to knowledge of that relationship.

In a poem praising the glories of baptism, Traherne suggests that same thing in far less psychologically sophisticated terms. He writes that baptism recreates the child with the capacity to become what God intends. In that state of the "first and second Adam," he is able to see "The Father Son and Spirit" in all the works of Creation. And in doing so, he rejoices, "I am a Tree, I am a Glorious Sun."[45] Wonder marries the identity of the person and the object into a new morally significant relationship or communion.[46] That union becomes the relationship through which the communication of goodness and Divine Love can be perceived, and our moral response formed.[47] It is no overstatement to speak of the formation of moral identity in terms of marriage. Traherne relies on language that he used to preside

---

43. Naess, *Ecology, Community, and Lifestyle*, 5.

44. Naess, *Ecology, Community, and Lifestyle*. The themes of play, climbing, and moral identification can be found in Naess's monograph.

45. Traherne, *Commentaries of Heaven*, 455. This passage is from his poem titled, "The Glory of Baptism," in his subsection "Observations" on the subject of "Baptism" in his incomplete encyclopedic work.

46. The same perspective is echoed in Whitman's poem, "Assimilations," which is part of "Leaves of Grass." It begins: "There was a child went forth every day; And the first object he looked upon, that object he became; And that object became part of him for the day, or a certain part of the day, or for many years, or stretching cylces of years" (Whitman, *Poetry and Prose*, 147). It continues to chronicle the kind of moral identification that a child makes with objects in their environment.

47. Matar has begun to explore Traherne's notion of union in Matar, "Individual and the Unity of Man."

over acts of holy matrimony.[48] After someone perceives God's Love as the active, efficient cause of a creature's being:

> now she can exalt a creature above all the things in Heaven and Earth, in herself : esteem it most dear, admire it, honor it, tender it, desire it, delight in it, be united to it, prefer it, forsake all things for it, give all things to it, die for it.[49]

Entering into the theatre of love "wherby all Beings Exchange themselvs for each others Sake to one another, and are united together" is a marriage, in that the communication of vital spirits between objects results in an extension of moral identity, and mutually dependent identification.[50]

At this point, it must be realized that Naess's theory of inter-subjectivity[51] is based on Spinoza's philosophical monism which posits that inter-subjectivity is possible because we share a substantial unity with God.[52] While this kind of inter-subjective monism has been deployed in at least one model for environmental education with children,[53] this approach is theologically problematic. Spinoza mingles categories of substance to the point that the created realm can share the actual substance of God, and nature is a "monad" or mode of the Divine substance. This was highly problematic in his own day, as it is in ours. However as a contemporary of Traherne, Spinoza was trying to overcome the same epistemological bifurcation that Traherne recognized. This epistemological trend leads McColley to believe most of the seventeenth-century poets, led by John Milton, were "monist animists" writing against Baconian empiricism.[54] However, I have already demonstrated that Traherne's relationship to Baconian empiricism is much more complex than her thesis allows. Also, she fails to acknowledge the range of pneumatological options that lie between nominalism and

---

48. The parish record of his marriages as well as baptisms in Credenhill are recorded in Traherne, *Centuries, Poems, and Thanksgivings*, 1:xxv.

49. Traherne, *Centuries, Poems, and Thanksgivings*, 1:214.

50. Traherne, *Kingdom*, 381.

51. The concept is called "identifisering" in Norwegian. See Naess, *Ecology, Community, and Lifestyle*, 10.

52. I refer here to the quote contained in a footnote, wherin Baruch de Spinoza "proves" we can conceive of no other essence but God's, and therefore, nature must be a "mode" of the Divine essence. See Spinoza, *Complete Works*, 225n29.

53. Mercon and Armstrong, "Transindividuality and Philosophical Enquiry," 251–64.

54. This basic thesis is presented in McColley, *Poetry and Ecology*.

Spinozan monism, including participation.[55] Nabil Matar[56] demonstrated that Traherne's notion of unity and individualism is much more complex than McColley allows. Traherne does not risk the kind of substantial elisions that are the hallmark of Spinoza's philosophy. He remains very orthodox as to the substantial difference between the Creator and creatures. However, according the quotes above, he fully realizes the depth of inter-subjectivity that is possible through the work of the Holy Spirit, as is the case in baptism.

This notion of unification is important, because Traherne is not suggesting a simple kind of moral extensionism which seeks to apply moral status to natural objects. This kind of extensionism is illustrated by Peter Singer's work on animal rights.[57] His kind of moral extionism is a cognitive extension of the ego, whereby we grant rights similar to human rights to species or individual animals. This kind of moral extension does not actually require any relational interaction with the object, and is not necessarily derived from a formative experience with nature.[58] Rather, Traherne suggests that our physical relationship to created Objects develops an extended identity in which our notion of the self depends upon the care of the other creature. Or as MacIntyre puts it, our relationships of care should now be extended to include those parts of creation which were the object of our contemplation. This kind of moral identification which Trevarthen and other psychologists suggest, and to which MacIntyre comes to late in his career, is part of Traherne's Christian ethics in a very simple way. He writes, "A man would little think, that by sinking into the Earth he should come to heaven."[59] This kind of moral identification transports us to "heaven," that is to say into the full "wisdom" and "glory" of our created, human identity. An inter-dependent, social identity is our true nature as God's living, moral creature and as well as the social purpose for having been created.

Because God is love, and the objects of our contemplation are the thousand forms which spring from the fountain of God's love, we can "know" our "duty" to Love, as God is Love by forming our identity in relationship to these common Objects of love.

---

55. The presence of participation as a pneumatological concept at work in Traherne's writing is explored in Allchin, *Participation in God*; *Profitable Wonders*.

56. Matar, "Individual and the Unity of Man."

57. Singer, *Animal Liberation*.

58. Anne Peterson demonstrates how many contemporary eco-philosophical and eco-theological theories are simple forms of cognitive extension, such as Singers, which still do not solve the "problem" of cognitivism, because these kinds of moral extensions do not necessarily require any relational change. Peterson, *Being Human*, 207.

59. Traherne, *Christian Ethicks*, 209.

> We are made to love both to satisfy the necessity of our active nature, and to answer the beauties in every creature: and it is our Duty like God to be united to them creature. By love our Souls are married and solder'd to the all. We must love them infinitely, but in God, and for God: and God in them: namely all His excellencies manifested in them. When we dote upon the perfections and beauties of some one creature, we do not love that too much, but other things too little.[60]

By love we are drawn to Objects of love. By love our souls are "solder'd to the all," and in that unification our identity is formed in love. In the end, this quote reinforces the dual nature of the child whose identity is formed in such a theatre of love. While much has been written about his Edenic theological anthropology of the child, his position affirms a very realistic perspective on the inter-subjective nature of the child's moral identity. The child is both dependent upon moral formation, and at the same time a moral agent. John Wall, who has written widely on the nature of the child and the philosophy of childhood, puts it succinctly when he writes that children might best be described ontologically as "fallen angels."[61] This resonates with Traherne's celebration of the fact that human beings were made between ants and angels. In light of our reading of *Kingdom*, we remember the moral significance of his claim that "God made man more by making him less."[62] The child is both a product of love, and an agent who can innately love. A young child is fully in need of being in loving relationships for their moral development, and yet a child is fully capable of loving the other creature with whom they relate.

Trevarthen suggests it is a principle of the child's human condition that they are capable of perceiving love as the moral foundation of caring communication in a social relationship with another creature. "It seems these impulses of a social self with potentiality for a conscience are alive early in infancy, far earlier than have been assumed by a dominant social-learning theory."[63] Trevarthen expands this notion in his chapter, The Self Born in inter-subjectivity: The Psychology of an Infant Communicating" in Ulric Neisser's *The Perceived Self, Ecological and Interpersonal Sources of Self Knowledge*. The titles alone suggest the force of Trevarthen's point that the child's notion of the "Self" is both "ecological" and "interpersonal," and is developed in the inter-subjective theatre. Trevarthen writes:

60. Traherne, *Centuries, Poems, and Thanksgivings*, 1:88.
61. Wall, "Fallen Angels," 160–84.
62. Inge, "'Poet Comes Home," 335–48.
63. Trevarthen, "Innate Moral Feelings," 2.

> It is in the nature of human consciousness to experience being experienced: to be an actor who can act in relation to other conscious sources of agency, and to be a source of emotions while accepting emotional qualities of vitality and feeling from other persons by instantaneous empathy. This interpersonal self, this person who breaks the private integrity of the ecological self, splitting its egocenter and reconstituting it as a part of a communication dipole or multipole, is fundamental to the human condition.[64]

Here Trevarthen confirms a point, made by Merleau-Ponty and J.J. Gibson before him, that is crucial for comprehending my reading of Traherne's moral theory. While it is in our nature to experience our own internal mental cogitation, it is also natural to "experience being experienced" by other beings. The experience of being experienced by another moral agent is a crucial step to breaking the egocentricity of the "ecological self" and developing the "social Self." But this is another place that Trevarthen, Gibson and Merleau-Ponty all diverge from "the dominant social-learning theory" of constructivists like Piaget and Kohlberg. Children do not just break the egocentricity of the ecological self when they develop the cognitive sophistication to "decenter" themselves from their environment by grasping moral conventions. Moral formation does not require this kind of radical discontinuity between the natural and moral self. The kind of moral epistemology that is necessary for expanding the ego-centric self can be experienced in the ecological location.[65] For this reason Trevarthen, like Gibson, believes that ecologically centering the self-in-relation is necessary to breaking the egocentricity of the ecological self. The experience of being experienced in that environmental "theatre" is a part of developing empathy, and it is an "affordance," or a "capacity" which infants possess. The child should be located in the phenomenal "theatre" of other "conscious sources of agency" to develop this "social Self." In this way, the inter-subjective "theatre" between humans and natural creatures is "fundamental to the human condition." This position reflects Traherne's notion that the "theatre" of creatures, or natural Objects:

> sustains you and all objects that you may continue to love them. Without which it were better for you to have no being. Life without objects is sensible emptiness, and that is a greater misery

---

64. Trevarthen, "Self Born in Intersubjectivity," 121.

65. This notion was addressed in chapter 4, under the topic of "wonder." Wonder is the way that children perceive this kind of moral epistemology in place.

than Death or Nothing. Objects without Love are the delusion of life[66]

Without this "theatre" between ourselves and nature's objects, it would be better to have no being because our being would not be fully formed. We would miss a fundamental means of perceiving the "Duty" of love for which we were created. In this same meditation, Traherne suggests this kind of moral formation is so central to our human condition that we are drawn "violently" towards the ministry of other natural creatures.

> The Objects of Love are its greatest treasures: and without Love it is impossible they should be treasures. For the Objects which we love are the pleasing Objects, and delightful things. And whatsoever is not pleasing and delightful to us can be no treasure: nay it is distasteful, and worse than nothing, since we had rather it should have no being. That violence wherewith sometimes a man doeth upon one creature, is but a little spark of that love, even towards all, which lurketh in his nature.[67]

Our social nature to Love is part of the natural force that draws us to contemplate the significance of the object. Children possess that native force which compels their ecological self into that phenomenal theatre where they can experience being experienced. That theatre into which we are naturally, violently compelled is the very theatre in which our egocentrical selves experience being loved. That theatre is where we perceive the fact that we are cared for.

Traherne is suggesting that becoming fully human (that is becoming an empathetic, inter-subjective being) depends upon entering into a theatre of other significant creatures. Their ecological care for us teaches us about our own need to care. God's creatures are morally significant in their own right. But they also play a role in developing a human being's moral identity as a "social self." In order to achieve their full glory as human beings, children need to be in morally significant, loving relational matrices that engage their rational and embodied ways of knowing they are cared for so that we can care in turn. And so do we who wish to become like a child. If we retire into the theatre of creation with a sense of wonder that unifies our empirical senses and our contemplative thought, creation can administer the kind of communion that helps us to achieve our full glory as human beings. In this way, it could be said that creation fulfils the mediating role of a priest. And Traherne says just that.

66. Traherne, *Centuries, Poems, and Thanksgivings*, 1:88.
67. Traherne, *Centuries, Poems, and Thanksgivings*, 1:88.

Ministry of the Earth

Traherne writes that in his early years as he explored the Hereford woods, "The Earth did undertake / The office of a Priest."[68] From across Traherne's meditations, we can collect a litany of references to creation's ministry:

> The World serves you, as it teaches you more abundantly to prize the love of Jesus Christ.[69]

> The whole world ministers to you as the theatre of your Love. It sustains you and all objects that you may continue to love them.[70]

> The Sun serves us as much as possible, and more than we could imagine. The Clouds and the Stars minister unto us, the World surrounds us with beauty, the Air refresheth us, the Sea revives the earth and us. The Earth itself is better than gold because it produceth fruits and flowers.[71]

> It raiseth corn to supply you with food, it melteth waters to quench your thirst, it infuseth sense into all your members, it illuminates the world to entertain you with prospects, it surroundeth you with the beauty of hills and valleys. It moveth and laboureth night and day for your comfort and service; it sprinkleth flowers upon the ground for your pleasure; and in all these things sheweth you the goodness and wisdom of a God that can make one thing so beautiful, delightful and serviceable, having ordained the same to innumerable ends.[72]

Traherne frequently writes that when you placing yourself in creation, you realize that you are cared for. The way that creation ministers to you with food, water, infuses sense, surrounds you with beauty, labours night and day "for your comfort and service" shows you that you are cared for in all creation. At first reading, this kind of a reading appears anthropocentric. However, after our reading of *Kingdom*, we understand that Traherne is struck by the overwhelming mutuality that exists within creation. Traherne

---

68. This excerpt is from the poem "Dumness" (Traherne, *Centuries, Poems, and Thanksgivings*, 2:44).
69. Traherne, *Centuries, Poems, and Thanksgivings*, 1:105.
70. Traherne, *Centuries, Poems, and Thanksgivings*, 1:88.
71. Traherne, *Centuries, Poems, and Thanksgivings*, 1:7–8.
72. Traherne, *Centuries, Poems, and Thanksgivings*, 1:60.

actually reflects a critical part of Trevarthen's theory. Trevarthen suggested that a child's "experience of being experienced" by other "conscious sources of agency" is critical to forming a child's inter-subjective identity. Read in this light, Traherne's passages are not merely anthropocentric. They reveal his belief that when a child is aware of being cared for by creation, that child is being formed in the morally significant mode of mutuality. He knows that a child's awareness of his deep "ecological self" affords them a relationship which helps them to become an inter-subjective self that encompasses the love of the Object and the Love of God. Because creatures offer such a significant relational nexus, Traherne counsels the faithful to "Place yourself therefore in the midst of the world as if you were alone, and meditate upon all the services which it doth unto you."[73]

Darcia Narvaéz is a moral psychologist who has studied the impact of various relational matrices on the formation of a child's moral identity. Most significantly she studies the maternal/infant matrix. Her research explores the kind of moral formation that occurs in direct, sensory "context interaction" of care taking relationships.[74] Hers is not a cognitive theory of how children derive moral decisions, but rather a theory about how a child's moral disposition is formed.[75] Her research shows that "early emotional experiences" are the root of "motivational orientations."[76] Early experiences of caring and being cared for help a child develop their capacity to develop through three ever increasing moral operations. Narvaéz confirms that "The mammalian nervous system is incapable of self assembly."[77] Human beings must be neurologically prepared to apprehend higher moral functions. Ultimately, feeling cared for is the most significant way to develop a moral disposition to care. This is because by nature humans have a "neurobiological

---

73. Traherne, *Centuries, Poems, and Thanksgivings*, 1:59–60.

74. Narvaéz and Hill, "Relation of Multicultural Experiences," 43; Nucci and Narvaéz, *Handbook*.

75. Her "Triune Ethics Theory" (TET) suggests that human beings have three ascending moral capabilities. These ascend from the "Ethic of Security" (reptilian stages of fight/flight/freeze/territory, etc., which prioritizes security over other moral behaviors), the "Ethic of Engagement" (which is Darwin's telos for mammals that includes maternal care, audiovisual communication, lust, care and play), and the "Ethic of Imagination," which, through the frontal lobes, is the height of evolution. Narvaéz writes: "Thinking without feeling as some brain damaged patients do leads to a disruption in judgement because to make good judgment one must feel the meaning of the judgement" (Narvaéz, "Triune Ethics," 104). How similar is this to Traherne's "for to feel is as glorious as to see," in his introduction to *Christian Ethicks*? See Narvaéz, "Triune Ethics," 95–119.

76. Narvaéz, "Triune Ethics," 96.

77. Narvaéz, "Triune Ethics," 102.

substrate to moral personality" which includes "epigenetic imprinting on brain structure and the affects of caregiver emotional co-regulation or its absence."[78] Narvaéz confirms that experiencing relationships of care form a child's "capacitie" to care, and be peaceable.

Research like hers provides a collective witness to the way in which the embodied act of caring is highly communicative. Through routine acts of caring a child can intuit moral information prior to their ability to cognitively deduce moral norms. Non-verbal communication makes an impact, an imprint on the brain which prepares the child's capacity to care. According to Narvaéz, the optimal conditions for moral development involve early "feeling" experiences that provide a foundation for the moral development of higher levels of moral operation. With proper contact and care the child can increasingly develop a basis for compassion, care and peaceability. Without adequate careful contact the infant can lack a host of chemical stimulants that develop the parasympathetic and sympathetic nervous system, which are the empirical powerhouse for moral reasoning.[79]

Her research confirms Trevarthen's statement that "Infants have the ability for communication in them, and this grows from within as well as by entering into dialogues with others. The way a young infant behaves when face to face with the right kind of available person supports a theory of innate inter-subjectivity, a theory that I proposed on the evidence of descriptions of mother-infant interactions."[80] But while Narvaéz and Trevarthen present a formidable case for the morally formational influence of the maternal/infant matrix in early experiences of care giving, neither addresses the question of alternative sources of care giving when a mother or care-giving parent is absent. It is at this point that I believe Thomas Traherne's own biography displays its most distinctive witness regarding the importance of the earth's ministry in the moral formation of the child.

The Earth as Othermother

Thomas Traherne was most likely orphaned as a young child. I say "most likely" because he never actually writes about his parents. But before the age of 4, Thomas was sent to live with an Uncle in the Herfordshire countryside.[81] The biographical fact that Thomas was orphaned or displaced as a

78. Narvaéz, "Triune Ethics," 112.
79. Narvaéz, "Triune Ethics," 103.
80. Trevarthen, "Self Born in Intersubjectivity," 159.
81. While the fact remains that Traherne's childhood before his entry into Brasenose College, Oxford, is simply undocumented at this point, Gladys Wade makes several

young boy is incredibly significant, and often overlooked by many Traherne scholars. He was sent to a new home as a child, and as if the boundaries of his "self" weren't challenged enough by being a boy, it was challenged by being an orphaned child in the midst of Civil War. He did not have the early experiences that Narvaéz speaks of in terms of a maternal matrix of care. Based on the facts that he was without his mother and that he never writes about her, we can assume that he did not have many of the maternal relationships of care that are morally formative according to theories of maternal attachment.[82] As an orphan, it seems young Thomas discovered the morally formative nature of another nurturing relational matrix—with creation.

He recalls that his most formative moments of free play in the Herefordshire countryside occurred around this time. At this early age he was inspired by the "whispering instinct of Nature" to intuit God as "infinite in Goodness and a perfect Being in Wisdom and Love."[83] He observed the forests, skies and cornfields of Herfordshire,[84] and peered into a reflecting pool.[85] In his poem entitled "Poverty," we can see that as a young child Thomas also gazed into the nature of poverty and riches by contrasting the built environment of his Father's poor house with a rich relative's posh dining room in which he found himself quite alone.[86] We can't be sure that another adult played a nurturing role in his life. But we can be sure that he felt alone in his new world, and nature provided him with the experience of being cared for in all the earth. As sure as young Thomas was without a significant maternal caregiver, Thomas's inter-subjective identity was impressed upon him by "another mother."

The concept of "Othermothering" is based on the notion that a broad network of relationships influences the formation of a child's moral identity. Anna Peterson explores the moral significance of "othermothering" in her book *Being Human*.[87] If a child misses one significant relationship, care

---

convincing points as to the likelihood that Traherne was orphaned. The biographical details that Traherne provides for his own life seem to confirm this trajectory, and in light of the current study, it makes all the more sense that he would turn to the solace of care giving wherever he found it. Wade and Parker, *Thomas Traherne*.

82. Here I am referring to Narvaéz's use of Bowlby's theory of maternal attachment, on which modern psychologists base a mammals ability to develop an Ethic of Engagement. See Narvaéz, "Triune Ethics," 101.

83. Traherne, *Centuries, Poems, and Thanksgivings*, 1:119.

84. Traherne, *Centuries, Poems, and Thanksgivings*, 1:111.

85. Traherne, *Centuries, Poems, and Thanksgivings*, 1:119.

86. Traherne, *Centuries, Poems, and Thanksgivings*, 1:119.

87. Peterson, *Being Human*, 237.

can, of course, be known in relationship to another. Peterson follows Mary Midgely's observations of the animal world that non-kin altruism, which is the experience of care from other caregivers who are not in your family, greatly increases the transmission of pro-social, cooperative behavior to the ones who receive care from the other-mothers.[88] Peterson demonstrates the consensus that "other-mothering" relationships result in a child's increased notion of a morally relational self.[89] The more "othermothers" a child can have, the broader the child's inter-subjective, identification with pro-social virtues of dependence may be.[90] In young Thomas's life, the earth's ministry was that of an "othermother" who cared for him in a manner that left a deeply pro-social, inter-subjective identification with virtues of dependence. And like all mothers, or other significant caregivers, creation's influence was not always positive in the affective sense.

Because his contemplations came to him during times of free play, he was often alone. Being alone, he felt at times a "certain want and horror" at the wideness and dangers of creation.[91] He also seemed in awe of the tension between his perceived childhood vulnerability in the face of nature and the fact that he was yet alive. His awareness of this exquisite paradox led him to wonder about the sublime significance of the earth's ministry. Traherne did not fear the strength and breadth of the natural world. Nor did his vulnerability make him skeptical of God's love or justice. Even the sight of natural things that were scary for such a young child yielded "liquid clear satisfactions" about his place in creation.[92]

---

88. Peterson, *Being Human*, 164. Peterson is referring to the work which Mary Midgley elaborates in Midgley, *Ethical Primate*; *Beast and Man*.

89. Peterson, *Being Human*, 180.

90. Frans De Waal has shown that morally significant acts of non-verbal communication are not confined to the human species. De Waal has devoted his life to the study of primates. De Waal explores the way that sympathy, quid pro quo, rank, authority and other social ethics function in the animal world in de Waal, *Good Natured*. Not surprisingly, De Waal demonstrates that non-verbal acts, particularly those between mothers and infants—such as food sharing, mouth feeding, holding, and other nurturing behaviors—are the means for transmitting important behavioral, social, and ethical concepts—such as justice and conflict resolution—to offspring and other offspring who are not genetically related in de Waal, *Peacemaking Among Primates*. Related to the theme of our study, sociologist Barbara King reminds us that morally significant non-verbal communication occurs within inter-species relationships as well. She reflects on the way in which our prehistoric and historic relationship with non-human creatures has impacted human sociality. Of course, interspecies relationships, particularly those between animals and young children, are mostly based on non-verbal communication. However, they are highly communicative. See King, *Being With Animals*.

91. Traherne, *Centuries, Poems, and Thanksgivings*, 1:68.

92. Traherne, *Centuries, Poems, and Thanksgivings*, 1:123.

As an orphan living among the horrors of the Civil War, perhaps Traherne's primary knowledge of caregiving did not come from a mother or another human care giver. Perhaps not experiencing that necessary and formative level of care-giving through his language based human relationships led him to realize even more deeply the "other-mothering" that creation is capable of providing if we place ourself deep enough into a non-verbal relational nexus with other creatures as Objects of love. This would no doubt confirm Traherne's own experience that children, even those who do not have a capacity for language, have the ability to form an inter-subjective identity between the self, creation and the Creator. Through a wondrous identification with creation's non-verbal communication of mutuality that occurs within the theatre of a caring relationship, children can develop an inter-subjective moral identity based on the virtues of dependence.

Conclusion

In this chapter, I demonstrated the importance that natural Objects of God's creation play in Thomas Traherne's moral theory, and his methodology of retiring into creation. Traherne believed the natural Objects that we perceive are morally significant in themselves because they are all created by the efficient cause of God's love. Creatures naturally communicate the love of God. Against both empiricism and rationalism, he affirms that "knowledge" of the true "value" of these objects is gained by being immediately present with them. For us to truly "see" these Objects, which we have perceived with our senses, we must enter into a physical "theatre" where we can behold the Object in love, as a creature of God's love.

In addition to grasping the moral significance of each creature, this ecological theatre provides the non-verbal, relational nexus in which the human being can cultivate its innate social nature into its true moral identity as a creature of God. The "theatre" provides the phenomenal field in which an inter-subjective identity can be developed. Psychologists such as Colwyn Trevarthen and Darcia Narvaéz confirm that our pro-social nature is indeed innate, but developing the empathetic virtues of dependence requires a certain methodology that includes early experiences of being cared for in time and space. This "experience of being experienced" helps a child expand their moral identity to include those creatures, which are perceived as care givers. I demonstrated that this method of inter-subjective formation operates within Traherne's own biography, and subsequently, his moral theory. This provides further explanation for Traherne's methodology of "Retirednes," which prescribes his parishioners and readers to go out among creation as a child, and experience the depth to which you are cared for in all the earth. By doing so, the child can be morally formed into the natural creature of love that she truly is.

The notion that the "ecological self" is a primary location for breaking the ego-centrism of the self-centered moral identity is a notion that has taken shape in response the behavioralist and constructivist theories of Piaget and Kohlberg. Against those constructivist moral theories that suggest moral formation requires a discontinuity with our nature and ecological location, psychologists, philosophers and theologians have begun to speak about the relational nature of moral formation. The child's natural social and ecological relationships can provide a base developing the virtues of dependence, such as empathy, and can be experienced long before the conventional cognitive stage of maturity.

I have demonstrated that this theory was already present, for many of the same reasons, in the writings of Thomas Traherne. He knew that true "knowledge" of God's creatures can be perceived in time and space through our natural, relational nexus in creation. He knew that creation's care provides the child with the experience of being experienced. By placing yourself in the presence of creation's Objects, we can begin to see the way we are cared for, and understand our great "interest" in sharing love among all of the Creator's creatures. This care, or "interest" is fundamental to developing virtues of dependence and care based on the pro-social principles that are innate to our loving identity as creatures. This is the reason that "interest" provides the third rationale for his method of retirement. In the next chapter, I will explore this third and final aspect of Traherne's theory of "Retirednes"—our Interest.

5

Retirednes

Interest as the Motivation for Moral Formation

Introduction

TRAHERNE'S MORAL THEORY PLACES humans among the living, moral beings.[1] As such, the human creature is able to (a) apprehend creation's communication, and (b) respond with moral movements. In chapter 3, I outlined the first point concerning the natural "Principles" by which Traherne believes human beings can perceive moral knowledge through communion with creation. In chapter 4, I discussed the common "Objects" of love that create the theatre of moral formation. Those chapters explained how we enter into a theatre to perceive the communication of moral epistemology. Now I will explore part (b), which asks the question, what is the epistemological content that motivates us towards a moral response? How does being in close communion with the "flow" of creation's communication leads us to respond with moral action?

To that end, I will continue my reading of *Inducements to Retirednes*, and consider the notion of "Interest," which is the third aspect of "retirement." I will demonstrate that perceiving the common "interest," or interdependent care, that we share among creatures motivates us to our moral "duty." These new manuscripts demonstrate that cogitation is not the only means towards knowledge of our moral duties. Rather, our communion with creation "moves" us in a way that our caring, humble and merciful responses "flow." I will use Merleau-Ponty's concept of "motives" as the critical context to evaluate the significant features of Traherne's theory. I will contrast his notion of interest with that of Immanuel Kant's, and demonstrate that Traherne both anticipates the split between empiricism and rationalism, and holds together a holistic moral theory similar to that which

---

1. See chapter 3, where I explore this aspect of Traherne's moral theory regarding the moral status of human beings.

psychologists and phenomenologists will use to repair the split nearly three hundred years later.

Perceiving Our "Interest"

In chapter 3, I outlined the three "rules" that provide the structure for Traherne moral theory. The first rule relates to his understanding of human nature, which he names "Adam's principles." Based on these principles, Traherne affirms that human beings can naturally apprehend the flow of God's goodness as it is revealed in creation. The second "rule" relates to the fact that goodness is revealed when we truly properly behold the "objects" of God's work. When we properly employ our human sense of wonder in a spatio/temporal theatre with created objects, we can "know" the inherent value of a creature, and the caring ministry that they provide to us. The third "rule" is that of "Interest." When we perceive the care that flows between ourself and an object of God's creation, we can come to know our interdependent "Interest" in that object. I will demonstrate why Traherne believes knowledge of our mutual "Interest" is the catalyst that moves us to moral actions. But we first need to distinguish Traherne's notion of "Interest" from other forms of enlightened self-interest that took centre stage in the moral sense theories of Hume and Smith, as well as the utilitarian metrics of centuries following. So we must understand Traherne's definition of "Interest."

Traherne believes that when we truly wonder about a creature, we learn to "see evry object in those two colours of Interest and Treasure."[2] When he writes of a person's interest in an object, he is referring to "the Relation of his Nature to the object on which he thinketh."[3] His references to the "Nature" of things is normally deployed in contradistinction to the preternatural, or economic value of an object.[4] By identifying "Interest" as a significant aspect of the natural relationship between a human being and another creature, Traherne directs us towards a kind of knowledge that has a specific moral quality. He believes that through their transpirational influence, creatures communicate knowledge about the way in which we naturally care for one another *qua* creatures. In *Inducements* he puts it in the following way:

> Of all the Delights which Retirement affordeth the Greatest is to see Gods Goodness so infinitely infinitand so Great to all. Who

---

2. Traherne, *Inducements to Retirednes*, 33.
3. Traherne, *Inducements to Retirednes*, 30.
4. For a full analysis of Traherne's understanding of the blasphemy related to assigning a 'natural' object a market value according to a 'preternatural' metric of worth, see Hawkes, *Idols of the Marketplace*.

> hath made evry one the Comprehensor, Evry one the End, and evry one the Head of all the rest. For by this Means he becometh infinit in Beauty and Delight to evry one, and giveth him self wholy unto each. By this Means his Wisdom appeareth in all its Glory, whose Luster is so Great, that He deviseth a Way wherby he giveth him self to one, and by so Doing enricheth another: For he Createth one for the sake of all, and by Crowning Him enricheth all. . . . The Services of the world by Reduplications pleasing him in an infinit Manner.[5]

Every creature is the "Comprehensor" of "Beauty," "Delight," and the very "Wisdom" of making each creature "the Head" of all the rest. Because every creature contains natural goodness relative to the Divine goodness which created it, every creature communicates the good means by which they care for other creatures. At the same time, they communicate their need to be cared for as an eternally significant "End." This "Wisdom" is part of the great circulation or communication of God's Goodness. Each creature communicates this goodness through the "Services of the world" that nurture every creature's nature. Here we have returned to a theme introduced in chapter 3. By retiring into close communion where we receive the transpiring influences of another creature, we begin to "know" the ecological benefits, or "Services" that each creature offers to all other creatures. Today, we might call these "Services" the biological and ecological benefits of biodiversity. In the following passage, Traherne calls it the "Beauty and Serviceableness of [creation's] parts":

> The WORLD is unknown, till the Value and Glory of it is seen: till the Beauty and the Serviceableness of its parts is considered. When you enter into it, it is an illimited field of Variety and Beauty: where you may lose yourself in the multitude of Wonder and Delights.[6]

Here, again, he invokes our wonder that can help us apprehend the communication of the moral value of ecological "serviceableness." Until we apprehend the "Beauty and Serviceableness of its parts" we can not say that we fully know creation and its goodness.

> [God's] goodness is manifest in making that beauty so delightful, and its varieties so profitable. The air to breathe in, the sea for moisture, the earth for fertility, the heavens for influences, the Sun for productions, the stars and trees herewith it is adorned

---

5. Traherne, *Inducements to Rerednes*, 32.
6. Traherne, *Centuries, Poems, and Thanksgivings*, 1:60.

> for innumerable uses. Again His goodness is seen, in the end to which He guideth all this profitableness, in making it serviceable to supply our wants, and delight our senses.[7]

Traherne knows that the biological, mineral and astronomical cycles work for the health of the whole ecosystem. He also delights in the fact that these ecological benefits demonstrate the attributes of God, in whose goodness they were created.[8] When we behold a creature in its proper, ecological place, it will show us the harmony of creation's diversity. To apprehend knowledge of our true, natural relationship to creatures, we must retire close enough to the Rivers, seas, and fields and other creatures to "Know it by their Influences."[9] That kind of knowledge is clearly related to the melange of empirical causality or "scientific" observation and cognitive faculties that constitute our natural wonder. This is perhaps best demonstrated by the contemplations recorded in "Thanksgivings for the Glory of God's Works," which is too long to reproduce in its entirety. In it, Traherne includes myriad parts of creation including the great "veins" of minerals and "precious stones," "perfumes and spices," "fruits and flowers," "clouds and vapours," "wheat and rye," "springs and rivers," the planets and celestial bodies, the seasons, pastures, agricultural lands, wilderness, a list of "Fowls and Fishes, Beasts and creeping things." He declares that we are to contemplate all "Creatures in Heaven and Earth" so that we can "Understand their Natures / See their Beings / Know their Excellencies / Take Pleasure in them / behold their Centres / Know their uses / See every property, Every excellence."[10] We perceive an empirical sense of perfumes, fruits, creeping things, birds and "vapours." We must exercise observational methods in order to behold the centre of planets. And he would certainly rely on a Cartesian kind of mental cogitation in order to imagine the "Natures" of "Creatures in Heaven." However, here they are all presented in a poetic list of the various ways we can know the nature, excellencies and diverse purpose of creatures. He further demonstrates his desire to "know" excellencies in the diversity of creation in his catalogue of creation, which we have previously explored in *The Kingdom of God*. By repeatedly assuring his reader that "all things serve you best in their proper places," he recalls our attention to the interdependent "interest" in the health of the whole creation.[11]

---

7. Traherne, *Centuries, Poems, and Thanksgivings*, 1:66.
8. Traherne, *Centuries, Poems, and Thanksgivings*, 1:60.
9. Traherne, *Inducements to Retirednes*, 34.
10. Traherne, *Centuries, Poems, and Thanksgivings*, 2:249.
11. Traherne, *Centuries, Poems, and Thanksgivings*, 1:19.

Inducements to Retirednes urges us to retire into these communicative relationships with creatures, because to achieve the fullness of our glory as human beings, "we must conceiv rightly concerning the Nature of, and our Interest to Things . . . and by frequent Examination be made familiar with the Verity of them. A Great Part of our Estate is before our Eys."[12] One epistemological goal of meditating on another creature is to discern our mutual interest. However, as I suggested above,[13] this mutual interest, even at the level of biological services, is qualitatively different from the Hobbesian self-preservation of a century before. And it is not a simple precursor to the enlightened self-interest of Locke and Smith. Traherne is fully aware that this notion of interest is the very thing that has exercised moralists of all generations. Each arrives at different moral theories precisely because they have different understandings of what constitutes our "interest," and therefore, what kind of knowledge influences our moral decision making. In his critique of Dr. Twisse's writings, Traherne suggests that Dr. Twisse is right in confessing:

> that Men may erre in designing the right End, as also in designing the right Means; and that these Errors are to be discovered, by that Science wherunto the consideration of the End as the Means belong, but not naming what science that is, he leaveth the Rule very obscure. Which in so intricate a Matter truly is most inconvenient, especialy for that it is a Matter of such great Importance.[14]

As we saw in the previous chapter, a true, natural, embodied and grace-filled sense of wonder is the only kind of "Science" that can lead the child or adult to live in God's image. Traherne writes:

> If we live in his Image, and throughly prize all things as he doth We shall prize all his Works not only for the Benefit and Service they do to us; but more abundantly for the Service which they do to others. For he prizeth Nothing in the Visible World immediately for his own, but others sakes.[15]

---

12. Traherne, *Inducements to Retirednes*, 33.

13. I addressed this issue in chapter 3, where I demonstrated the offense that Traherne took to Hobbes's notion of self-preservation as the only real "law of nature." My discussion there related to Hobbes, *Leviathan*. For further reading on Hobbes's understanding of self-interest as the "law of nature," see Zagorin, *Hobbes and the Law of Nature*.

14. Traherne, *Sober View*, 71.

15. Traherne, *Sober View*, 60.

Our true "Interest" is not a selfish or biologically self-interested concept. We prize the "Service which [creatures] do to others" even "more abundantly" than the service that they provide to us. In chapter 2, I showed that Traherne's notion of true love was complex, in the sense that when the communication of Divine love is operative, there can be no distinction between self-love and the love of another. As demonstrated, this was the basis of his critique against Hobbes's notion of our selfish nature. For Traherne, the notion that self-interest and selflessness are somehow opposed is simply a false dichotomy of the way God exercises love. Traherne states that God's interest is ultimately united to the interest and well being of all creatures, and to think otherwise is an effect of sinful detachment from God's purpose for creation.

> It is a trick that Satan taught them, but God was never Acquainted with it, to divide his own Interest from that of others. His Interest is most promoted in that of his Creatures, and only in their it is secured. His Interest and his Creatures is united inseparably, and in Exalting them, he is himself Exalted.[16]

In the same way, our "Interest" in ecological benefit, or the perception of creation's natural goodness, is equally precluded from selfishness. If we do not have the interest of other creatures in mind when we perceive our interest, then we are not actually "Interested." We are merely selfish. We recognise our true "Interest" when we grasp that:

> God's infinit Wisdom doth not appear only in making a River Spring out of the Ground, or run into the Sea; but by making it profitable to Trees and flowers in the Way between, Serviceable to many luxuriant fields and Beautifull meadows and populous villages and Townes and Cities, being usefull to Birds and Beasts and Fishes, yea to men in themselvs and in all these so likewise doth his Wisdom appear in making the Stream and Current of his Decrees, from the very fountain Head, in all the Tracts of Time between that and the ocean of Glory infinitly Delightfull to all Spectators in being Serviceable all along to innumberable Ends.[17]

In this passage, the moral purpose of perceiving this scene of ecological beneficence is to comprehend the way in which all creatures are cared for by the flow, or flux of God's loving Wisdom. Traherne makes this point explicit in later centuries.

16. Traherne, *Kingdom*, 297.
17. Traherne, *Sober View*, 72.

> Since therefore all things depending so continually upon His care and love the perpetual influx of His almighty power is infinitely precious and His Life exercised incessantly in the manifestation of Eternal Love, in that every moment throughout all generations He continueth without failing to uphold all things for us. We likewise ought to show our infinite love by upholding Heaven and Earth, Time and Eternity, God and all things in our Souls, without wavering or intermission : by the perpetual influx of our life. To which we are by the goodness of all things infinitely obliged. Once to ease is to draw upon ourselves infinite darkness, after we have begun to be so illuminated : for it shows a forgetfulness and defect in love, and it is an infinite wonder that we are afterward restored.[18]

The perpetual influx of God's care into creation, and by extension God's loving care for us, demands our constant influx of care for creation. Our participation in this circulation of care depends on "the perpetual influx of our life" towards the end of caring for all creatures. Not to care for creation reveals a "defect" in our love, as well as a "forgetfulness" of the principles of our human nature and our identity in relationship to creation and a caring Creator. Following from this point, he believes not to care for creation would be an ultimate act of apostasy.

> Should God give Himself and all worlds to you, and you refuse them, it would be no purpose. Should He love you and magnify you, should He give His Son to die for you, and command all Angels and men to love you, should he exalt you in His Throne, and give you dominion over all His works, and you neglect them it would be to no purpose. Should He make you in His image, and employ all His wisdom and power to fill Eternity with treasures, and you despise them, it would be in vain. In all these things you have to do; and therefore your actions are great and magnificent, being of infinite importance in all eyes; while all creatures stand in expectation what will be the result of your liberty.[19]

Reminiscent of the Apostle Paul, Traherne knows that creation is waiting for us to care for it in the way that it cares for us (cf. Rom 8:19). A goal of the Christian life is to honour God by realizing creation cares for us, and in turn care for creation. Contemplating biodiversity is a valuable part of forming a faithfully caring character. In the natural theatre of love that

---

18. Traherne, *Centuries, Poems, and Thanksgivings*, 1:101.
19. Traherne, *Centuries, Poems, and Thanksgivings*, 1:192.

is our being-in-creation, we can perceive the knowledge that we are each cared for, and in turn care for one another. At this point, I can be more precise about the ethical significance of what Traherne believes we should be aware of. This definition of "Interest" is the moral content that Traherne believes is communicated via creation's influences.

However, our response, which creation so eagerly anticipates, is qualitatively different from the care that creatures provide. Revisiting section III of *Sober View*, we recall that the "serviceableness" which non-living or necessary creatures provide are not moral. They are the necessary function of a non-moral being who was created good.

> As the shining of the Sun, or the Blowing of the Wind is Good for Several Ends, it is profitable and subservient to the Benefit of Man and the Welfare of Creatures, being suitable to the End for which it is ordained. And thus it sheweth forth his Glory that made it so to Act, tho it Worketh of Necessity But this is all its Goodness, it neither Knoweth nor intendeth what it doth, and therfore is but an Inferior and Mechanical Agent: Whose Operations are neither Wise nor Holy. . . . Nothing is Moraly Good but what is Righteous. That is, which floweth from one that is sensible of what is right, purlely from his Love to virtue, in respect to obligations and Rewards; freely, without compulsion or Constraint; having a desire of being Beautifull, and pleasing to som Lawgiver, Benefactor, Lord or Creator; or at least Good to some other object in a delightfull manner.[20]

In this treatise, he is trying to combat the perspective of Dr. Twisse who staunchly defended the Calvinist notion of pre-destination. In this debate Traherne takes the side of Anglican theologian Dr. Sanderson. Traherne insists that pre-destination is a more complicated notion than simply determining whether some people are specially elected for salvation. Traherne suggests pre-destination is problematic from the standpoint of moral theology. Humans are certainly not pre-destined for election in the Calvinist sense, because that would make us merely necessary agents. If we were elected by God's will, our participation in God's goodness would be an involuntary act, as when a stone holds the soil or the sun when it shines. However positively life-giving that situation would be, Traherne laments that we would no longer be at liberty to respond to our duty in righteousness. In that case we would cease to be moral beings. This is similar to his argument against the emerging atheistic empiricism that developed into the moral sense theories of David Hume and Adam Smith. Moral actions

---

20. Traherne, *Sober View*, 58.

are not simply the mechanical, causal result of our having been struck with the atoms of a plant or rock's transpiring influence. There is indeed something that happens within our selves when we perceive that communication which motivates our moral movements. Traherne goes on to state:

> For whereas God determineth to Creat Grace in the Heart of his Elect in the very Act as he is meerly passive, he is involuntary: wheras Righteousness is a Wise and Voluntary Motion and operation of the Soul, wherby the person that is converted becometh Righteous because he cooperates with God, and maketh use of the Ability which God giveth him of his own Accord: being desirous to answer all those obligations that are laid upon him, and prizing, or loving the Beauty of those Duties that are set before him.[21]

Traherne is certain that the communication of that necessary, natural goodness, properly perceived, moves us to moral action. While we do not simply react to necessary motions, we are also not left alone to our mental capacity to conceive moral "obligations" or deduce our "Duties." The perception of our reciprocal "Interest" revealed by the care of another creature is the knowledge of God's natural goodness that teaches us, or moves us towards our moral duty. This is a significant point in understanding Traherne's moral theory.

> The works of contentment and pleasure are of the Day. So are the works which flow from the understanding of our mutual serviceableness to each other: arising from the sufficiency and excellency of our treasures, Contentment, Joy, Peace, Unity, Charity, &c., whereby we are all knit together, and delight in each others happiness.[22]

Traherne suggests that if we can perceive this kind of communication that creation is constantly offering, requisite "duties" will necessarily flow into our action. The fourth century of his meditations begins by reminding his reader that "besides contemplative, there is an active happiness, which consisteth in blessed operations."[23] The "blessed operations" are those ethical practices that flow from the moral knowledge that was perceived in contemplative communion with God through creation.

> The world serves you in beautifying and filling [your soul] with amiable ideas; for the perfecting of its stature in the eye of God.

---

21. Traherne, *Sober View*, 68.
22. Traherne, *Centuries, Poems, and Thanksgivings*, 1:17.
23. Traherne, *Centuries, Poems, and Thanksgivings*, 1:169.

> ... For He is all eye and all ear. Being therefore perfect, and the mirror of all perfection, He hath commanded us to be perfect as He is perfect. And we are to grow up into Him till we are filled with the fullness of His Godhead. We are to be conformed to the Image of His glory: till we become the resemblance of His great exemplar. Which we then are, when our power is converted into Act, and covered with it, we being an Act of KNOWLEDGE and WISDOM as He is: When our Souls are present with all objects, and beautified with the ideas and figures of them all.[24]

Nature's necessary acts of care fill us up with "amiable ideas." Recalling our earlier discussion, ideas are not merely the Lockean intellectual representations of objects. For Traherne, "Ideas" can be carried by the vital spirits that are transmitted through a creature's transpiration. We can receive ideas when we retire into the physical theatre with other creatures where our exhalations can physically impact our knowledge of one another. The perception of vital ideas "converts" our power to reason "into Act." Here Traherne describes the moral moment in which we are motivated to participate in the righteousness of God. We perceive our interest through the communication of their vital ideas, and being "covered" by these influences from other creatures, we become "an Act of KNOWLEDGE and WISDOM" as God is.

Traherne insists that empirical communications are necessarily, but not sufficiently, part of our moral process. So, Traherne is no mere empiricist. But he also suggests that a creature's transpirational, empirical influences communicate to our very atoms. The intersubjective experience forms us in a sense of the dependent virtues. So he is no simple rationalist. Traherne believes that our natural communication and communion with nature tells us something about our common "Interest," and that knowledge can move us, or motivate us to grasp our duties and perform our blessed operations. Here lies an important difference with Immanuel Kant's moral theory. Moral knowledge is continuous, or at least related to our created nature, and our embodied context. Before I move on to consider the ethical significance of this "motive," I will say a brief word about Traherne's fundamental difference with Kant's moral theory.

Comparing Traherne and Kant on Our "Interest" in Nature

Immanuel Kant also grappled with the question posed by the moral empiricists. What is the relationship between our empirical senses and our moral

---

24. Traherne, *Centuries, Poems, and Thanksgivings*, 1:99.

response? Like Traherne, he was sure that our moral duty was not a mere response to physical stimuli. Like Traherne, he also maintained that our interaction with nature was somehow morally significant. However, the manner in which Kant tried to solve this moral *aporia* was significantly different from Traherne. Kant set the course of modern moral theory in an entirely different direction from what Traherne believed to be true.

In the midst of the eighteenth-century Enlightenment, moral empiricists such as David Hume and Adam Smith were extending the logic of Hobbes's moral skepticism. They were using empirical science to form a basis from which moral philosophers would be skeptical of the notion that there was a Divine source of moral knowledge present in nature. Partly in order to free morality from skepticism and the influence of passionate or physical emotions, Kant emphasized that morals transcend our empirical reality, and can only be properly known through our human cognitive, rational function.[25] For Kant, the moral order was not necessarily continuous with created order, our nature, or our embodied context. Basically extending a Platonic notion, Kant affirms that morals exist as a rational category prior to our experience of them. Therefore, we can rationally or cognitively access them through mental exercise and derive our own duties, or maxims from a categorical imperative.[26] This rationalist justification provides a philosophical platform from which the senses can be disassociated from moral reasoning. Morals existed as categorical imperatives that were not subject to human senses.

> Thus every empirical element is not only quite incapable of being an aid to the principle of morality, but is even highly prejudicial to the purity of morals, for the proper and inestimable worth of an absolutely good will consists just in this, that the principle of action is free from all influence of contingent grounds, which alone experience can furnish. We cannot too much or too often repeat our warning against this lax and even mean habit of thought which seeks for its principle amongst empirical motives and laws; for human reason in its weariness is glad to rest on this pillow, and in a dream of sweet illusions (in which, instead of Juno, it embraces a cloud) it substitutes for morality a bastard patched up from limbs of various derivation, which looks like anything one chooses to see in it, only not like virtue to one who has once beheld her in her true form. To

---

25. Kant's theory of the categorical foundation for morality is worked out in Kant, *Groundwork of the Metaphysic of Morals*.

26. Kant explores the relationship between practical and moral knowledge in Kant, *Metaphysics of Morals*.

> behold virtue in her proper form is nothing else but to contemplate morality stripped of all admixture of sensible things and of every spurious ornament of reward or self-love. How much she then eclipses everything else that appears charming to the affections, every one may readily perceive with the least exertion of his reason, if it be not wholly spoiled for abstraction.[27]

Here we see that regardless of what Kant goes on to believe about the metaphysics that support a categorically imperative moral, or the duties that we are able to deduce from those moral imperatives, he believes that no sensible interaction with nature can provide the "motives" for discerning moral duties. We must strip virtue of "all admixture of sensible things and of every spurious ornament of reward or self-love." We must remain disinterested if we are to discern moral duties.

Perhaps Kant did preserve religious morality from the growing atheistic skepticism of science. But in doing so, he supported the idea that human beings must remain "disinterested" from the natural world in order to exercise their moral function. In his *Critique of Judgement*, he writes:

> everything which is to give disinterested pleasure to the merely reflective Judgment must bring with the representation of it, subjective and, as subjective, universally valid purposiveness—although no purposiveness of the form of the object lies (as in the case of the Beautiful) at the ground of the judgement.[28]

Kant is sure that if anything is to be a universally valid moral judgement, it must be valid when the subject is completely disinterested in the effect of the moral form.

In her work devoted to the aesthetics of the natural environment, Emily Brady graciously interprets Kant's "disinterestedness" as impartial, non-instrumental, or not subject to "sensory gratification."[29] Brady is keen to demonstrate that Kant differentiates knowledge that we gain through scientific enquiry from the emotions that are derived from our sensory interaction with nature. However, we cannot avoid the fact that for Kant moral reasoning must be "disinterested" in our interaction with nature.

A sympathetic reading of Kant's position like Brady's, reveals that he did not completely divorce moral reasoning from our interaction with the natural world.[30] Kant does relate our perception of the natural world to

---

27. Kant, *Metaphysics of Morals*, 39.
28. Kant, *Critique of Judgment*, 68.
29. Brady, *Aesthetics of the Natural Environment*, 34.
30. David Carr provides a very balanced critique of Kant's moral theory, particularly

moral knowledge through his notion of the sublime. In the fear that the human being feels in the presence of the "terrible" aspects of nature, (large, overhanging rocks, storm clouds, etc.) the human realizes the sublime, or a greater sense of order.[31] Kant does not deny that morality is related to the created order. However, our sensibility to, or communication with creatures in the landscape is not what leads to moral knowing. Kant writes that nature is merely the "schema" for causing our imagination to try and understand why we feel a sensation of terror in nature's presence. Kant believed that once we start to attune our mind to that sensation,

> Reason exerts a dominion over sensibility in order to extend it in conformity with its own realm (the practical). . . . In fact, without development of moral ideas, that which we, prepared by culture, call the sublime, presents itself to the uneducated man merely as terrible.[32]

For Kant, our sensory perception of nature is not the means by which the created order communicates any notion of our moral duties. Our senses merely create the scenario in which our rationality can override our emotional fear of nature. Brady suggests that, for Kant, our relationship to nature leads to a recognition of fear wherein "we discover our strength as moral beings, not against or superior to nature, but as having a kind of independence (while also part of it). This engenders a feeling of respect for both nature, in its might, and ourselves, as moral beings."[33]

While Traherne does give thanks to God for the human being's rational ability, and reason that plays such a key role in our moral identity, it is this notion of rational independence that distinguishes Traherne's moral theory from Kant's influential form of rationalism. In the quote above Kant suggests our only purposeful interest in a natural object is to strengthen our individual will as independent rational, moral beings, whereby "the idea of the will of every rational being as a universally legislative will."[34] This kind of moral exercise is something that the "uneducated man," and presumably

---

the implications that his theory has for educational philosophy. He is very clear that Kant is not solely responsible for the disassociation that I am referring to, however, his theories are responsible for a great shift in educational philosophy. I will address this later in this chapter. See Carr, *Educating the Virtues*. Emily Brady also provides a very fair estimation of Kant's concept of the sublime, especially as it relates to our interaction with nature. Yet, even with her very fair analysis, her thesis does not contradict my reading of Kant. See Brady, *Aesthetics of the Natural Environment*.

31. Kant, *Critique of Judgment*, 78.
32. Kant, *Critique of Judgment*, 78.
33. Brady, *Aesthetics of the Natural Environment*, 37.
34. Kant, *Metaphysics of Morals*, 44.

pre-operational children are not capable of experiencing.[35] Even in Kant's own defence of his theory of the sublime aesthetic, he makes this startling claim:

> It will be said that this account of aesthetical judgments, as akin to the moral feeling, seems far too studied to be regarded as the true interpretation of that cipher through which Nature speaks to us figuratively in her beautiful forms. However, in the first place, this immediate interest in the beautiful is actually not common; but is peculiar to those whose mental disposition either has already been cultivated in the direction of the good or is eminently susceptible of such cultivation.[36]

Kant does not believe it is an essential principle of human nature to be able to apprehend moral content through our relationship to nature. Rather, he believes moral reasoning is done through a highly "cultivated" cognitive assent to rational thought. Our perception of nature is the prelude to a rational exercise in which the object itself, even a natural creature, is not actually morally significant. Identifying such a cognitive basis for rationalizing moral knowledge reinforces a moral "disinterest" in creation.

Perhaps the greatest consequence of this moral "disinterest" in a natural object is the fate of the object itself. In order to support the notion that we should remain disinterested in an object in order to arrive at a moral judgement, Kant actually affirms that the object about which the subject is making a judgement does not contain any morally purposive objectivity. He believes that "no purposiveness of the form of the object lies (as in the case of the Beautiful) at the ground of the judgement."[37] In chapter 3, we named this as the rationalist "reduction" of phenomenal objects which Husserl and Merleau-Ponty critiqued. Kant suggests a person might judge an object to be beautiful because it represents some transcendental form of beauty, but not because the object is actually beautiful. If I look at an object and believe it is actually beautiful as an object, and therefore love it, then I am merely interested, which means my admiration is no longer a moral act. The object does motivate us to moral duties. Only our rational reflection on a mental representation of an object can lead us to morality. For Kant, morality cannot actually be communicated via nature. Once we apprehend its moral significance, the object is of no value or interest. Kant writes:

---

35. Kant, *Critique of Judgment*, 78.
36. Kant, *Critique of Judgment*, 107.
37. Kant, *Critique of Judgment*, 68.

> The song of birds proclaims gladsomeness and contentment with existence. At least so we interpret nature, whether it have this design or not. But the interest which we here take in beauty has only to do with the beauty of Nature; it vanishes altogether as soon as we notice that we are decieved and that it is only Art—vanishes so completely that taste can no longer find the thing beautiful or sight find it charming.[38]

Kant's quote stands in stark contrast to this passage from Traherne:

> The world therefore serveth you abundantly in teaching you your duty. They daily cry in a living manner, with a silent and yet most loud voice, We are all His gifts " We are tokens and presents of His Love. You must therefore esteem us according to the beauty and worth that is in us, and the love from whence we came. Which to do, is certainly the most blessed thing in all the worlds, as not to do it is most wicked and most miserable.[39]

There are several reasons that Traherne differs from the moral theory that Immanuel Kant would develop a century later. As I have suggested these have to do with the role of sensory perception in moral reasoning, and the autonomy or heteronomy by which the human involves their environment in moral reasoning. But in the context of the current chapter, the most significant distinction between their moral theories relates to Kant's notion of disinterest and the moral status of the object.

Traherne and Kant both see the growing conflict between our knowledge of God's goodness and our empirical knowledge of the world around us. Kant attempted to guard moral epistemology from skeptical empricism by relegating moral reasoning to rationalism that insists if we are to derive pure duties, we must not allow for any notion of self-interest. While "protecting" the Divine source of moral epistemology, Kant actually exacerbated the dis-continuity between the natural and the moral order, and therefore the bifurcation of knowledge that Traherne was striving so hard to unite. A century before Kant, Traherne believed that the way in which living, moral human beings could apprehend our duties and be motivated to respond in gratitude and love was to take supreme "Interest" in the way creation cares for us and moves our embodied, reasoning soul to care. For Traherne, an empirically based, sensory filled communion with actual morally significant creatures was of supreme "Interest" to our moral formation.

---

38. Kant, *Critique of Judgment*, 107.
39. Traherne, *Centuries, Poems, and Thanksgivings*, 1:72.

> GOODNESS and Lov are absolute Beings, yet is Nothing in the world more Relativ then they. Were the Sun Divested of its Relations to the Earth and Seas, to the Stars and Skies, to Birds and Beasts, and Fishes and Men, and Angels what would it become? Take away it Relation to Trees and Herbs, you abolish part of its Goodness. Take away its Relation to God, you remov it all. Its Emanations and Influences make it Good, and if it be not Good to other things it is good for Nothing. It relateth to GOD, and me, and thee, and evry Thing, and in all its Relations to GOD and Me, it relateth unto thee, and in all Relations unto all, it relateth unto Evry one. So doth the Kingdom, wherin the Sun is but a base and Inferior Light, and a Shadow only of what is more Divine. It is more Min, and more precious to me, then if twere mine alone; Becasue it is evry ones it is my Perfect Joy, being infinitly Beautiful in its Relation to God, to God the Father, to GOD the Son, and to GOD the Holy Ghost. More good abundantly becaus of its Communication of it self to this Angel, to that Seraphim, to the other Cherubim, to Evry Saint and Holy Creature, whom I love, as I lov my self; and the more good, the more I enjoy it.[40]

For Traherne, the creature is good because it does actual good for the life of other creatures, whether or not it is represented as such in the human cognition. Their goodness, which is love in action, is integrated into the good that it does for other creatures. Its physical, and empirical relationship to other creatures is a source of its goodness which interests human beings for the goodness that we stand to receive, as well as the goodness that it offers in relationship to other creatures. The creature's relationship to God is the very thing that makes it beautiful, and the creature's relationship to me and other creatures is the very thing that communicates God's love in action. Our interest in this relationship of natural, innate goodness leads us to grasp the Shadow of something "more Divine." Our apprehension of that communicative relationship leads us to perceive beauty and motivates us to dutiful acts of love. Our deep interest in God's works, or our interest in and love of creatures *per se*, moves us to various forms of moral action:

> What those Works are in their Nature we must learn by his [God's works], whose Essence is the fountain of all Goodness, Knowledge, Righteousness and Holiness. It is an Easy matter to prove that Love is the Cause and the End of Things. For nothing but Love could move God to give a Beginning and Being to Creatures. . . . This is the Grand Duty which both his Nature and

---

40. Traherne, *Kingdom*, 431.

ours enjoyns. All Obligations are laid upon us to perform it, and all Rewards to Crown it. It is in one Act the fulfilling of all Laws, and the doing of Right to all Creatures. For tis to Prize them according to their Value in God, and Delight in them according to the Delightfulness that is in them. Which being done to all the Things in Heaven and in Earth, their Beauties and Services and Excellencies being seen, it is Good and Righteous towards them. The Excellency of which Action, or Good Work, will appear in the Order which compared with other things, by Nature it is Seated in.[41]

Divine love moves God to create. Perceiving the ways that we are cared for by other creatures in the ecological field moves us towards acting on our moral duties in a unified moral moment of body and soul. While Kant sequesters us to disinterested cogitation in order to generate knowledge of our duties, Traherne invites us into a relationship with a creature where we can take interest in our God given motive to love.

The Motivation to Care

The claim that perception of being cared for by creation *moves* us to fulfil our "duty" to care brings us back to the topic of motivation. Traherne's use of the word, "move" to describe the effect of perception is ethically significant. We can see in the quote above that there is a unitary flow, or continuity between our act of perceiving an object, knowing that object, and subsequently making our moral response. Traherne's moral theory is based on this unified motion. While the eighteenth and nineteenth century ushered in a competing philosophical schools which tried to persuade that our moral action was either the empirical effect of physical motions that resulted in moral sentiments, or the result of cognitive exercises, both empiricism and rationalism alienated our interaction with the natural world from the process of moral reasoning. Because they believed that physical interactions were the cause moral sentiments, empiricists were skeptical that there was a natural moral order. Therefore, as Hume famously put it, there is no way to derive a moral ought from what exists in nature. Our moral judgments are ever only our reasonable act of making decisions according to what we perceive as benevolent (Hume), or sympathetic (Smith). On the other side, because they believed our rational cogitations led us to grasp universal moral categories, rationalists were skeptical that the natural world with all of its sensory passions was a necessary part of moral reasoning. If moral reasoning was an

---

41. Traherne, *Sober View*, 59–60.

act of deduction from rational categories, there is no need to derive a moral ought from what exists in nature. Rational beings are perfectly capable of "knowing," deriving our moral duties according to our individual rationality, or social deliberation about what is right. For the rationalist, moral judgments are the result of our intellectual cogitations, which opens the door for existentialism, utilitarianism and modern rights based moralizing. Given that these two positions defined the major opposing views throughout the eighteenth and nineteenth centuries, it is no surprise that the twentieth century would usher in an attempted repair in the form of phenomenology. Merleau-Ponty demonstrated that while both moral causality (empiricism) and moral intellectualism (rationalism) were necessary, neither was sufficient for understanding the perception of moral knowledge. Empricism and rationalism, as such, are insufficient moral theories because:

> one treats man as the result of the physical, physiological, and sociological influences which shape him from outside and make him one thing among many; the other consists of recognizing an acosmic freedom in him, insofar as he is spirit and represents to himself the very causes which supposedly act upon him.[42]

Empirical theories of moral sentiments suggest that our moral judgements are simply the result of physical interactions with objects, as if culture or beliefs do not shape our moral judgements. Rationalist theories suggest that our moral judgements are purely the result of our free, rational deduction, which can be made in isolation from our bodies or environment, although not from culture or language. Merleau-Ponty preferred to talk about moral "motives" precisely because moral judgements can not be the product of simple emotional causality or by simple rational deduction.

> In perception we do not think the object and we do not think ourselves thinking it, we are given over to the object and we merge into this body which is better informed than we are about the world, and about the motives we have and the means at our disposal for synthesizing it.[43]

Instead, the whole complex of human interaction, physical, psycho-spiritual and rational, "motivates" or "moves" us toward moral action. This idea relates very well to our discussions in chapters 3 and 4 regarding the way early childhood relational matrices of care nurture the child's natural substrate for developing a morally expanded disposition to care.[44] Merleau-Ponty writes:

42. Merleau-Ponty, *Sense and Non-Sense*, 71.
43. Merleau-Ponty, *Phenomenology of Perception*, 275.
44. This refers back to our discussion of Trevarthen and Gibson (chapter 3) and

> if we reflect on the way our body is actually moved by the world, we arrive at the phenomenon of motivation, in which we see ourselves as moved by things of which, in many cases, we are only vaguely (if at all) aware. The objects and situations that we encounter in the world thus act on us through an ambiguous and indeterminate motor significance. Our natural encounter with a thing is "packed with small perceptions that sustain it in existence. . . . Confronted by the real thing, our comportment feels itself motivated by "stimuli" that fill out and vindicate its intention.[45]

This is Merleau-Ponty's definition of "motivate" or "move" that I detect in the writings of Traherne. There are two reasons that it makes sense to find this concept of moral motivation operating in Traherne's theory. The first reason is conceptual. As I have demonstrated, he is keenly interested in overcoming the bifurcation of knowledge that would see the empirical science, or "New Philosophy," taught in alienation from moral knowledge. While Traherne did not know "empiricism" and "rationalism" *per se*, as Merleau-Ponty did, Traherne clearly saw the logical extension and the grave consequences of the epistemological split that was emerging.

Traherne intended to maintain an epistemological relationship between the empirical communication of creatures, and our moral response. He was trying to guard against the bifurcation, and Merleau-Ponty was trying to repair it. But both were viewing the same philosophical *aporia* from opposite sides, and employed similar notions of moral motivation. In *A Sober View*, Traherne affirms that rational cogitation or deduction are not sufficient to determine the "Rule" that we "know God by."[46] He writes that this kind of knowledge "is not in Logick to be found." Knowledge about the "Nature of [God's] Ways" must be perceived in a whole suite of embodied thoughts and sensible experiences. They are found "By Mercies and Judgments and Miracles and Revelations and Parables and Proverbs and Similitudes and Secret Motions Convictions and Inspirations."[47] He reflects on the secret motions that are revealed in God's creation. He reaffirms that this "World of Evidences" of "God's Goodness"[48] are part of the knowledge that God uses "to direct or Comfort us by."[49] This "direction" is our motivation,

---

Narvaéz and MacIntyre (chapter 4).

45. Merleau-Ponty, *Phenomenology of Perception*, 391.

46. This phrase is written in a marginal comment in Traherne's secondary script, which suggests a later commentary on the text. See Traherne, *Sober View*, 71.

47. Traherne, *Sober View*, 72.

48. Traherne, *Sober View*, 73.

49. Traherne, *Sober View*. This phrase comes from the same marginal comment that

because "all our Natural and Substantial Duties Flow from the Goodness and Love of God, they being all so Congenial to Mans interest and Happiness that nothing more is desireable to him."[50]

Secondly, both Merleau-Ponty and Traherne believe that natural creatures are crucial motivators in our perception of moral knowledge. Empiricism understands the creature as a mechanical object, in which we view the creature with a mere investigative gaze. Kant's version of rationalism disregards the creature as a morally insignificant object. At best, the natural world might be a fearful reminder of our need to cogitate. At worst, any "interest" in our relationship to a creature can distract us from our cognitive moral exercise. Whether empirical or rational both methodologies distort the value of the object *qua* creature, and can only claim to know about an object, instead of actually knowing an object. Additionally, and more to the question of motivation, both theories disregard the fact that the object plays a fundamental role in our perception. In both theories, there is a discontinuity between the moral and natural order. We have seen that for Merleau-Ponty, every object in the perceptual "field" is epistemologically significant. And there is continuity between moral motivation and the natural context. The experience of perceiving knowledge in that phenomenological field motivates us.

> I give ear, or look, in the expectation of a sensation, and suddenly the sensible takes possession of my ear or my gaze, and I surrender a part of my body, even my whole body, to this particular manner of vibrating and filling space known as blue or red. Just as the sacrament not only symbolizes, in sensible species, an operation of Grace, but it also the real presence of God, which it causes to occupy a fragment of space and communicates to those who eat of the consecrated bread, provided that they are inwardly prepared, in the same way the sensible has not only a motor and vital significance, but is nothing other than a certain way of being in the world suggested to us from some point in space, and seized and acted upon by our body, provided that it is capable of doing so, so that sensation is literally a form of communion.[51]

Our "being in the world" is "communion" because our vital and motor perception of the moral significance of objects is not just symbolic or rational. For Merleau-Ponty, the sacrament offers an example of the way in which

---

highlights Traherne's purpose for this section.

50. Traherne, *Sober View*, 66.
51. Merleau-Ponty, *Phenomenology of Perception*, 245.

an embodied means of knowing can become the vehicle for creation's communication of grace, and ultimately, knowledge of God. This is the kind of proformative communication that empiricism does not make room for, and rationalism "withholds." Merleau-Ponty is explicit about the fact that intellectualism, or rationalism witholds something from our perception. "Taking this view [that sensation is literally a form of communion], it becomes possible to attach to the notion of 'significance' a value which intellectualism withholds from it."[52] But the sacrament resonates with physiognomic, kinetic, energetic, and cognitive knowledge of the phenomenon that occurs among those creatures in communion. The sacramental objects communicate the real presence of God's grace and motivate those in communion who are "prepared" to perceive. In the same way, the phenomenal field resonates with physiognomic, physical, cognitive and emotional information to those who are prepared to enter into that theatre. All parts of the phenomenal field, things seen and unseen, contribute to our perception.[53]

Traherne's concept of motivation is very similar to that which Merleau-Ponty used in his repair of the epistemological *aporia* a few centuries later. While he continues to praise the rational and spiritual inspiration that comes from marvelling at the infinite depths of space, his is equally moved to moral action by retiring into his geocosmic place, with its sacramental ability to resonate with moral significance.[54] He is moved by perceiving the care of seen and unseen creatures in his local phenomenal field. Quite literally, he is moved by the fields of the earth which:

> raiseth corn to supply you with food, it melteth waters to quench your thirst, it infuseth sense into all your members, it illuminates the world to entertain you with prospects, it surroundeth you with the beauty of hills and valleys. It moveth and laboureth night and day for your comfort and service; it sprinkleth flowers upon the ground for your pleasure; and in all these things sheweth you the goodness and wisdom of a God that can make one thing so beautiful, delightful and serviceable, having ordained the same to innumberable ends. It concocteth minerals, raiseth exhalations, begetteth clouds, sendeth down the dew and rain and snow, that refresheth and repaireth all the earth.[55]

52. Merleau-Ponty, *Phenomenology of Perception*, 246.

53. This point is demonstrated in chapter 4, where I consider Traherne's notion of perception.

54. Inge, *Christian Theology of Place*. Inge discusses the difference between space and place.

55. Traherne, *Centuries, Poems, and Thanksgivings*, 1:60.

Traherne perceives the role that every being plays in the health of that system, from animals to vegetation to microscopic bugs to the influences of light and water particles. Every creature in the phenomenal field has the potential to teach us something about our mutual interest in the "care of a Creator, more than any station of quiet could do."[56] The "influence" of each creature has the potential to motivate us to respond in a way that is not merely derived from a cognitive "station of quiet." Each creature actively communicates the motor presence of God's love to those who are prepared to enter into this communion.[57]

> All that they do, being Still imputable to the Holy Spirit, because the Holy spirit is the LOVE of the Father and the Son, which proceeding from them appeareth to the Understanding in the Means of Grace and Dwelling in them (for they that see it receive it).[58]

The Holy Spirit, being the essence of God, is love. Therefore, when we apprehend this loving communion we perceive the Holy Spirit. All that we do is a participation in the communication of the Holy Spirit. He writes that "Certainly therefore by the Philosophy of the Scripture there are som infused Habits of Grace and Virtu that may be given,"[59] that constitute our "Spiritual Seeing."[60] That is to say, the Holy Spirit is the philosophical explanation for our embodied way of perceiving the truth of God's love that activates creation's interdependent care. That sacramental nature of our communion with each creature reveals the natural goodness which is an effect of God's love. For those who are prepared to participate in this communion of God's active love, creation's care can motivate us to a moral response.

In the end, Traherne's reason for taking up the theological debate about predestination is far more fundamental than the desire to weigh in on a doctrinal squabble between Calvinists and Anglicans. His reason for wanting to resolve the question about predestination is so that people would not be worried about the soteriologial quandry, but rest assured that they are loved and rest in the communion with creation in which they can know they are loved. The final page of *A Sober View* reveals this purpose. He

---

56. Traherne, *Centuries, Poems, and Thanksgivings*, 1:60.

57. Allchin has written extensively on the sacramental nature of Traherne's relationship to creation. His work is groundbreaking, and helps to lay the groundwork for understanding the ethical implications of creation's nature as a vehicle for grace. See Allchin et al., *Profitable Wonders*.

58. Traherne, *Sober View*, 134.

59. Traherne, *Sober View*, 107.

60. Traherne, *Sober View*, 108.

exhorts his reader to "be sure I say to believ firmly that Esau was once an Object of God's Love and that every man Primitively and Originaly is so."[61] To believe otherwise about our natural state is the result of sin.

> The first thing the devil persuaded our first Parents in Paradise was that God did not love them Enough: That he envied their Perfection, and kept som thing from them that it was good to know. And ever sence he tempteth us to unbelief. And chiefly assaulteth our Father here. He cannot endure that we should believe that God is Love.... Besides all which this Opinion hindereth the knowledg of God in the World.[62]

He fears that "Some men have formed such a GOD that even a Saint him self cannot love him: as if they went about to sow the Seeds of Enmity between God and Man."[63] By retiring into creation, and observing the "interest" with which creation cares for each creature, we can perceive the knowledge that God's goodness creates each creature and each creature is therefore loved. Out of Divine goodness, God did not "keep anything from us" that we must know, because God's loving care is completely revealed in creation's care for us. With that hindrance of envy and uncertainty removed, we are motivated to respond to that loving care.

His concern with the ethical implications of pre-destination explains why Traherne took up this doctrinal question in *A Sober View*. Otherwise the treatise seems rather out of place among the rest of his writings which seem so little concerned with doctrinal apologetics.[64] The reason for dismissing the notion of predestination as a special election is that he knows every creature is the result of goodness. This simple truth is the basis for his belief that we are meant to apprehend knowledge of God's love, and be motivated to moral action by our communion with each creature. God's love must be active, which results in the creation of natural goodness, and the way that necessary creatures care for one another. Therefore he is certain that retiring into that "flow" or "influx" of God's love into creation will motivate us to love, and move us toward our blessed operations, which are the motive acts of care that naturally flow from that knowledge. In a marginal comment in his manuscript, Traherne seems to revel in the notion that

---

61. Traherne, *Sober View*, 195.
62. Traherne, *Sober View*, 195.
63. Traherne, *Sober View*, 186.
64. The obvious exception to this being Traherne, *Roman Forgeries*. This was an early apologetic regarding the way in which the Roman Catholic Church had abused the interpretation of early church documents.

"This is Excellent because that Mystery is now Reduced from Apprehension to practical duty."[65]

Above, I recognized that Traherne believed there is a symmetry between God's grace and our nature. Because God's loving presence is communicated in a way that we can naturally perceive, our participation in the mystery of communion with God's righteousness moves us from apprehension to the fulfilment of our duty. At the end of this quote, he claims that if we knew this principle of our nature by which all creatures can participation in God's righteousness, "we should all be Holy."

> Now GOD is so Gracious that if we examine his Laws, they require us to live a Godlike Life, and that is the Whole Sum and Substance of the Commandment. For they would have us to be Righteous as God is Righteous and Wise as he is Wise and Holy as he is Holy; and not to be so, is to live contrary to Nature. For nature it self willeth us to prize the Best and most Excellent Actions so highly, as not for any less or inferior God's to desert the same; and when we do thus we are Holy. For Holiness is the Zeal of our soul to righteous Actions. And God therefore is infinity Holy, because he is Holy towards all Things, abhors Profaness and Remissness in any thing, and would not for all worlds swerv a tittle from what is Righteous in any operation. And by this Attribute the Holiness of all Creatures throughout all Eternity is his Delight. . . . Did we Know the Principles of our own Nature, we should all be Holy.[66]

In other words, "We then ourselves, if we understood our Inclination, have the seeds of all Righteousness within us, forasmuch as by the Best and most Eligible Actions we are made most Glorious and most Acceptable. Righteousness of Esteem is that wherby we do Right to things in our Apprehensions; or that wherby we render them their Due esteem."[67] Knowledge of the full esteem of each creature is a source of motivation towards the "Grand Duty" and our other various "blessed operations." Traherne writes:

> This is the Grand Duty which both his nature and ours enjoyns. All Obligations are laid upon us to perform it, and all Rewards to Crown it. It is in one Act the fulfilling of all Laws, and the doing of Right to all Creatures. For tis to Prize them according to their Value in God, and Delight in them according to the Delightfulness that is in them. Which being done to all the

---

65. This comment is recorded in Traherne, *Sober View*, 140n7.
66. Traherne, *Sober View*, 149.
67. Traherne, *Sober View*, 150.

Things in Heaven and in Earth, their Beauties and Services and Excellencies being seen, it is Good and Righteous towards them. The Excellency of which Action, or Good Work, will appear in the Order which compared with other things, by Nature it is Seated in.[68]

Our moral actions, which are "Good and Righteous" towards creation, are "one Act" with the perception of God's goodness. This explains why Traherne states so vigorously and repeatedly in *The Kingdom of God* that "[God's] goodness alone is an Oracle interpreting the sence and meaning of all the World."[69] By that oracle:

> Thus we see what Influence the goodness of God has upon all his Kingdom. Should we proceed further, and shew what concerns it hath in others, and the consequences therof, it were Easy to discover how all our Duties spring from this Infinit and Eternal Goodness, both towards God, our selves, our Neighbor, and to all his Creatures.[70]

Perceiving the "interest" creation motivates us to extend care towards "ourselves, our Neighbor and to all his Creatures." Retiring into creation motivates us to fulfil our moral duties, and is a method of discovering our moral identity.

Conclusion

I have outlined Traherne's theory of "retirement." Based on his understanding of human principles, the moral nature of objects, and the fact that our mutual interest motivates us to respond to creation's care, retiring into creation is a method of moral formation that matches the nature of human perception with the creation's communication of the Creator's goodness. Because retirement is a method based on an embodied notion of perception and motivation, it can serve as a pro-formative pedagogical method of moral formation for children.

In the next chapter, I will leave Traherne's historical context and compare his theory of moral epistemology to questions regarding the moral formation of children in our age. I will outline the contemporary moral consequences of disconnecting children from their natural environment, and the current revival of notions of moral formation in theological ethics.

68. Traherne, *Sober View*, 60.
69. Traherne, *Kingdom of God*, 299.
70. Traherne, *Kingdom of God*, 301.

In this critical context, I will interpret the pedagogical implications of Traherne's moral theory. More specifically, I will propose the role that environmental education might play in the moral formation of our children as peaceable, living, human creatures.

6

Cultivating the Careful Child
The Pro-formative Role That Ecology Plays in Educating Caring Children

Introduction

TRAHERNE'S METHODOLOGY OF "RETIREDNES" urges us to "go out among them" in order to discern their Creator, and our moral response. The preceding chapters have focused on Traherne's empirical understanding of "how" Objects communicate knowledge of God's goodness, his anthropological understanding of "how" human beings perceive their communication, and his philosophical and theological understanding of "how" that moral epistemology motivates us to respond with moral actions. Up to this point, I have analysed the epistemological significance of his theory based on the bifurcation between empiricism and rationalism in his own day, and recent trends in the philosophy of human perception and developmental psychology. But in this last chapter I will consider the pedagogical significance of his theory. I will demonstrate that his notion regarding the role that ecological place plays in the formation of the child's interpersonal identity places him among a current conversation about moral formation of children.

First, I will outline the relationship between Traherne's moral theory and his critique of pedagogical methods of education. Secondly, I will trace the symmetry that lies between Traherne's moral theory and current trends in the philosophy of moral education. Specifically that his yearning for a unified theory of knowing the love of God gave him reason to teach that we should embed our sense of self in our naturally created place. I will conclude by drawing a comparison to some programs of proformative moral education that are based on the notion of care, specifically place-based environmental education.

In many ways, this chapter runs a certain risk by attempting to cross the interdisciplinary lines that exist between moral theology and educational philosophy. However, the division between moral theology and pedagogy did not exist in Traherne's day. I will show that the separation between the two has created our contemporary dilemma over methodologies of moral education. I will juxtapose Traherne's discontent with the pedagogical problems that arose from a bifurcated moral theory in his lifetime alongside the questions that educational philosophers are raising today about the moral formation of children. In doing so, I hope to demonstrate the congruency between Traherne's methodology for the moral formation of children, and contemporary attempts to cultivate the moral formation of the whole, natural, wonderful child.

The Pedagogical Question: Teaching to Care

To this point in my study, I have analysed the theological and philosophical basis for Traherne's moral theory. But Traherne's theory of "retirednes" also has pedagogical implications. Beyond theological proofs, Traherne provides pastoral counsel to his readers who desire to engage in moral renewal, or "rejuvenation," as Denise Inge calls it.[1] Traherne's theory of "retirednes" answers a question that moral educators have been asking for centuries. As educator David Carr puts it, moral educators want to know "how morality gets 'inside' the individual."[2] How we believe morality "gets inside" determines the pedagogical method. For those who take Christ's calling seriously become as a child and be motivated to "blessed operations of goodness," Traherne encourages us to "go out" and retire among creation.

But Carr points out that the question of "how morality gets inside the individual" is actually secondary to a question regarding social theory and the basic understanding of human nature. Generally, pedagogical theories are based on some theory of human nature and the nature of society.[3] I demonstrated that Hobbes believed that human beings were naturally selfish and inclined to violence. Most Enlightenment philosophers followed this notion that human beings were atomized individualists. For these kinds of "conflict theorists,"[4] the moral order is not a continuation of the created

---

1. Inge, *Wanting Like a God*, 248. This point is also adressed in Newey, *Children of God*, 19–38.

2. Carr, *Educating the Virtues*, 112. This is also the perspective of Darcia Narvaéz's studies, which were considered in chapters 4–5. Her research field—that of moral psychology—is not concerned with the content of morality but rather the way in which moral dispositions are formed in early childhood. See Narvaéz, "Triune Ethics," 95–119.

3. Carr, *Educating the Virtues*.

4. Carr, *Educating the Virtues*, 115. Again, such narratives of social conflict recall Milbank's rejoinder that an "ontology of violence . . . is only a mythology" that can and should be exchanged for theories based on an ontology of peace (Milbank, *Theology*

order. Therefore, the moral order of justice and peace which was derived through rational cogitations and political consent originated from "outside" of our created nature. Even David Hume believed that, though benevolence was a basic moral response to life, people were nonetheless individuals who needed to act benevolently in order to construct some form of social order. For the empiricists, emotivists, utilitarians, and rationalists of the Kantian or Burkean mold, a basic selfishness of our human nature needs to be overcome with some moral constraint if we were to maintain peaceableness. Based on their theories about society and human nature, moral pedagogy was tasked with overcoming some defect in our being, and morality gets inside the individual through various rational methods of catechetical or humanist education that are discontinuous with our nature.

However, against the violent backdrop of Hobbes, and the horrors of the English Civil War and the Protectorate which suggested Hobbes was correct, I demonstrated that Traherne believed creation fundamentally communicated God's goodness. He observed in the natural order, that if maintained in proper relationship, difference works in the "interest" of every creature. Traherne's empirical observation of ecological mutual interest points to an underlying theological point. By suggesting that differences ultimately create harmony, he gives ontological primacy to mutuality and peace. Because creation is naturally good, the peaceable moral order can be derived from within our nature. It need not come from dis-continuous, disembodied rational notions, rather, it can come from a deep perceptive attention to creation. In the midst of a war filled childhood, Thomas remembers that creation:

> taught me that I was concerned in all the world : and that in the remotest borders the causes of peace delight me, and the beauties of the earth when seen were made to entertain me : that I was made to hold a communion with the secrets of Divine Providence in all the world.[5]

By referring to nature as a reference point for moral discernment, Traherne makes a radical statement about the social theory which underwrites his pedagogical theory of "retirement." Traherne believed that in our proper, cooperative, natural state, creation generally cared for the well-being and peaceableness of all creatures.[6] Because he believes this about our natural,

---

and *Social Theory*, 278–79).

5. Traherne, *Centuries, Poems, and Thanksgivings*, 1:123.

6. The theory that animal populations and environments naturally existed in a state of cooperation and mutuality was introduced by Kropotkin, *Mutual Aid*. This theory of mutuality was demonstrated as a rejoinder to the effects of Social Darwinism that

Divinely created disposition, he believes that the way "morality gets inside the individual" has something to do with observing this care in nature. It must be remembered that he was not naïve. Living through the siege of Hereford left him well aware that we are capable of horrors. But, he felt that our violence and brokenness is the result of sinful privations, not a deprived nature. He laments that "it had been the easiest thing in the whole world to [teach me]" about God's love and the felicity that is to be learned by being among nature.[7] Yet "our Parents Carelessness at first obliterated the Love with ought to allure us."[8] And he continues to believe that:

> our misery proceedeth ten thousand times more from the outward bondage of opinion and custom, than from any inward corruption or depravation of Nature : And that it is not our parents' loins, so much as our parents' lives that enthrals and binds us.[9]

He believed that social conventions and certain educational practices distract the child's attention away from their natural tendency to learn about peaceableness. In this light, I will demonstrate the pedagogical implications of Traherne's moral theory. Traherne believes that moral education, or the pedagogical task of learning about "causes of peace" involves a continuation of our nature, not a discontinuity with our nature.

Character Education and Care Ethics

The editors of the scholarly edition of Traherne's *Ethicks*, suggest that Traherne's virtue theory has little to add to the moral theology of his day.[10] I believe this assessment is only true because Traherne ultimately did not try to present a new theory of the virtues. He declares in the opening pages of his *Ethicks* that he will not present the virtues as per normal, because that has been done sufficiently in the past.

> I need not treat of Vertues in the ordinary way, as they are Duties enjoyned by the Law of God; that the Author or the whole

---

resulted from the violent basis on which Darwin's theory of natural selection operated. Traherne's own demonstration of mutuality suggest the kind of "ontology of peace" that Milbank suggests needs to challenge the myth of violence as being our ontological nature.

7. Traherne, *Centuries, Poems, and Thanksgivings*, 1:116.
8. Traherne, *Sober View*, 144.
9. Traherne, *Centuries, Poems, and Thanksgivings*, 1:115.
10. This perspective of Marks and Guffey is introduced in chapter 2.

Duty of Man hath excellently done: nor as they are Prudential Expedients and Means for a mans Peace and Honour on Earth; that is in some measure done by the French Charron of Wisdom ... my Office is to carry and enhance Vertue to its utmost height, to open the Beauty of all the Prospect and to make the Glory of GOD appear, in the Blessedness of Man, by setting forth its infinite Excellency: Taking out of the Treasuries of Humanity those Arguments that will discover the great perfection of the End of Man, which he may atchieve by the capacity of his Nature:[11]

Rather than provide a revised virtue theory, which was the method of popular tracts such as *The Whole Duty of Man*, and the scholarly scholastic work of "the French Charron of Wisdom" Eustache de St. Paul, he presents an ethical theory that is related to our human nature, "the Treasuries of Humanity" which I outlined in the last three chapters.

Traherne does rearrange the virtues somewhat. He moves justice from among the cardinal virtues to a Divine virtue, expands Prudence to differentiate Prudence in matters of art and in matters of God, and adds Meekness and Humility to the less principle virtues. These are important alterations to the model virtue theories of his day. But he basically assumes the standard scholastic groupings of Divine virtues, theological virtues, cardinal virtues and the lesser virtues.[12] He never feels the need to justify the moral reason as to why we should be loving, prudent, merciful, etc. I believe this is why Traherne does not treat the notion of vices in his *Ethicks*. He admits, "I do not speak much of Vice, which is far the more easier Theme."[13] Even though he thinks it easier, he is not interested in innovating with regards to moral judgements about what actions are right and good. Rather, Traherne is concerned with how Christians come to be moral beings. His is interested in the pedagogical question, of how the morals "get inside the individual." He wants to equip us to care-fully consider creation's communication. In this way, Traherne aligns with the current goals of "character ethics."

In *Handbook of Moral and Character Education*, Darcia Narvaéz and Larry Nucci discuss the differences between "moral education" and "character education" in today's educational philosophy.[14] Broadly defined, "moral education" is concerned with the development of moral reasoning. "Moral educators" tend to be guided by Kantian "rationalist" categories of

---

11. Traherne, *Christian Ethicks*, 3.

12. Paul Cefalu has demonstrated the Thomistic influences in Traherne's poetry and prose (Cefalu, "Thomistic Metaphysics and Ethics," 248), but the scholastic influence is clearly demonstrated in the form and content of Traherne's *Ethicks*.

13. Traherne, *Christian Ethicks*, 3.

14. This definition is covered briefly in Nucci and Narvaéz, *Handbook*, 2.

justice or fairness. Moral educators are also generally constructivists who base their pedagogical methods on the work of Piaget. As demonstrated earlier, I would not classify Traherne among the "moral educators," since he displays such clear differences from the Kantian/Piagetian genealogy, and explicitly states he is not concerned with outlining a new theory of moral judgements. "Character education," on the other hand is broadly defined as those virtue-based approaches that "incorporate an emphasis on the attachment to groups," and the role that socialization plays in forming the moral identity or disposition of the moral agent. Character ethicists begin with an Aristotelian genealogy, and are associated with the more recent work of Emile Durkheim. Based on the congruences that I have demonstrated between Traherne's writing and the work of developmental psychologists and character educators such as Darcia Narvaéz, it should be clear that I would categorize Traherne among today's character ethicists. However, my categorization is supported even further by the goal which Traherne makes explicit in his *Ethicks*. Traherne explores the "treasury" of human nature that disposes us to our social and peaceable moral disposition. I have shown that *Kingdom* and *Inducements to Retirednes* outline those principles that make humans social beings, as well as the natural society in which we can deploy our nature towards our moral edification. According to the parameters that Narvaéz and Nucci provide, Traherne's practical advice to "be present now with all the creatures among which you live" is a social prescription that relates to the methods of character education. Even more so, our moral formation depends upon that socialization with creation. "You are never what you ought till you go out of yourself and walk among them."[15] By inducing us to retire among creation, he is prescribing a method of character education.

But furthermore, Narvaéz and Nucci recognize "care ethics" as a subcategory within the field of character education. "Care ethicists" are largely concerned with emotions, and those who focus on attachment theory and "spiritual education" are normally categorized as "care ethicists."[16] There is no room in the space of this thesis to parse the differences between care ethicists and other character ethicists. But the basic category applies for two reasons. First, I have demonstrated that Traherne believes the nature of the relationship to creation "motivates" the moral being to action. Second, I have demonstrated that one of the main moral motivators in his theory is "care." Not only do "blessed operations" flow from the perception of being cared for, but he clearly believes that the way to teach this kind of perception

---

15. Traherne, *Centuries, Poems, and Thanksgivings*, 1:94.
16. Nucci and Narvaéz, *Handbook*, 2.

is to place your self in the environment of caring creatures. For all of these reasons, I am associating Traherne among the character educators, and more precisely among those who focus on an ethic of care. This categorization is helpful in understanding the pedagogical implications of Traherne's theory about how morals "get inside the individual."

Traherne's "Care Ethics"

In section IX of *A Sober View*, husbandry serves as a motif of care. Traherne conceives of the world as "a Vineyard as well as a Talent which evry Heathen ought to use. Evry man living as a Husbandman in that Vineyard: He ought to plough it by Meditation, to adde unto it the Soyl of Holy Thoughts: to consider who made it, who gave it him, and to what End?"[17] To care for the vineyard we must consider it care-fully. Careful consideration of the vineyard renders true knowledge of its "End." We will "see" is the mutual serviceableness and care that the vineyard provides each creature. Careful consideration of the trees, the sea, the moisture, the influences of the Sun and Starts and all creatures reveals gratitude, obedience and love. And as I have shown before, our careful consideration reveals the knowledge that we are cared for by the vineyard. It reveals to the care-ful cultivator that he "is a vine him self, and not only a vine Dresser."[18]

Significantly, Traherne applies this parable to every "Heathen." "Evry man" could participate in this kind of care-ful consideration of creation because God has "given us such Excellent Natures, Ordained us to live in his Image, prepared such Beautifull Works for us to Discharge and to walk in."[19] The "capacity" for a unified perception of creation is a one of our human principles because we were created in the image of God which can lead us to "see" the end of every being through a unified, care-ful, considerate mode of perception which we have discussed to this point.[20] It is therefore "our principal duty . . . to keep our Ey open and our Consideration awake."[21] The human's "Desire of Wisdom" is related to the principle of wonder, or the "inquisitive Nature" to know the care that is inherent in creation. In other words, humans naturally want to carefully consider other beings in order to discern our mutual interest, and that innate wonder is the gift of having been care-fully created in God's image. Care-ful consideration of creation

17. Traherne, *Sober View*, 93.
18. Traherne, *Sober View*, 94.
19. Traherne, *Inducements to Retirednes*, 26.
20. Traherne, *Sober View*, 61.
21. Traherne, *Sober View*, 134.

is continuous with our nature, and as a significant relationship of care, it nurtures our moral formation and motivation.

In chapter 3 I suggested that carefulness, or attentiveness to creatures in the phenomenal field, turns our natural sense of wonder about creation into the moral motivation to care for creation.[22] Merleau-Ponty wrote about the connection between attentiveness and our ability to make moral judgements. He knows that mere empiricism "cannot see that we need to know what we are looking for," and "intellectualism [or rationalism] fails to see that we need to be ignorant of what we are looking for."[23] Both empiricism and rationalism confuse perception with scientific and rational consciousness. Neither empiricism or pure rationalism can "grasp consciousness *in the act of learning*" because they both assume we know what we are looking for when we encounter an object.[24] Note the pedagogical implication of his quote. Merleau-Ponty knows that in order to perceive the epistemological significance of the object we behold, we have to be attentive to its inherent significance, not merely what we want to know about it. Pedagogically, empiricism and rationalism suggest that the actual act of being attentive to the object's significance "creates nothing."[25] The act of being attentive to the object is not morally significant because, as you will recall, the object is not necessarily morally significant in itself. On the contrary, Merleau-Ponty affirms that the observer's care-ful attentiveness to the object is morally significant because it is part of our perception. If we are care-ful in our consideration of, or attention to, the object we are more likely to "know" it.

To demonstrate this theory, he recalls Head's experiments with patients who had damage to the central nervous system that caused "a local weakening of attention" in one area of the brain. The patients could feel the sensation (such as a pin prick), but could not identity the location of the contact. As a result, the patients failed to respond to stimuli. They could not translate their perception into a response because their condition prevented them from being able to pay attention to the spatio/temporal realities of the perceptual field. This kind of disorder represents a "disintegration of the

---

22. While articulating the role that wonder plays in perception in de Waal, *Lost in Wonder*.

23. Merleau-Ponty, *Phenomenology of Perception*, 33.

24. Merleau-Ponty, *Phenomenology of Perception*, 33.

25. "Perceptual consciousness is confused with the exact forms of scientific consciousness and the indeterminate does not enter into the definition of the mind. In spite of the intentions of intellectualism, the two doctrines, then, have this idea in common that attention creates nothing, since a world of impressions in itself or a universe of determining thought are equally independent of the action of the mind" (Merleau-Ponty, *Phenomenology of Perception*, 33).

sensory field which no longer remains stable while the subject perceives."[26] Merleau-Ponty insists that our attention to the flux of information that comes from the phenomenal field allows the human being to integrate perception with motivation. He writes, "Attention first of all presupposes a transformation of the mental field, a new way for the consciousness to be present to its objects."[27] The role of attention is to prepare the body to acquire a certain kind of knowledge. It is not to simply to recall knowledge of which you are already aware (which he calls "paying attention"). Attention is a posture where the person is open to perceive whatever information is being given. We have to be "attentive" to learn something new or unexpected. Without it, we are likely to not perceive the object at all, or our response towards the object will be disintegrated from our perception of it. In either case, we will not fully "know" or "see" the object. Thus careful attention is:

> the active constitution of a new object which makes explicit and articulates what was until then presented as no more than an indeterminate horizon. At the same time as it sets attention in motion, the object is at every moment recaptured and placed once more in a state of dependence on it. It gives rise to the "knowledge-bringing event."[28]

Attention to the phenomenal field "sets in motion" the chain of moral meaning making. Attention transforms our "investigative gaze" to the posture of being-in-the-world which allows us to actually see objects in the phenomenal field, and perceive the information which they communicate. This is what Traherne means by giving "careful" "consideration." We must apply attentive consideration in order to perceive the way creatures care for us in their being. This is the same kind of attentiveness and carefulness that underwrites Arne Naess's counsel to be present in nature. Attention to the spatial temporal relationship is what inspires the child to fully perceive objects. Naess recalls visiting the sea as a four year old, and marvelling at a tidal pool. His attention was drawn to "the overwhelming diversity and richness of life" and "the tiny beautiful forms which 'nobody' cared for, or were even unable to see."

> These reflections instilled within me the idea of modesty—modesty in man's relationships with mountains in particularly and the natural world in general. As I see it, modesty is of little value if it is not a natural consequence of much deeper feelings,

---

26. Merleau-Ponty, *Phenomenology of Perception*, 33.
27. Merleau-Ponty, *Phenomenology of Perception*, 33.
28. Merleau-Ponty, *Phenomenology of Perception*, 35.

> a consequence of a way of understanding ourselves as part of nature in a wide sense of the term. This way is such that the smaller we come to feel ourselves compared to the mountain, the nearer we come to participating in its greatness.[29]

Paying careful attention to the phenomenal field provokes our moral sensibility, and prepares the human to perceive the natural communication of care. For Naess, this set into motion the formation of modesty, and the formation of his inter-dependent moral identity as a being-in-creation. Because children naturally do this well, the pedagogical implications are immediate, and they were obvious to Traherne as well. In the image of God, children were naturally given this "talent" to carefully consider the "vineyard." When we encourage a child's attentive relationship to the "works of God" we nurture this "talent," and cultivate the substrate for moral development to be "set in motion." He writes, "That we are capable of all these is manifest, because we are made in his Image. And being so made we live contrary to Nature, when we live not like God."[30] But like all "talents," Traherne reminds us that we can live contrary to our nature, and choose to not carefully use this gift.

> For to him that hath, (that is hath a Gift, and Care to use it) shall be given but from him that hath not, shall be taken away even that which he hath. What he hath without care of improving it, tho it be but little, shall be taken away.[31]

When we choose to not employ our "inquisitive Nature" in care-ful consideration of creation we are choosing to live contrary to our nature, and therefore contrary to the image of God that is in us. This is the source of great apostasy and a root of our sinfulness. Care-lessness of creatures and creation leads to a lack of moral formation, which is discontinuous with our nature. "Man's Greatest Ineptitude is seated in a Carelessness, or will it self, to stir up or make use of those Noble Principles that lie in his Nature."[32] The failure to nurture the natural careful consideration of a child has moral consequences.

Traherne believes our falleness results from care-lessness, or being inconsiderate of creation. "Inconsideration separates the Soul from the most Glorious Objects."[33] It was demonstrated above that Traherne believes it was

---

29. Naess, *Ecology, Community, and Lifestyle*, 3.
30. Traherne, *Sober View*, 149.
31. Traherne, *Sober View*, 94.
32. Traherne, *Sober View*, 94.
33. Traherne, *Sober View*, 92.

the heart of Satan's deceit to convince human beings that our interest lies somewhere else than the careful consideration of fellow creatures. This is the manner in which he interprets Adam's original sin. Because Adam was created with this Image of God, which is to carefully consider the way he is cared for in all creation,

> there was all the reason in the World that Adam should stand, and continue Upright in the Estate of Innocency: yet he fell, and therin sind against all Obligations and Interests whatsoever: because he was inconsiderat, and by that Omission deserted Reason, which is a Sad . . . of his Posterity becoming Apostates unto Reason ever since.[34]

Again, "inconsideration" of creation is a discontinuity with our nature. Because Adam's original sin was to stop carefully considering creation, he understands that:

> By Inconsideration Sin came into the World, and the long dark Entery that keepeth it in, till it become Aged, is Inconsideration. Inconsiderateness being the very Path that leadeth unto Hell.[35]

This notion of consideration and care establishes another facet to Traherne's view of the moral condition of the child. The child does not enter the world in a pre-lapsarian state of grace.[36] However, the child is naturally careful, in the sense that we have established. It is one of our natural "Principles" to approach the world as a stranger, just as Adam.[37] While still fully participating in the human condition, a child has the natural "capacity" to carefully consider creation because they naturally wonder about each communicative creatures in their new environment.[38] A child's fall from this Adamic state of consideration happens when they are convinced at an early age that they should turn their attention from God's works, towards baubles and preternatural fineries. In his poem *The Apostacy*, Traherne writes:

> To do as Adam did;

---

34. Traherne, *Sober View*, 88. This passage is particularly plagued with Traherne's penchant for poor spelling. There is also a gap in the manuscript, which is designated by an ellipsis.

35. Traherne, *Sober View*, 92.

36. I demonsrated this point in chapters 2–3, but in this regard, my reading follows this notion of Newey's analysis of the same in Newey, *Children of God*.

37. See chapter 3, where I consider Traherne's understanding of the "Principles" of our human nature.

38. See chapter 3, where Traherne prefigured the "stranger" in *Kingdom* as as child coming to the created world as Adam.

> And not to know those superficial Joys
> Which were from him in Eden hid:
> Those little new-invented Things,
> Fine Lace and Silks, such Childish Toys
> As Ribbans are and Rings,
> Or worldly Pelf that Us destroys.
> For God,
> Both Great and Good,
> The Seeds of melancholy
> Created not: but only foolish Men,
> Grown mad with customary folly
> Which doth increase their Wants, so dote
> As when they elder grow they then
> Such Baubles chiefly note;
> More Fools at Twenty Years than Ten.[39]

Apostasy is associated with being led away from our natural carefulness, into a state of carelessness about God's works. Traherne's apostasy was perpetuated by his own education.[40] As demonstrated in chapter 1, Traherne's critique of his education was that it sought to teach moral epistemology in a manner that actually distracted the child from their natural ability, and therefore contributed to the destruction of that innate, pro-formative foundation for moral perception. He realized his university education alienated the search for empirical knowledge from the perception of moral knowledge. He claims "We studied to inform our Knowledge, but Knew not for what End we so Studied. And for lack of aiming at a Certain End, we Erred in the Maner"[41] To him, this manner of investigative science was "*Aliena.*"

Reflecting on his childhood, Traherne became aware that his alienation began when he was tempted away from his natural carefulness of his nature and ecological location. His education represented a discontinuity with his natural "principles." Pedagogical or social methods that tempt a child away from their natural carefulness towards a fetishization of preternatural value, or language and conventions as sources of moral knowledge effectively "murder" the child's nature. That is, they suggest that the development of a moral identity requires a cognitive dis-continuity with their nature and ecological identity. In *The Apostacy*, Traherne grieves his own "infanticide."

---

39. Traherne, *Centuries, Poems, and Thanksgivings*, 2:95.

40. See chapter 1, where I consider how the conflict between Traherne's scholastic grammar school education and his Paracelsian/Baconian education at Oxford created a realization that there was a growing gap between these kinds of knowledge. That birfurcation made for a "bad" education.

41. Traherne, *Centuries, Poems, and Thanksgivings*, 1:111.

> But I,
> I knew not why,
> Did learn among them too
> At length; and when I once with blemisht Eys
> Began their Pence and Toys to view,
> Drown'd in their Customs, I became
> A Stranger to the Shining Skies,
> Lost as a dying Flame;
> And Hobby-horses brought to prize.
> The Sun and Moon forgon,
> As if I unmade, appear
> No more to me; to God and Heven dead
> I was, as tho they never were:
> Upon som useless gaudy Book,
> When what I knew of God was fled,
> The Child being taught to look,
> His Soul was quickly Murthered.[42]

The cognitive pursuit of moral conventions, or "customs," demanded a departure from the natural means by which God communicates goodness through creation. This discontinuity from his natural capacity to perceive goodness made him feel that he had been "unmade." His created nature having been "murdered," "God and Heven" themselves seemed "dead," and were "No more" to him. It would be difficult to find more powerful language to suggest this kind of education does not respect our created nature.

These strong words amount to a fundamental critique of the emerging pedagogical theories in his day. As I demonstrated in chapter 1, Traherne received his education in a time of great reform. He seems to have gleaned some of the educational reformers' views on the need to relate pedagogical methods to the natural principles of childhood. Several times he refers to the seventeenth-century Moravian priest and educational reformer Comenius who wrote "My aim is to show, although this is not generally attended to, that the roots of all sciences and arts in every instance arise as early as in the tender age, and that on these foundations it is neither impossible nor difficult for the whole superstructure to be laid; provided always that we act reasonably as with a reasonable creature."[43]

Interestingly, psychologists and moral educators have levied a similar critique of current methods of moral education. Colwyn Trevarthen makes a critique of modern methods of moral education that are based on cognitive, empiricist, emotivists and behavioralist notions of moral education.

---

42. Traherne, *Centuries, Poems, and Thanksgivings*, 2:97.
43. Comenius, *Comenius's School of Infancy*, 52.

Each of these moral theories, which are based on a less than relational understanding of human nature, "are reluctant to allow innate or prefabricated motives that would be capable of directing awareness of a coherent self—especially the specialized motives that are required to detect another human subject and to interact immediately, intimately, and productively."[44] Trevarthen suggests here that these modern methods of moral education do not allow for the kind of attentiveness to the relational field for which we are naturally "wired."[45] Like Traherne's education, they are not a continuous with our natural, created, inter-subjective self.

Based on her own research about the child's need for relationships of caregiving, Narváez's Triune Ethics Theory (TET) constitutes a critique of modern methods of moral education similar to Trevarthen's. In her *Handbook of Moral and Character Education*, she concurs that rational, constructivist and linguistic forms of moral education generally fail to realize the "neurobiological substrate to moral personality."[46] Current constructivist methods such as those that are based on the theories of Piaget and Kohlberg generally fail to take seriously that a child's relationship to caring objects are critical to moral formation. Thomas Wren argues that this is the case because contemporary methods of moral education are based on Kant's rationalism. The influence of Kant's theory has vast implications for the role that direct experience of creation plays in moral formation, especially for young children. As demonstrated in the last chapter, Kantian moral agency requires a rational, objective distance from creation, or discontinuity with our embodied nature. Rather than unifying moral knowledge with sensory perception, Kant's distinction between moral, practical and aesthetic knowledge drives the western child deeper into himself to cognitively grasp the knowledge of virtues. Moral education in the Kantian tradition understands moral education as a process of "in-forming" the child of moral

---

44. "We wade in much tramped-about, muddied waters, full of semantic eddies, when we enter a debate on the rationality of interpersonal life for any stage of development. Use of the widely accepted terms for cognition, chosen as they are to describe the thoughts in a unitary, isolated Cartesian thinker solving problems, generates profound misapprehensions of human relating and its emotional regulation. . . . The conservative mainstream of cognitive psychology is as reluctant as was behavioristic psychology to allow innate or prefabricated motives that would be capable of directing awareness of a coherent self—especially the specialized motives that are required to detect another human subject and to interact immediately, intimately, and productively" (Trevarthen, "Self Born in Intersubjectivity," 160).

45. "All education, and indeed all special education or therapy to compensate for disorders in their development or social support, depends upon responding to the communicative expressions of learners with emotions of sympathy that respect their initiatives and intuitions" (Trevarthen, "Innate Moral Feelings," 17).

46. Narváez, "Triune Ethics," 112.

conventions. In broad strokes, Piaget based his theory on this notion, and outlined the cognitive stages in which a child could grasp rationale conventions of moral thought such as justice. In other words, he process of getting morals "inside" the child is not a continuation of our embodied, natural and social experience. David Carr outlines the way that Kantian pedagogical theories of Piaget competed with those of Emile Durkeheim for the heart and soul of twentieth-century educational philosophy. Durkheim's theories represented the notion of moral formation by which the substrate for moral identity was formed through the social experience. While I cannot fairly discuss the development of educational philosophy in the space of this chapter, the current paradigm of educational philosophy demonstrates Carr's point that Piaget's constructivist moral theory has dominated educational philosophy for the past century.[47] Wren suggests that for this reason, Kant's "shadow" hangs over all modern philosophies of character education and moral formation.[48]

However, based on current research that we have explored in previous chapters, he believes "we can sense movement in a new direction."[49] Narváez and Nucci's volume shows that since the twentieth century, many pedagogical methodologies have emerged as way to overcome the perceived deficiencies of Piagetian forms of constructivist moral education that rely on cognitive methods of "teaching" any number of virtue theories. Moral educators Kessler and Fink attest to the current trend among educational philosophy that believes for children, ethics must be continuous with, and integrated into some embodied sense of identity.

> Imprinting at the cognitive level is not enough. The best character education programs out there know this now. When we are looking at character from the perspective of the soul, it is perhaps more useful to speak of educating for "integrity."
>
> The divided self is still capable of moral action. We can and should teach our children impulse control, and the ethical capacities to distinguish right from wrong and to respect the commandments hallowed by great traditions. But we must also help young people discover an inner experience that is alighted with an outer life of action without harm. While it is not always simple and seamless, young people can develop an inner core of being peace, compassion and respect, from which the doing

---

47. Carr provides a detailed exploration of the differences between the theories of Durkheim and Piaget in Carr, *Educating the Virtues*, 183.

48. This is Wren's assertion in his chapter on the "philosophical moorings" of moral education in Nucci and Narváez, *Handbook*, 25.

49. Trevarthen, "Self Born in Intersubjectivity," 160.

and choosing of caring, fair, and just behaviors can flow in an undivided self.

Connection—meaningful, deep connection—is, I believe, the root of such compassion, attachment and bonding. . . . Students who feel deeply connected don't need guns to feel powerful.[50]

These educators agree that virtue theories are necessary, but not sufficient for moral formation. Moral formation requires attention to significant relationships.

Carol Gilligan was one of the first to suggest that relationships of embodied care are the most formative in her seminal work, *In a Different Voice*.[51] Rather than depending on rational, abstract, and in her opinion masculine methods of teaching notions of justice, Gilligan demonstrates that the relational orientation towards interdependence and care is not only more dominant in the female orientation to the world, but is contained within the natural methods of early childhood moral formation.[52] Returning to the question of how morals "get inside" the child, Gilligan arrives at a different understanding of moral education from the cognitivists because she maintains a different understanding of human nature. While theories such as Piaget and Kohlberg posit rational notions of justice as a mark of moral strength, Gilligan asserts that dependence and care are naturally human strengths. This is the "different voice" from which her ethic of care arises. Therefore, if moral education was embedded in the child's existing, natural relationships of care as the method of moral formation, then young children can engage in inter-subjective, moral formation without needing to "decenter" from their natural ecological identity.

Following Gilligan's notion that early moral formation occurs "in a different voice," methods of moral formation that are based on an ethic of engagement rather than a programme of "moral education" have recently emerged. Nell Noddings developed Gilligan's notion in her book, *Educating Moral People*, which is subtitled *A Caring Alternative to Character Education*.[53] She suggests that moral education curricula based on virtue theory should be exchanged for the creation of care based relationships in every aspect of the child's education. Education, in her opinion, should draw a child's attention to the multiple relationships in which they are cared for, and in which they can play the role of caretaker. Young children can be

---

50. Nucci and Narvaéz, *Handbook*, 453.
51. Gilligan, *In a Different Voice*.
52. Gilligan, *In a Different Voice*, 171.
53. Noddings, *Educating Moral People*.

caregivers to their pets, younger siblings, toys, parents, grandparents, neighbours, friends and the natural environment in which they live. Of all of these relationships the child's ability to care for the natural environment stands out for our purposes. By turning the child's attention towards their interdependent relationship with creation, Traherne also sought to teach ethics in another voice.

Teaching Virtue in Another Way

I have demonstrated that with a few exceptions, Traherne felt no need to change the content of Christian virtue theory, and basically accepted standard theories that were alive and well in his age. His main question was not about the content of a theory of virtues, but of educating the virtues. As he promised in the beginning of his *Ethicks*, and in the beginning of his *Centuries of Meditations*, Traherne was striving to teach these virtues in a different way. Virtue theory had been taught through the humanistic manner of catechetical memorization for centuries, and was a particular hallmark among the Calvinistic Puritans in Traherne's grammar school experience.[54] Of course, Traherne later learned that the relationality he so yearned for is revealed in the words of Christian Scripture. But at the time, he thought "the gaudy Book" of words were no way to teach a young child about their moral identity.[55]

> The Sun And Moon forgot,
>
> As if unmade, appear
> No more to me; to God and heven dead
> I was, as tho they never were:
> Upon som useless gaudy Book,
> When what I knew of God was fled,
> The Child being taught to look,

---

54. Basil Willey suggested that in response to the Calvinist tendency towards Divine Command theory and their focus on the written word of Scripture, the Cambridge Platonists strove to maintain epistemological unity between faith and reason by suggesting that goodness which was revealed in Christ can be known in the created order. Because that moral content was so obvious to the divines of the seventeenth century, there was no real argument over what constituted morality. Willey suggests that they wanted "not so much a means of knowing what we ought to do, as wills to do that which we may know." The formation of the moral will was their main concern. This debate about revelation and reason, catechesis and moral formation that was raging in Traherne's time continues among Christian ethicists of today. See Willey, *English Moralists*, 188.

55. Traherne, *Centuries, Poems, and Thanksgivings*, 2:97.

His Soul was quickly murthered.[56]

Disconnecting a child from their natural, wondrous relationship to God in creation was "murder" instead of moral education. We must reconnect them to that morally significant relationship with creation that naturally prepares a child to "feel" their "glory" as a creature of God. In continuation with their natural principles, the ministry of the earth will help the child apprehend their duty towards creation. Traherne induces us to retire into a relational nexus with creatures that seems more at home with Gilligan and Noddings ethic of care, than Piaget's constructivist programmes that are based in Kant's disembodied notions of rational duties.

In the introduction to *Ethicks*, Traherne tells us that his project is not to approach the topic of moral education "in the ordinary way, as they are *Duties* enjoyed by the Law of God" as the moralists of his day have done.[57] In other words, he will not set out to demonstrate virtue through the explication of laws, rational, political, temporal, Divine or otherwise. Rather, he sums up his whole project by saying it is "my business to make as visible, as it is possible for me, the lustre of [vertue's] *Beauty, Dignity*, and *Glory*: By shewing what a necessary Means Vertue is . . . how naturally Vertue carries us to the Temple of Bliss, and how immeasurbly transcendent it is in all kinds of Excellency."[58] Traherne's contribution to moral theology is through teaching retirement as a practical theology. Traherne proposes something that resonates with our natural identity to perceive the glory of those virtues. "And (if I may speak freely) . . . to open the Beauty of all the Prospect, and to make the Glory of God appear, in the Blessedness of Man, by setting forth its infinite Excellency: Taking out of the *Treasuries* of *Humanity* those Arguments that will discover the great perfection of the End of man, which he may atchieve by the capacity of his *Nature*."[59] Towards that goal, Traherne laments that normally,

> Vertues are listed in the rank of Invisible things; of which kind, some are blind as to deny there are any existent in Nature: But yet it may, and will be made easily apparent, that all the Peace and Beauty in the World proceedeth from them, all honour and Security is founded in them, all Glory and Esteem is acquired by them. For the prosperity of all the Kingdoms is laid in the Goodness of God and of Men.[60]

56. Traherne, *Centuries, Poems, and Thanksgivings*, 2:97.
57. Traherne, *Christian Ethicks*, 3.
58. Traherne, *Christian Ethicks*, 3.
59. Traherne, *Christian Ethicks*, 3.
60. Traherne, *Christian Ethicks*, 4.

While virtues can be deduced from laws, temporal or divine, they can distract the child from their natural means of forming a moral identity based on the peace that naturally exists in the Kingdom. In other words, through our natural capacity to perceive the beauty of Peace that proceeds from the Creator and exist "in Nature." These moral virtues can be learned in continuation with the principles of our nature, and the natural context of our ecological location in the peaceable kingdom.

If the affects of a "bad education" result in the death of the child's natural ability to care, surely a Christian moral education should help redeem that natural, human sensibility. Traherne writes that our "principal Work is to Open, Engage and incline the Heart to turn it from that vanity Aversness and forgetfulness and to fill it with an Affection Love of Pondering to make it delight in Meditating upon the Laws of God, and naturaly to chuse Holy Objects."[61]

For those who have lost this natural carefulness, part of redemption relates to re-engaging the human being with creation so that the heart will be inclined to once again perceive this communication in the sensible way that fallen human beings created with the image of God between Ants and Angels are capable.[62] "For as Man is Greater then the Angels in that he can beget the Divine Image, so is he likewise entrusted with a Greater Power in their Care and Education."[63] Traherne certainly saw this as his task for redeeming adults to this child-like state of carefulness. This kind of education, or re-education is the way to counteract the inconsiderate way in which he "was corrupted; and made to learn the Dirty Devices of this World. Which now I unlearn, and becom as it were a little Child again, that I may enter into the Kingdom of God."[64]

Again, the childhood to which we return is not a state of soteriological purity. That was the proper work of Christ. "But Since Christ hath merited, it is necessary that thou Act Naturaly."[65] Christ has redeemed creation, and therefore the continuity that exists between the goodness of our created nature and our perception of God's goodness in creation. The Christian is one who returns to this natural "glory" of our human wonder, and is once again carefully aware of the sacramental nature of their relationship to creation.

61. Traherne, *Sober View*, 95.

62. See chapter 2, where I provided the rationale by which human beings, in our fallen state, are blessed to live between Ants and Angels, because we can reason about God's love, and yet are blessed to know the joy of sensing that moral epistemology through our relationship to other creatures.

63. Traherne, *Sober View*, 85.

64. Traherne, *Centuries, Poems, and Thanksgivings*, 1:111.

65. Traherne, *Sober View*, 140.

Referring to Traherne's poem "Thanksgiving for the Body," David Brown affirms that the resurrection of Christ redeems our "awareness" of God's love that is "deeply embedded" in creation.[66] He follows Traherne in suggesting that the Christological and Pneumatological redemption of the body involves a re-tuning or returning of our senses to a careful awareness of the sacramental resonance that creation communicates. The careful creature retires into creation where it is "natural again for man to love and rejoyce in God. . . . His Wonder and Gratitude being now as natural as ever."[67] Our moral duty to care can flow when our natural carefulness is "rejuvenated," as Denise Inge puts it, or returned to "une revivisance" as Ellrodt suggests.[68] To this end, Traherne understands "our principal Duty being to keep our Ey open and our Consideration awake."[69] In thanksgiving for reclaiming our childlike ability to perceive creation's care, we can spend our days returning this blessing to our children, and educating them to not lose their natural care-fulness.

> Especialy considering how Great Treasures they are to God that are the Divine Image. For herby Men are enabled to become Blessings and Treasures to their Children, while they Cooperat with God and to the Parents Care the Child oweth his Eternal Salvation: and in their fidelity to be infinitly Pleasing to the Almighty, in safely returning what was committed to their Trust as a Pledge of their Creators favor.' How great a Favorite is he esteemed to whom a King entrusts the Bringing up of his Child![70]

Traherne joyfully affirms that this kind of moral formation of children is a central task of the Church and parents alike. He writes:

> Even in these very Children he sheweth his Care and Tenderness over them. For to the Intent he may make the Parents fidelity secure to whom he committeth them, he requireth their Souls at their hands and under the Pain of Eternal Torments chargeth them to be faithfull. He also implanteth a double Affection in them, that the very Parents might feel the Punishments of the Children or Partake in their Glory: And that by double and Treble Walls the Discharge of this Duty might be fortified. All that is done unto them he accepteth as done unto himself. No

---

66. This notion underwrites Brown's whole thesis, but he specifically relates Traherne and the redemption of the body in Brown, *God and Grace of Body*, 12–13.

67. Traherne, *Sober View*, 133.

68. Ellrodt, *L'Inspiration personnelle*, 349.

69. Traherne, *Sober View*, 134.

70. Traherne, *Sober View*, 85.

> King can be more Circumspect in the Deposition of his Heir. He telleth them, Lo now I put persons into your Hands, in whom you may express all the Greatness of your Love to me. Pay all the Respect which ye owe me here. Here is a Person capable of your Gratitude, and upon him I devolve all your Affections.[71]

Having navigated the crisis that came of his own education and upbringing, Traherne possesses a keen insight into the necessity, responsibility and gift that is being involved in the moral education of children. The goal of Christian teachers and parents alike was to help their children incline their hearts to carefully "Chuse Holy Objects" for consideration, and to orient their sight towards God's works, so that we nurture their ability to perceive the way that God's creatures cared for them. Christian education must be partly "in-formative." Whether that education is training in the investigative sciences or the catechetical comprehension of doctrine and scripture, the pursuit of knowledge must respect the continuity between the Creator's Goodness, and the goodness of creation. Traherne believed that the main goal of Christian education, or at least that component which makes for a "good" education, should be "pro-formative." A pro-formative education helps a child maintain their natural sense of care by exercising the natural principles of their human being. The "good" education does not teach scientific and moral epistemology as discontinuous *aliena*. A "good" education should help children discern their deep interest amongst creatures, and the way that they are cared for in all the world. The "good" education is one that maintains the continuity between our natural created place and our moral response to the goodness of that ecological place. This kind of education helps the child utilize their natural gifts as a creature. It nurtures their ability to carefully engage their natural place, and "feel" their moral duty to care for that place.

Our Contemporary Problematique and Some Proposals regarding Placed-Based Moral Formation

Traherne's last few years were spent writing his pedagogical inducements for the moral formation of his patrons and parishioners. He yearned for the faithful to re-embed their knowledge of what is real and good through retirement among God's works, and reclaim the end for which we were made—to "see" God and subsequently enjoy the world aright.[72] While it is

---

71. Traherne, *Sober View*, 86.
72. Traherne, *Centuries, Poems, and Thanksgivings*, 1:5.

obvious that Traherne found happiness, joy, and rapture in recovering his own ability to apprehend creation's communication, he knew this was not the case for most children. And he personally knew that a disconnection from nature has tragic consequences. This view is reflected in the contemporary critique of moral education.

In his book *Last Child in the Woods*, Richard Louv considers the western cultural trend in which a growing percentage of a child's family life, recreation and education occur in isolation from the natural world. This trend gives rise to a childhood condition he calls "Nature Deficit Disorder."[73] The "Disorder" is a kind of "Cultural Autism"[74] that results from a child's isolation from the natural world. Jane Clark, a professor of kinesiology at the University of Maryland uses the phrase "containerized kids" to describe the vast numbers of children who are growing up without direct access to the natural, non-human world.[75] Louv broadly connects complex social issues related to urbanization, concern for security, and privatization of land to the list of reasons that children are increasingly isolated from direct experiences of nature. While the effects of these cumulative forces are multivalent, Louv hints that the modern concept of moral epistemology, in which the senses are ignored as a necessary component of moral and human formation, has Cartesian roots. In his book, *The Environment and Christian Ethics*, Michael Northcott suggests a longer genealogy by which the divorce of scientific and moral knowledge begins with nominalist, Protestant theology and proceeds through Francis Bacon, Descartes, Newton, Hume and Kant towards the rise of modern utilitarianism which identifies morality in increasingly subjective terms of "pleasure and pain, of like and dislike."[76]

Northcott suggests that by the end of the Enlightenment, the fact that morality was located "exclusively in human interiority reflected the philosophical and scientific evacuation of meaning and purpose from the cosmos."[77] He writes that "This new morality dislocates the sense of self from the natural order of the biophysical world, including the embodied character of human identity."[78] According to this modern notion of moral epistemology where the moral order is discontinuous with the natural order, it seems possible and indeed morally acceptable that our children would grow up in isolation from their natural environment. Louv agrees that when

73. Louv, *Last Child in the Woods*.
74. Louv, *Last Child in the Woods*, 64–65.
75. Louv, *Last Child in the Woods*, 35.
76. Northcott, *Environment and Christian Ethics*, 71.
77. Northcott, *Environment and Christian Ethics*, 71.
78. Northcott, *Environment and Christian Ethics*, 71.

children grow up in isolation from nature, the arête of human flourishing is stifled, leading to a demonstrable "cultural autism" in recent generations of children. He gives voice to a whole generation of children who are being educated in an increasingly synthetic world. And perhaps unknowingly, Louv's diagnosis locates the issue of the moral formation of children among theological ethicists who, like Traherne, are trying to articulate the relationship between contact with the created order and the formation of Christian virtues.

I have already demonstrated the way in which Alisdair MacIntyre came to believe late in his career that inter-subjective relationships develop virtues of dependence that are an integral part of forming a complex moral identity. MacIntyre also suggests that rather than learn moral concepts, children are dependent upon the experience of relationships to form an integrated moral identity which then equips the child to make decisions about what is "good."[79] A complex moral identity helps children develop imaginations about possibilities for future moral action.[80] Within the field of ethics, MacIntyre suggests moral formation is a key motivation for making moral judgements about "good" behavior. However, in MacIntyre's account, children are often understood as the objects of care in these relationships, not moral agents themselves.

Rowan Williams affirms a similar perspective on moral formation, but with respect to the moral agency of children. Williams writes that the moral formation of a child cannot be simply about "bolting on" cognitive components of moral education to a child's experience of life.[81] Rather, it must be related to the natural life of the child and the context in which that life is lived. Williams affirms that we can help form the moral identity of our children by getting them in touch with the relational "icons" that make up the child's experience of the world. This would include the natural environment as well as all the relationships in which the child can either receive or give care. Such a formative relationship helps equip children with the ability to imagine the "good" as a moral response because they "know" what it means to be cared for. Williams's account of moral formation resembles

---

79. MacIntyre, *Dependent Rational Animals*, 96.

80. This resembles Trevarthen's analysis: "Core motivating processes determine temporo-spatial patterns of exploration of enviromental affordances and the selective pickup of information to guide actions, thereby determining what will be learned and what can be remembered for later use. . . . The appearance of efficient communication of motives in the first phase of an infant's postnatal life suggests that human learning is founded on a particular kind of curiosity, one that is designed to be regulated intersubjectively, between minds" (Trevarthen, "Innate Moral Feelings," 3).

81. Williams, *Lost Icons*, 37.

Traherne's in the sense that he writes about the importance of drawing the child's considerate attention to those "icons" or images that reveal care. In Williams's perspective, worship, and specifically the sacraments, are necessary "icons," but the location of worship may be important as well.

In his book, *A Christian Theology of Place*, John Inge suggests that the place in which the sacramental life is experienced is one such icon for consideration. Inge contends that the notion of place, both natural and built, has been generally ignored in contemporary virtue ethics. When place is considered, the commentary does not adequately address the importance of the sacramental community's location.[82] Inge relies on a report by Roger Hart that the environment in which a child is formed heavily influences their ability to imagine moral alternatives. By improving the child's environment, Hart contends, "Children would learn to see a range of outcomes from their environmental manipulations."[83] Inge's use of sacrament and place is remarkably similar to William's icons of moral formation in that the "icons" of creation assist the child in forming a moral identity that includes care as one of the moral responses. However, Inge laments, "I am not aware of these recommendations being taken up anywhere."[84]

The reality is these "recommendations" are being taken up by many educational philosophers and environmental educators. The role of place-based education played a role in the writings of influential educator, Paulo Freire. For Freirie, the goal of education is the formation of the human being. He shows that the "banking model" of education, in which the dominate culture donates, or extends "knowledge" to the uneducated, is an in-formative method. This resembles the standard cognitive, constructivist model of education where knowledge is transmitted as cognitive bundles. Freire believes this pedagogical method is oppressive because it does not allow the person to discover any meaningful knowledge that is continuous with their own life. This kind of knowledge actually represents a discontinuity with the learner's cultural and natural location, and dislocates them from their environment. They might know facts and information, but Freire argues that the student has not really learned anything because they have not entered into any meaningful relationship, which defines the difference

---

82. Inge, *Christian Theology of Place*, 134. This concept is also demonstrated in Gorringe, *Theology of the Built Environment*. However, Gorringe is concerned with the built environment rather than the natural one. While the built environment does play a significant role in the moral formation of Thomas Traherne, I am mostly concerned with his contemplation of the natural environment.

83. Inge, *Christian Theology of Place*, 133.

84. Inge, *Christian Theology of Place*, 133.

between human "knowing" and animalistic "knowing."[85] For Freire, the goal of education is to enter into a dialogue which brings the learner to the *prise de conscience* that awakens our awareness, or our attention, that he calls "conscientization."[86] When a person is in this state of attention, they perceive meaningful relationships to their neighbours, embedded in their ecological context. At that point, they make social meaning, or knowledge that is continuous with their nature and context. Looking at the world from the context of those meaningful relationships, the learners can become conscious of "generative words" which arise out of that context.[87] Becoming conscious of those "generative" themes, then they can begin to "know." Freire is clear that this kind of education is not based in "bolted on" theories of cognitive idealism, or social, economic, or scientific materialism.[88] This kind of education is real humanism.[89] That is, it is a pedagogical method that respects the human being's nature and the "ecological" contexts of their meaningful relationships. It is a method of formation based on the notion that knowledge "gets inside" a person through the experience of natural meaningful relationships rather than being radically disconnected from them.

Recently, educators have extended Freire's theories to the realm of eco-literacy and environmental education.[90] Based on UNESCO's Tbilisi Declaration of 1978, programmes in environmental education have oriented programmes in ecology and biodiversity towards an awareness that our relationship to our local ecology impacts our biological social, cultural, aesthetic and moral self-awareness.[91] One of the goals stated in the Tbilisi

85. Freire, *Education for Critical Consciousness*, 154.
86. Freire, *Education for Critical Consciousness*, 148.
87. Freire, *Education for Critical Consciousness*, 43. These generative words are the words, either colloquial words or standardized words, which have meaning in the given situation. After considering a context, for instance, a picture of a familiar social situation or scene, the group decides on a "generative word" that embodies the meaning for that group. In this way, the teacher avoids importing words from another cultural context that may not have meaning in the context, or may distract the group from the meaning that is important in this context.
88. Freire, *Education for Critical Consciousness*, 146.
89. Freire, *Education for Critical Consciousness*, 156.
90. Specifically, the application of Freire's notion to ecopedagogy can be found in Corcoran et al., *Young People*, 107–12. But Freire's influence is also felt in the following texts on eco-pedagogy: Grey, "Ecological Theology and Education," 8–122; Kahn and Kellert, *Children and Nature*; Kahn, *Critical Pedagogy*.
91. Colwyn Trevarthen affirms this notion of the relationship between the scientific and moral elements of the natural sciences: "The creations of science and all its applications in society are necessarily moral. . . . The unnatural separation and lack of communication between Science and the Humanities that emerged with Newton's

Document is that environmental education should include local knowledge and contextual discovery, and help the learners acquire "knowledge, values, attitudes" in addition to practical skills. In other words, value laden knowledge and affected attitudes, i.e., a moral response to knowledge of the student's relationship to the local environment, are formed continuously with the child's ecological place. Many studies have been written on the way that individuals who participate in programs to learn about their local environment increase their ability to articulate concepts of justice and peaceableness.[92] And as this current study is written, we are far enough from the Tbilisi Document to have had at least one significant longitudinal study of the effects of environmental education on patterns of future studies.[93] These studies show that when environmental education places students in a meaningful environmental context in which they can develop significant moral knowledge regarding ecological care, the experience sometimes affects the child's vocational choice. In Freirian terms, the local ecological place becomes a "generative" theme for forming a child's notion of care, and a vocational sense of what it means to be human. Once again, this demonstrates the point made in chapter 4, that the child's "ecological self" is not necessarily a hindrance to developing allocentric behavior as Piaget and Kohlberg suggested. If the child's natural, "ecological" self is situated in their local environment, it becomes a means to help the child experience being experienced, and to sense being cared for. This kind of environmental education can be a highly significant form of moral formation in continuity with the child's nature.

In Freire's terminology, this is an example of a true education that is formational, or pro-formative, rather than in-formative.[94] This view, like Traherne's, respects the natural, relational principles of the human being rather than being discontinuous from it. Pedagogical theories must not seek to only teach information, but rather to increase the natural capacity of the learner to "know." In this regard, he comes very close to the pedagogical import of Traherne's theory. We only really "know" the virtues of love and

---

materialism in the eighteenth century, now again dominating government planning for educational services and policies in Universities throughout the 'developed' world, is destructive of fundamental moral responsibilities and the adaptation of services of science and technology to social needs" (Trevarthen, "Innate Moral Feelings," 18).

92. Andrzejewski, *Social Justice*; Johnson and Mappin, *Environmental Education and Advocacy*.

93. The study that I refer to is Farmer et al., "Elementary School Environmental Education," 33–42; James et al., "From Play in Nature." Other non-longitudinal studies of this kind can be found in Harrison, "Why Are We Here?," 3; Reis and Roth, "Feeling for the Environment," 71–87.

94. Freire, *Education for Critical Consciousness*, 125.

care by entering into a significant relationship with the creature, the object of love. However, Freire's theory relates to Traherne's in another significant way. For Paulo Freire, the purpose of education is never to build the capacity to produce, and domesticate the individual against their nature. Rather, the purpose of education is to nurture the child's natural capacity to "know," and therefore set them free to be fully human.

While environmental educators and educational philosophers do not necessarily have in mind Christian concepts of moral formation,[95] theories of this kind have been advanced by Christian ethicists such as Michael Northcott.[96] Northcott sees the importance of ecologically and liturgically embedded relationships as the location of moral formation. When liturgically situated, contemplation of creation can lead to a faithful attentiveness to the Divine basis for human and ecological good. The Christian contemplative tradition offers a way to derive Trinitarian ethics of care from a liturgically embedded sense of place.

> In the common life of worship in local communities of place Christians rediscover the primordial unity of all persons and creatures which is affirmed in the resurrection of Christ. From their participation in the Trinitarian divine nature through Christ and the Spirit, Christians learn to attend to the common goods and the intricate inter-relationships which constitute the diversity and the sustaining energy and nutrient flows of created order.[97]

Liturgy, as a pedagogical method of making moral meaning, should also be continuous with our ecological location, rather than rationally or spiritually disassociated from it. Liturgically, socially and ecologically embedded relationships become the natural location for the "making" of a moral identity. He writes that:

> welfare resides in the building of richer relationships between persons and all creatures, and between creatures and the Creator. Enriching relationships . . . is therefore the true source of human and ecological flourishing. Resituating the self-in-relation describes the core task of the contemplative community. And hence such communities in Christian history have not only been centres of prayer and worship, but also of care and compassion for the poor and the sick. And they have also been

---

95. Although some clearly do, as is the case with Bergmann, *Nature, Space, and the Sacred*; Dunn, "Ecology, Ethics, and the Religious Educator," 34–41.
96. Northcott, *Environment and Christian Ethics*; *Moral Climate*.
97. Northcott, *Moral Climate*, 184.

places where work on the soil, and the stewardship of creation, have been restored to their central place in the arts of human making.[98]

Like Gilligan, Noddings, and Freire, Northcott reminds us that the relationship and the location in which the relationship occurs is significant to our ability to make meaningful culture, find moral motivation, and discover the "true source" of human and ecological flourishing. Our discernment of the Trinity's will for the flourishing of life should be done in continuity with our ecological, natural place in creation. One particular entry in Traherne's *Church's Year-Book* demonstrates he agreed that locating life and liturgy in our ecological place is truly an "icon" for moral formation.

The Rogation Formation

The *Church's Year-Book* was intended to be a compendium of mediations, litanies, confessions, and intercessory prayers for each festival day in the Church year. Traherne's year book went unfinished due to his early death. But he completed his entry for Rogation Week. Rogation Week is the festival in which the parishioners walk the boundaries of the parish, giving thanks to God for the land on which the community lives, and asking for God's blessings on the harvest that will come from the land. Just as the Church "leadeth us in the Circuit of [God's] Mercies"[99] through the liturgical year, in Rogation Week, "she now leads us by the Hand to the Sight and Possession of Temporal Delights and Earthly Blessings."[100] Rogation falls 40 days after Easter. And in "so Convenient a Season" as Springtime we are able to enlist our "lively Sight and Sence of the Benefits which He hath prepared abroad, and by giving which He hath magnified the Greatness of His Wisdom and Love to us."[101] This season of blossoming is the perfect time for the parishioners to physically walk the land and see "the Visible Beauties of His Works, beneath, which in their proper Season com also to be Remembered," as God's love and goodness, which "Sanctifies the Land in all our Eys."[102]

This seems to be a standard praise to God for the gifts of the land. However Traherne makes another, unnecessary defence of Rogation Week. Traherne writes that:

---

98. Northcott, *Moral Climate*, 186.
99. Traherne, *Church's Year-Book*, 63.
100. Traherne, *Church's Year-Book*, 63.
101. Traherne, *Church's Year-Book*, 63.
102. Traherne, *Church's Year-Book*, 63.

> The keeping of these days was not Novel Superstition, but a Venerable Institution of Pious Antiquity, As S. Augustine witnesseth in his Sermon on Ascension Eve: and in another concerning Rogation Sunday.[103]

Traherne acknowledges what St. Augustine before him knew, that rogation time is not a Christian institution, *per se*. Seed time and fertility rites are present in nearly all times, cultures and religions. However, Traherne praises the fact that the "[Holy] Church hath Wisely set apart these Rogation Days, as an Extraordinary Time," which can be used to "Implore God's Blessing upon the Fruits of the Earth, which are then all in Springing."[104] Traherne likely feels the need to make this defence of Rogation because, during the Interregnum, festivals that were not explicitly delineated in Scripture were outlawed. Traherne laments:

> Pity then it is, that out of pretended fear of Superstition, Men should Neglect Primitiv and Excellent Devotion: or out of fals Groundless fear, Endeavor to Disannul such Heavenly Constitutions. There are some things that Carry so much Light and Beauty in them that they need not be written in a Law, being Asserted by Reason and taught by Nature.[105]

Traherne is making the case that not everything which contributes to the Christian life need come from the "Law," which is both a reference to the Bible as such, and specifically to the Ceremonial Law of Moses, to which Traherne actually devotes his longest manuscript. Using the example of David's regulations regarding the tabernacle, he demonstrates that all of the dancing, celebrating, decorating and processions "were not Ordained nor commanded by a Law, yet being the Product of a Clear Reason, Adding to the Splendor and Glory of their Church and Conferring more to the Visible Honor of God upon Earth, David allowed it, and Rejoyced in it."[106] But Traherne really wants to say that those natural things which have "Light and Beauty in them," and yet lay outside of the Law, rationality, or the Divine Command moral theories, can be signs of God's grace.[107] The natural things of creation have significant import for the formation of our Christian moral

---

103. Traherne, *Church's Year-Book*, 62.
104. Traherne, *Church's Year-Book*, 62.
105. Traherne, *Church's Year-Book*, 64.
106. Traherne, *Church's Year-Book*, 64.

107. Traherne's attempt to explore the sacramental nature of social and even agricultural phenomenon might be an early attempt to engage in what Milbank calls a "thick" or "deep" theological exploration of social phenomenon as a means of demonstrating the underlying ontology of peace.

identity when our relationship to God is embedded in our relationship to the creatures of the land, and land itself in which we "live, and move and have our being."[108] This is another example that things of our nature, and things which can be "taught by Nature," can be continuous with our moral formation. To that end, he prays that "the Church with Reason Institut Festivals" which:

> adde an Exterior Beauty, as well as an Interior within the Temple, that both without and within, in the fields and in the Churches, God being Honored, a Contemplating Ey might have the fuller Prospects, throughout all the Land seeing the Sitting of His Servants, and the Majestie of His Service beneath the Roof, and the Goings of His Hostes abroad, in the Open Sun. Where by Ocular Demonstration they might view His Works, and see His Glory which they hear of in the Temple, and learn to hav a Sacred Esteem even of the very Fields, because they are His who made the Heavens. That all the World might appear to be the House of God, by the Universality Variety and Beauty of His Servants, and their Ministry.[109]

The variety and beauty of creation in Rogation time lead us to honour God in the fields as much as we do in the temple. Those with a "Contemplating Ey" can see natural goodness when they hold a "Sacred Esteem even of the very fields." Traherne ends this section with a quote from "Learned Hooker" who writes, "It grieveth me that Things of Principal Excellencey, should be Bitten at by Men, whom God hath Endued with Graces, both of Wit and Learning for Better Purposes."[110] Walking the parish fields and boundaries in thanksgiving to God and in prayer for the land is one of the ways that we are taught by nature. Furthermore, Traherne suggests there are "Better Purposes" to glean from this rogation time pilgrimage. After the introduction to the nature and purpose of Rogation Week, he includes a section entitled "Acts of Adoration and Thanksgiving." This section is a mixture of his peculiar spatially poetic writing and prose that describes the way our immersion in the land benefits our moral formation.

First he praises God for the Divine being which sustains life, and "for whom all Creatures labour, under Whom all are Obedient, to Whom all Relate."[111] He outlines the relational nexus that is created between God and all creatures on the land. Among those creatures that are part of our

---

108. Traherne, *Church's Year-Book*, 63.
109. Traherne, *Church's Year-Book*, 65.
110. Traherne, *Church's Year-Book*, 65.
111. Traherne, *Church's Year-Book*, 66.

significant relationships are those among the variety of "Inanimate Creatures," including the celestial bodies in the "Heavens," water, mineral "Elements," and "Mixt Bodies" which is a reference to compounds and metals. He also names "The Animate" beings who have life, "The Sensitiv" beings who have feeling and include all "Beasts, Birds and Fishes," "The Rational" who have understanding, "the Virtuous" ones who have grace, "the Vegetativ Life" which includes "Trees, Flowers, and Plants," and the "Spiritual Being and Intellectual Life" which is given to "all the Orders of Angels." This, and a whole litany of creation that follows, is the panoply of beings which make up the morally significant relationship that awaits us when we walk the land in Rogation time. Among this communion of creatures, Traherne gives thanks for the human being-in-creation, which God has given:

> Being, as to the Heavens:
> Life, as to the Plants:
> Sense, as to the Beasts:
> Understanding, as to the Angels.[112]

This thanksgiving recapitulates the notion that human beings are made somewhere between ants and angels. We are true "moral" beings because we are not merely sensate or rational, rather, we need both to have joy and be formed into our full self. Traherne praises several significant virtues of dependence that are formed in the human moral being-in-creation among this communicative, inter-subjective communion of creatures. He cites "charitable actions," "Compassion," "Thanksgiving," "Lov," "Joys," and "Peace" as the virtues which will stream from our "Divine and Heavenly Interest in all thy Creatures."[113] The peaceable communion of creatures which we encounter in our prayerful walk through our local ecology is "Part of the Beatifique Vision" by which Traherne discerns the fruits of "all thy Care."[114]

He knows the entire phenomenal field of creation, the land and every being bears witness to the Divine care. In anticipation he asks God to grant him the power, just as Job did before him:

> to Ask the Beasts of the field, for they shall teach me, and the fowles of the Air for they shall tell me, the Earth it self, and the Fishes of the Sea, for they shall Declare; that in all these Things thy Hand O Lord is seen, in whose Hand is the Soul of evry Living Thing, and the breath of all Mankind.[115]

---

112. Traherne, *Church's Year-Book*, 67.
113. Traherne, *Church's Year-Book*, 71.
114. Traherne, *Church's Year-Book*, 71–72.
115. Traherne, *Church's Year-Book*, 67. This is a reference to Job 12, to which this

Rogation Week is normally a time to pray for the cultivation of the land. But for Traherne, it is a time to learn from the beasts, birds, fishes, and even the earth itself who teach us the care of God. Rogation is the worshipful act of a community that is embedded in the relational nexus of the land. It nurtures us and provides us with a generative theme to cultivate our moral identity. Traherne knew this care as a child, when creation became his "othermother" and his tutor. His local ecology became a relational "icon" that revealed to him the ways of peace that was woven into the fabric of creation.

For the attentive child, an act of worship, discovering the mutual interest of an ecological community, and a learning experience about care-in-creation can become a form of place-based moral formation in the virtues of dependence and the ways of peace. According to this reading, we can understand the pedagogical implications of retiring in creation. It is a way to cultivate the caring child.

Conclusion

Perhaps a good way to summarize the content of this chapter is to suggest that pedagogy follows anthropology. The way we teach children necessarily depends upon our belief in the natural state of the child. Major shifts in ethical theories are all been based on a particular notion of human nature. And like all moral theorists, Traherne bases his theory of moral formation on a particular notion of human nature. However, his differs significantly from the selfish, atomized, or rationalistic version that underwrites many Enlightenment moral theories. Because his views of human nature and the nature of creation are fundamentally different, we should expect his view of moral education would also be different. Psychologist and educator Colwyn Trevarthen summarizes this point when he writes:

> The theory of an essential cooperative and creative nature of human motivation in infancy has a firm empirical foundation, and it accords well with certain ancient traditions of the humanities, as well as with the latest discoveries in brain science. . . . It shows we are born to make our intentions work to formulate "narratives" of agency in engagement with the "lived experience" of a conceptual world that is both absorbingly private and passionately social.[116]

---

section resembles as kind of litany of creation.

116. Trevarthen, "Innate Moral Feelings," 19.

As Trevarthen suggests, I have identified two items of "accord" between contemporary pedagogical theories of moral formation, and the "ancient traditions" upon which Thomas Traherne bases his notion of moral formation. First, that human nature, and that of creation, is essentially good, cooperative and caring. Second, through careful attention to the way in which the local biodiversity cares for us, the natural environment provides a meaningful context in which a child can be formed in an ethic of care.

I have outlined a convergence of perspectives in theology, educational philosophy and child psychology which suggests the need for a pedagogical basis for moral education that does not rely solely on the rational, positivistic, or linguistic basis for moral cognition. Constructivist theories tend to view morality as the product of cognitive methodologies which can be "bolted on" when a child is ready to comprehend such ethical sophistication. But from the perspective of an ethic of care, children can naturally and fully participate in the pro-formative relationships from the earliest age. In relationships of care-giving, the neurological basis for a child's moral framework is nurtured, and the virtues of dependence and interdependence can be experienced.

Traherne understood that the purpose of education is moral formation. Therefore the goal of his theory of "Retirednes" is based on the child's innate identity, or "glory" as a creature, and the fact that God's goodness is communicated through the way creation cares for the child. A care based relational nexus respects the child's innate sense of wonder, and does not deconstruct their natural, ecological identity in the great educational march towards rationality. In the early years, those pro-formative experiences help children form a relational, inter-subjective, "ecological" self-image. Or as Traherne would put it, the image of a creature who is cared for.

While rationalist theories of moral formation turn our attention towards the inward workings of our cognitive, moral judgements, Traherne urged his readers to turn their careful attention toward creation. Care-lessness towards our place within creation is what led to all manner of sinfulness and the lack of flourishing in the life for which we were created. In our age, when our children are becoming, as Louv suggests, more distracted from paying careful attention to their ecological location, I submit that Traherne's ethical theory of care-fulness finds as much moral import in our age as in his own.

Educators and psychologists such as Gilligan, Noddings, Narvaéz, Nye, Trevarthen and Carr suggest that care based relationships are essential to the pro-formation of virtuous dispositions. Theologians and moral philosophers such as MacIntyre, Northcott, Inge, and Williams suggest that creatures and the fabric of creation itself can provide a morally significant relational nexus in the context of Christian moral formation. Their theories accord with Traherne by suggesting that creatures can become "icons" of God's love if we help our children pay careful attention to our shared interest in caring for one another. Traherne believes that the "duty" of caring for creation is the result of having perceived the way in which we are cared for by a diverse, life giving creation.

> Since therefore all things depending so continually upon His care and love the perpetual influx of His almighty power is infinitely precious and His Life exercised incessantly in the manifestation of Eternal Love, in that every moment throughout all generations He continueth without failing to uphold all things for us. We likewise ought to show our infinite love by upholding Heaven and Earth, Time and Eternity, God and all things in our Souls, without wavering or intermission : by the perpetual influx of our life. To which we are by the goodness of all things infinitely obliged. Once to ease is to draw upon ourselves infinite darkness, after we have begun to be so illuminated : for it shows a forgetfulness and defect in love, and it is an infinite wonder that we are afterward restored.[117]

In terms of moral agency, not to care for creation reveals a great "defect" in our love, and a "forgetfulness" of who we are in relationship to creation and a caring Creator. Contemplation of creation provides the relational context in which we can attentively perceive the care which helps form us into caring creatures. Perhaps even Carol Gilligan and Nell Noddings[118] could not say it better. In our age when many virtue theories and ethics are moving from the cognitive focus on justice towards relational care as a basis for virtue, Thomas Traherne reminds us that a goal of the Christian life is to honour God by realizing we are cared for by creation, and in turn care for creation. To that end, contemplating biodiversity is a necessary component of forming a faithfully caring character. Traherne believes that in this theatre of God's love, the child can grow into the full "glory" of our natural human identity. And he believes that our ministry in helping cultivate the natural glory of a child through "the Care of Parents and Fathers of Famelies was to be continued in the World, and publickly celebrated in Divine Worship" was "annexed to the Covenant of Grace."[119] The cultivation of the careful child is part and parcel of God's means of Grace. So he urges us to administer that means of grace to the youngest of our children:

---

117. Traherne, *Centuries, Poems, and Thanksgivings*, 1:101.
118. Noddings, *Educating Moral People*.
119. Traherne, *Church's Year-Book*, 124.

By this ministry let nurses, and those parents that desire Holy Children learn to make them possessors of Heaven and Earth betimes; to remove silly objects from before them, to magnify nothing but what is great indeed, and to talk of God to them, and of His works and ways before they can either speak or go.[120]

---

120. Traherne, *Centuries, Poems, and Thanksgivings*, 1:117.

7

Conclusion

IN THIS STUDY I have demonstrated several significant aspects of Traherne's moral theory. Traherne affirmed that by virtue of having been created by the active love of God, creation is inherently good in its natural, ecologically cooperative state. By their motions and influences creatures communicate this goodness by reflecting and transpiring their "vital spirits." Human beings have an innate "capacity" to perceive, or "apprehend" this communication because humans were created to participate in this loving cooperation. When we retire into creation and engage creatures in their proper, ecological place with our child-like sense of wonder, we create a theatre in which this goodness can resonate in our being. In that close communion, we come to know the depth of care that creation provides for us and discern the love of our Creator. Sensitivity to that care motivates us to perform "blessed operations." Our sensitive perception and moral response is what makes us moral beings, separates us from the ants and makes the angels jealous.

His moral theory is also based on a particular understanding of human nature. Because we are created by the goodness of God, we are good by nature. Violence, discord and predation are very real parts of our sinful existence. But our deficiency does not arise from our nature. It arises from our unwillingness to be attentive to the goodness of God that is woven into the fabric of Creation. Forming a good, loving, wise and peaceable moral identity can begin as a young child by retiring into creation and establishing an attentive, significant relationship.

For all the scientific sophistication that Traherne deployed in his study of moral theology, his entire theory is founded on the fundamental principle that God is good. Because creation participates in that divine goodness, our faithful and scientific ways of knowing can work together as we seek to understand what is good. This theory is as simple as it is profound.

It is simple because it suggests that spending time playing in nature can be a significant component of forming a relational, caring, inter-subjective moral identity. As Chrysostom knew before Traherne, what comes into contact with a child's senses draws her attention and affects her perception of human nature. He knew that parents can bless their children by drawing the attention of their child towards the goodness of God's creation. And so did Traherne.

> For nothing is so easy as to teach the truth because the nature of the thing confirms the doctrine : As when we say the sun is glorious, a man is a beautiful creature, sovereign over beasts and fowls and fishes, the stars minister unto us, the world was made for you, &c. But to say this house is yours, and these lands are another man's, and this bauble is a jewel and this gew-gaw a fine thing, this rattle makes music, &c., is deadly barbarous and uncouth to a little child; and makes him suspect all you say, because the nature of the thing contradicts your words. Yet doth that blot out all noble and divine ideas, dissettle his foundation, render him uncertain in all things, and divide him from God. To teach him those objects are little vanities ... yet better and more glorious things are more to be esteemed, is natural and easy.[1]

These words ring true from a young man who was adopted from his rural home around the age of four and placed into the urban environment of Hereford city.[2] In this urban life of custom and culture, Traherne became a stranger to the skies and the ministry of the animals and fields. But after decades of education and years of service in the parish, Traherne was blessed to perceive again the truth of God's goodness that is revealed in the caring nature of creation. Like all good moral philosophies, Traherne realized that he already knew this truth from his childhood. But he found support for his theory in the science of his day. That is what makes his simple moral theory so profound.

Traherne witnessed the great intellectual alienations that were approaching. The senses would be disassociated from moral perception, scientific from moral knowledge, urban social life from creation, the Kingdom of heaven from politics of the earth. Traherne knew that these things must never be taught as "aliena," and that education played a key role in the formation of a moral identity that respected our created nature. We live on the opposite side of many of those great disassociations. On this side of the divide, we are re-discovering what it means to be "ecological" or "relational" beings through the social, psychological and natural sciences. We live in an age when educators and religious leaders are beginning to understand that these ideas must be re-associated with the lives of our children. They need

---

1. Traherne, *Centuries, Poems, and Thanksgivings*, 1:117.
2. Traherne, *Centuries, Poems, and Thanksgivings*, 1:xxxvii.

to experience a broad range of caring relationships in order to nurture the natural formation of their moral identity.

We do not have to wait to the age of reason to teach the virtues of justice, love and peaceableness. In fact, we must not wait that long. A child's Christian formation as a human being begins with taking them out to be present with all the creatures among which they live so that they can "hear them in their beings and operations praising God in a heavenly manner. Some of them vocally, others in their ministry, all of them naturally and continually."[3]

In this way we can refrain from dividing the child's nature, and help them associate with the rest of creation. We equip our children by teaching them from an early age that natural and moral knowledge are two parts of one unified science that contribute to a full understanding of what it means to be human. We inspire our children with that knowledge when we encourage them to perceive the mystery of love woven into creation. We bless our children by reminding them that "You are never what you ought till you go out of yourself and walk among them."[4] In an age when so many children are violently denied the experience of significant relationships of care by the effects of war, poverty, technological and economic pressures, we need to reconnect children to as many relational theatres as possible. Creation can become an "othermother" that demonstrates the care intended for their life and helps form the child's disposition to care for others.

As Traherne says, it would be a shame to ignore the possibility for moral formation that is so full of "Light and Beauty" out of "Superstition" about paganism. And on the contrary, rooting our notion of Christian moral formation in the natural seasons and cycles of the earth reclaims the spiritual significance of the land, seasons and creatures from any materialist claims Recovering the mysterious unity of knowledge is therefore an act of faith in the goodness of the Creator. As the Sufi mystic Ali al-Khawas wrote "There is a subtle mystery in each of the movements and sounds of this world. The initiate will capture what is being said when the wind blows, the trees sway, water flows, flies buzz, doors creak, birds sing, or in the sound of strings or flutes, the sighs of the sick, the groans of the afflicted."

Traherne reminds us that our Christian moral identity with all its virtues is not opposed to our nature. He asks, "what Creature could I desire to be which I am not Made?"[5] We were created to communicate the goodness of God's peaceable Kingdom as creatures. Choosing to go out among

---

3. Traherne, *Centuries, Poems, and Thanksgivings*, 1:95.
4. Traherne, *Centuries, Poems, and Thanksgivings*, 1:95.
5. Traherne, *Centuries, Poems, and Thanksgivings*, 1:35.

creation simply affords us the opportunity to be what we were created to become. Until we take our place among them, "all creatures stand in expectation of what will be the result of your liberty."[6]

---

6. Traherne, *Centuries, Poems, and Thanksgivings*, 1:193.

Bibliography

Akers, Matthew P. "From the Hexaemeral to the Physico-Theological: A Study of Thomas Traherne's Meditations on the Six Days of the Creation and The Kingdom of God Focusing upon the Cosmological Controversy." PhD diss., Drew University, 2008.

Allchin, A. M. *Participation in God: A Forgotten Strand in Anglican Tradition*. Wilson, CT: Morehouse-Barlow, 1988.

Allchin, A. M., et al. *Profitable Wonders: Aspects of Thomas Traherne*. Oxford: Amate, 1989.

Andrzejewski, Julie. *Social Justice, Peace, and Environmental Education: Transformative Standards*. New York: Routledge, 2009.

Bacon, Francis. *The New Organon*. Edited by Lisa Jardine and Michael Silverthorne. Cambridge Texts in the History of Philosophy. Cambridge: Cambridge University Press, 2000.

Bakke, Odd Magne. *When Children Became People: The Birth of Childhood in Early Christianity*. Minneapolis: Fortress, 2005.

Balakier, James J. "A Pre-Newtonian Gravitational Trope in Thomas Traherne's Centuries of Meditations." *English Language Notes* 39 (2001) 32–41.

———. *Thomas Traherne and the Felicities of the Mind*. Amherst, NY: Cambria, 2010.

———. "Traherne, Husserl, and a Unitary Act of Consciousness." In *Re-Reading Thomas Traherne: A Collection of New Critical Essays*, edited by Jacob Blevins, 201–220. Tempe, AZ: Arizona Center for Medieval and Renaissance Studies, 2007.

Bartholomew I. *Cosmic Grace, Humble Prayer: The Ecological Vision of the Green Patriarch*. Edited by John Chryssavgis. Grand Rapids: Eerdmanns, 2009.

Bergmann, Sigurd. *Nature, Space, and the Sacred: Transdisciplinary Perspectives*. Burlington, VT: Ashgate, 2009.

Berry, Thomas. "The Ecozoic Era." In *People, Land, and Community: Collected E. F. Schumacher Society Lectures*, edited by Hildegarde Hannum, 191–203. New Haven, CT: Yale University Press, 1997.

Blevins, Jacob, ed. *Re-Reading Thomas Traherne: A Collection of New Critical Essays*. Tempe, AZ: Arizona Center for Medieval and Renaissance Studies, 2007.

Bonhoeffer, Dietrich. *Creation and Fall: A Theological Exposition from Genesis 1–3*. Translated by Douglass Stephen Bax. Dietrich Bonhoeffer Works 3. Minneapolis: Fortress, 1997.

Brady, Emily. *Aesthetics of the Natural Environment*. Edinburgh: Edinburgh University Press, 2003.

Brown, David. *God and Enchantment of Place: Reclaiming Human Experience*. Oxford: Oxford University Press, 2004.

———. *God and Grace of Body: Sacrament in Ordinary*. Oxford: Oxford University Press, 2011.
Cantor, G. N. *Optics after Newton: Theories of Light in Britain and Ireland, 1704–1840*. Manchester: Manchester University Press, 1983.
Carr, David. *Educating the Virtues: An Essay on the Philosophical Psychology of Moral Development and Education*. Abingdon: Routledge, 1991.
Carus, Titus Lucretius. *De Rerum Natura: The Poem on Nature*. Edited by Charles Hubert Sisson. Abingdon: Routledge, 2003.
Cefalu, P. "Thomistic Metaphysics and Ethics in the Poetry and Prose of Thomas Traherne." *Literature and Theology* 16 (2002) 248–69.
Chittister, Joan. *Heart of Flesh: A Feminist Spirituality for Women and Men*. Grand Rapids: Eerdmans, 1998.
Clements, Arthur L. *The Mystical Poetry of Thomas Traherne*. Cambridge: Harvard University Press, 1969.
———. *Poetry of Contemplation: John Donne, George Herbert, Henry Vaughan, and the Modern Period*. Albany: SUNY Press, 1990.
Clucas, Stephen. "Poetic Atomism in Seventeenth-Century England: Henry More, Thomas Traherne, and Scientific Imagination." *Renaissance Studies* 5 (1991) 327–40.
Comenius, Johann Amos. *Comenius's School of Infancy: An Essay on the Education of Youth during the First Six Years*. Edited by Will Seymour Monroe. Boston: D. C. Heath, 1828.
Corcoran, Peter Blaze, et al. *Young People, Education, and Sustainable Development: Exploring Principles, Perspectives, and Praxis*. Wageningen: Wageningen Academic, 2009.
Cutsinger, James S. *Not of This World: A Treasury of Christian Mysticism*. Bloomington: World Wisdom, 2003.
Damon, William, et al. *Handbook of Child Psychology, Cognition, Perception, and Language*. Chichester: Wiley, 2006.
De Waal, Esther. *Lost in Wonder: Rediscovering the Spiritual Art of Attentiveness*. Norwhich: Hymns Ancient & Modern, 2003.
De Waal, Frans. *Good Natured: The Origins of Right and Wrong in Humans and Other Animals*. Cambridge: Harvard University Press, 1997.
———. *Peacemaking Among Primates*. Cambridge: Harvard University Press, 1990.
Debus, Allen G. *Science and Education in the Seventeenth Century: The Webster-Ward Debate*. Macdonald, 1970.
DeNeef, A. Leigh. *Traherne in Dialogue: Heidegger, Lacan, and Derrida*. Durham: Duke University Press, 1988.
Descartes, René. *Discourse on Method and the Meditations*. Edited by F. E. Sutcliffe. London: Penguin, 1968.
———. *Meditations and Other Metaphysical Writings*. London: Penguin, 2003.
Dicker, Georges. *Hume's Epistemology & Metaphysics: An Introduction*. Abingdon: Routledge, 1998.
Dowell, Graham. *Enjoying the World: The Rediscovery of Thomas Traherne*. New York: Morehouse, 1990.
Dunn, S. "Ecology, Ethics, and the Religious Educator." *Religious Education* 85 (1990) 34–41.
Edwards, Derek. *Discourse and Cognition*. New York: SAGE, 1997.

Eliot, T. S. *Selected Essays*. London: Faber, 1999.
Ellrodt, Robert. *L'Inspiration personnelle et l'esprit du temps chez les poètes métaphysiques anglais... Les Origines sociales psychologiques et littéraires de la poésie métaphysique au tournant du siècle*. Paris: J. Corti., 1960.
———. *Seven Metaphysical Poets: A Structural Study of the Unchanging Self*. Oxford: Oxford University Press, 2000.
Engel, Susan, and Margery B. Franklin. "Aesthetics: An Introduction." *Children's Environments Quarterly* 8.2 (1991) 2–3.
Farmer, J., et al. "An Elementary School Environmental Education Field Trip: Long-Term Effects on Ecological and Environmental Knowledge and Attitude Development." *The Journal of Environmental Education* 38 (2007) 33–42.
Fergusson, David, and Nigel Dower. *John Macmurray: Critical Perspectives*. Bern: Peter Lang, 2002.
Fisher, Saul. *Pierre Gassendi's Philosophy and Science: Atomism for Empiricists*. Leiden: Brill, 2005.
Francis. *Laudato Si, Praise be to You: On Care for Our Common Home*. San Francisco: Ignatius, 2015.
Freire, Paulo. *Education for Critical Consciousness*. New York: Continuum, 2005.
Fuller, Robert C. *Wonder: From Emotion to Spirituality*. Chapel Hill, NC: University of North Carolina Press, 2006.
Gazzaniga, Michael S. *The Bisected Brain*. New York: Appleton-Century-Crofts, 1970.
———. *The Social Brain: Discovering the Networks of the Mind*. New York: Basic, 1985.
Gibson, James Jerome. *The Ecological Approach to Visual Perception*. Abingdon: Routledge, 1986.
Gilligan, Carol. *In a Different Voice: Psychological Theory and Women's Development*. Cambridge: Harvard University Press, 1993.
Gorringe, Timothy. *A Theology of the Built Environment: Justice, Empowerment, Redemption*. Cambridge: Cambridge University Press, 2002.
Grant, Patrick. "Original Sin and the Fall of Man in Thomas Traherne." *Johns Hopkins University Press* 38 (1971) 40–61.
———. *The Transformation of Sin: Studies in Donne, Herbert, Vaughan, and Traherne*. Amherst, MA: University of Massachusetts Press, 1974.
Grene, Marjorie. "The Primacy of the Ecological Self." In *The Perceived Self: Ecological and Interpersonal Sources of Self-Knowledge*, edited by Ulrich Neisser, 112–18. Cambridge: Cambridge University Press, 1993.
Grey, Mary C. "Ecological Theology and Education." *Ecotheology* (1997) 8–122.
Gruenewald, David A., and Gregory A. Smith. *Place-Based Education in the Global Age: Local Diversity*. Mahwah, NJ: Lawrence Erlbaum, 2008.
Haddad, B. M. "Property Rights, Ecosystem Management, and John Locke's Labor Theory of Ownership." *Ecological Economics* 46 (2003) 19–31.
Harrison, Sam. "'Why Are We Here?' Taking 'Place' into Account in UK—Outdoor Environmental Education." *Journal of Adventure Education & Outdoor Learning* 10 (2010) 3.
Harvey, William. *On the Motion of the Heart and Blood in Animals*. New York: Prometheus, 1993.
Hawkes, David. *Idols of the Marketplace: Idolatry and Commodity Fetishism in English Literature, 1580–1680*. Basingstoke: Palgrave Macmillan, 2001.

Hedley, Douglas, and Sarah Hutton. *Platonism at the Origins of Modernity: Studies on Platonism and Early Modern Philosophy*. New York: Springer, 2008.
Heindel, Max. *The Rosicrucian Mysteries: An Elementary Exposition of Their Secret Teachings*. London: L. N. Fowler, 1916.
Heinz, Werner, and Margery B. Franklin. *Comparative Psychology of Mental Development*. Philadelphia: David Brown, 2004.
Hermes Trismegistus. *Divine Pymander*. 1889. Reprint, Pomeroy, WA: Health Research, 1996.
Hobbes, Thomas. *Leviathan*. Edited by A. P. Martinich and Brian Battiste. Peterborough: Broadview, 2010.
Hooke, Robert. *Micrographia Or Some Physiological Descriptions of Minute Bodies*. New York: Cosimo, 2007.
Huffman, William H. *Robert Fludd*. Berkley: North Atlantic, 2001.
Hume, David. *Moral Philosophy*. Edited by Geoffrey Sayre-McCord. Indianapolis: Hackett, 2006.
———. *A Treatise of Human Nature*. Sioux Falls: NuVision, 2008.
Inge, Denise. "A Poet Comes Home: Thomas Traherne, Theologian in a New Century." *Anglican Theological Review* 86 (2004) 335–48.
———. *Wanting Like a God: Desire and Freedom in the Works of Thomas Traherne*. London: SCM, 2009.
Inge, John. *A Christian Theology of Place*. Farnham: Ashgate, 2003.
James, J. Joy, et al. "From Play in Nature, to Recreation then Vocation: A Developmental Model for Natural History-Oriented Environmental Professionals." *Children, Youth, and Environments* 20.1 (2010) 231–56.
Johnson, Edward Arnold, and Michael Mappin. *Environmental Education and Advocacy: Changing Perspectives of Ecology and Education*. Cambridge: Cambridge University Press, 2005.
Johnson, Elisabeth. *Ask the Beasts: Darwin and the God of Love*. London: Bloomsbury, 2015.
Johnson, Samuel. *Lives of the Most Eminent English Poets: With Critical Observations on Their Works*. London: F. Warne, 1870.
Jordan, Jeff. *Pascal's Wager: Pragmatic Arguments and Belief in God*. Oxford: Oxford University Press, 2006.
Kahn, Peter H., and Stephen R. Kellert. *Children and Nature: Psychological, Sociocultural, and Evolutionary Investigations*. Cambridge: MIT Press, 2002.
Kahn, Richard V. *Critical Pedagogy, Ecoliteracy, & Planetary Crisis: The Ecopedagogy Movement*. New York: Peter Lang, 2010.
Kant, Immanuel. *Critique of Judgment*. New York: Cosimo, 2007.
———. *Groundwork of the Metaphysic of Morals*. Edited by Herbert James Paton. New York: Harper & Row, 1964.
———. *The Metaphysics of Morals*. Cambridge: Cambridge University Press, 1996.
Kaye, Kenneth. *The Mental and Social Life of Babies: How Parents Create Persons*. Abingdon: Taylor & Francis, 1984.
King, Barbara J. *Being With Animals: Why We Are Obsessed with the Furry, Scaly, Feathered Creatures Who Populate Our World*. New York: Doubleday, 2010.
———. *Evolving God: A Provocative View of the Origins of Religion*. New York: Doubleday, 2007.

Kohlberg, Lawrence. *The Philosophy of Moral Development: Moral Stages and the Idea of Justice*. New York: Harper & Row, 1981.

———. *The Psychology of Moral Development: The Nature and Validity of Moral Stages*. New York: Harper & Row, 1984.

Kropotkin, Petr Alekseevich. *Mutual Aid: A Factor of Evolution*. London: Heinemann, 1908.

Kuchar, Gary. "Traherne's Specters: Self-Consciousness and its Others." In *Re-Reading Thomas Traherne: A Collection of New Critical Essays*, edited by Jacob Blevins, 173–200. Tempe, AZ: Arizona Center for Medieval and Renaissance Studies, 2007.

Kurian, George Thomas, and James D. Smith, III. *The Encyclopedia of Christian Literature*. New York: Scarecrow, 2010.

Laistner, M. L. W., and John Chrysostom. *Christianity and Pagan Culture in the Later Roman Empire: Together with an English Translation of John Chrysostom's Address on Vainglory and the Right Way for Parents to Bring Up Their Children*. Ithaca: Cornell University Press, 1951.

Lewis, Clive Staples. *The Discarded Image: An Introduction to Medieval and Renaissance Literature*. Cambridge: Cambridge University Press, 1994.

Lindberg, David C., and Ronald L. Numbers. *God and Nature: Historical Essays on the Encounter Between Christianity and Science*. Berkley: University of California Press, 1986.

Littledyke, M. "Primary Children's Views on Science and Environmental Issues: Examples of Environmental Cognitive and Moral Development." *Environmental Education Research* 10 (2004) 217–35.

Locke, John. *An Essay Concerning Human Understanding*. London: T. Tegg & Son, 1836.

———. *Two Treatises of Government: And a Letter Concerning Toleration*. Edited by Ian Shapiro. New Haven: Yale University Press, 2003.

Loebach, Janet, and Jason Gilliland. "Child-Led Tours to Uncover Children's Perceptions and Use of Neighborhood Environments." *Children, Youth, and Environments* 20.1 (2010) 52–90.

MacIntyre, Alasdair C. *Dependent Rational Animals: Why Human Beings Need the Virtues*. Chicago: Open Court, 2001.

MacKinnon, Mary Heather, and Moni McIntyre. *Readings in Ecology and Feminist Theology*. Lanham: Rowman & Littlefield, 1995.

Marks, C. L. "Thomas Traherne and Cambridge Platonism." *Publications of the Modern Language Association of America* 8 (1966) 521–34.

Marshall, W. H. "Thomas Traherne and the Doctrine of Original Sin." *Modern Language Notes* 73 (1958) 161–65.

Martz, Louis Lohr. *The Paradise Within: Studies in Vaughan, Traherne, and Milton*. New Haven: Yale University Press, 1964.

Matar, Nabil I. "The Individual and the Unity of Man in the Writings of Thomas Traherne." PhD diss., Cambridge University, 1976.

———. "Thomas Traherne's Solar Mysticism." *Studia Mystica* 7 (1984) 52–63.

Matthews, Gareth B. *Dialogues with Children*. Cambridge: Harvard University Press, 1984.

———. *The Philosophy of Childhood*. Cambridge: Harvard University Press, 1994.

McAdoo, Henry Robert. *Anglican Heritage: Theology and Spirituality*. Canterbury: Canterbury, 1997.

McColley, Diane Kelsey. *Poetry and Ecology in the Age of Milton and Marvell*. Farnham: Ashgate, 2007.
McIntosh, Mark Allen. *Discernment and Truth: The Spirituality and Theology of Knowledge*. New York: Crossroad, 2004.
Merchant, Carolyn. *The Death of Nature: Women, Ecology, and the Scientific Revolution*. New York: HarperCollins, 1990.
Mercon, J., and A. Armstrong. "Transindividuality and Philosophical Enquiry in Schools: A Spinozist Perspective." *Journal of Philosophy of Education* 45 (2011) 251–64.
Merleau-Ponty, Maurice. *Phenomenologie de La Perception*. Paris: Gallimard, 1945.
———. *Phenomenology of Perception*. Abingdon: Routledge, 2002.
———. *Sense and Non-Sense*. Chicago: Northwestern University Press, 1964.
Midgley, Mary. *Beast and Man: The Roots of Human Nature*. Abingdon: Routledge, 2002.
———. *The Ethical Primate: Humans, Freedom, and Morality*. 1994. Reprint, London: Routledge, 1996.
Milbank, John. *Theology and Social Theory: Beyond Secular Reason*. Hoboken: John Wiley & Sons, 2008.
Miller, David. "Property and Territory: Locke, Kant, and Steiner." *Journal of Political Philosophy* 19 (2011) 90–109.
Miller, Jon. *Topics in Early Modern Philosophy of Mind*. New York: Springer, 2009.
Mintz, Susannah B. "Strange Bodies: Thomas Traherne's Disabled Subject." In *Re-Reading Thomas Traherne: A Collection of New Critical Essays*, edited by Jacob Blevins, 21–36. Tempe, AZ: Arizona Center for Medieval and Renaissance Studies, 2007.
Tempe, AZ: Arizona Center for Medieval and Renaissance Studies, 2007.
Naess, Arne. *Ecology, Community, and Lifestyle: Outline of an Ecosophy*. Edited by David Rothenberg. Cambridge: Cambridge University Press, 1990.
———. "Maturity, Adulthood, Boxing, and Play." *The Trumpeter* 21 (2005) 35–36.
Narvaez, D. "Triune Ethics: The Neurobiological Roots of Our Multiple Moralities." *New Ideas in Psychology* 26 (2008) 95–119.
Narvaez, D., and P. L. Hill. "The Relation of Multicultural Experiences to Moral Judgment and Mindsets." *Journal of Diversity in Higher Education* 3 (2010) 43.
Neisser, Ulric. *The Perceived Self: Ecological and Interpersonal Sources of Self Knowledge*. Cambridge: Cambridge University Press, 2006.
Newey, Edmund. *Children of God: The Child as Source of Theological Anthropology*. Farnham: Ashgate, 2012.
———. "'God Made Man Greater When He Made Him Less': Traherne's Iconic Child." *Literature and Theology* 24 (2010) 227–41.
Nicolson, Marjorie Hope. *The Breaking of the Circle: Studies in the Effect of the 'New Science' upon Seventeenth-Century Poetry*. Chicago: Northwestern University Press, 1950.
Noddings, Nel. *Educating Moral People: A Caring Alternative to Character Education*. New York: Teachers College Press, 2002.
Northcott, Michael S. "Children." In *God in the City: Essays and Reflections from the Archbishop's Urban Theology Group*, edited by Peter Sedgwick, 139–52. London: Mowbray, 1995.

———. *The Environment and Christian Ethics*. Cambridge: Cambridge University, 1996.
———. *A Moral Climate: The Ethics of Global Warming*. London: Darton Longman & Todd, 2007.
———. "A Place of Our Own?" In *God in the City: Essays and Reflections from the Archbishop's Urban Theology Group*, edited by Peter Sedgwick, 119–38. London: Mowbray, 1995.
Nucci, Larry P., and Darcia Narvaéz. *Handbook of Moral and Character Education*. Abingdon: Routledge, 2008.
Nygren, Anders. *Agape and Eros*. New York: Harper & Row, 1969.
O'Donovan, Oliver. *Common Objects of Love: Moral Reflection and the Shaping of Community*. Grand Rapids: Eerdmans, 2002.
Palmer, Joy, and Philip Neal. *The Handbook of Environmental Education*. Abingdon: Routledge, 1994.
Parry, Graham. *The Seventeenth Century: The Intellectual and Cultural Context of English Literature, 1603–1700*. London: Longman, 1996.
———. *Seventeenth-Century Poetry: The Social Context*. London: Hutchinson, 1985.
Peterson, Anna Lisa. *Being Human: Ethics, Environment, and Our Place in the World*. Berkley: University of California Press, 2001.
Piaget, Jean. *The Child's Conception of the World*. Lanham: Rowman & Littlefield, 1951.
Plumwood, V. "Nature, Self, and Gender: Feminism, Environmental Philosophy, and the Critique of Rationalism." *Hypatia* 6 (1991) 3–27.
Ponsford, M. "The Poetry of Thomas Traherne in Relation to the Thought and Poetics of His Period." New Castle: University of Newcastle upon Tyne, 1984.
Purver, Margery. *The Royal Society: Concept and Creation*. Abingdon: Routledge, 2013.
Reis, Giuliano, and Roth Wolff-Michael. "A Feeling for the Environment: Emotion Talk In/for the Pedagogy of Public Environmental Education." *Journal of Environmental Education* 41 (2009) 71–87.
Richards, Anne, and Peter Privett. *Through the Eyes of a Child: New Insights in Theology from a Child's Perspective*. London: Church House, 2009.
Roux, Sophie, and Dan Garber. *The Mechanization of Natural Philosophy*. New York: Springer, 2012.
Ruether, Rosemary Radford. *Gaia and God: An Ecofeminist Theology of Earth Healing*. New York: Harper Collins. 1994.
Russell, D. "Locke on Land and Labor." *Philosophical studies* 117 (2004) 303–25.
Salter, Keith W. *Thomas Traherne: Mystic and Poet*. Lyndhurst: Barnes & Noble, 1965.
Sherrington, Alison J. *Mystical Symbolism in the Poetry of Thomas Traherne*. Brisbane: University of Queensland Press, 1970.
Shiva, Vandana. *The Violence of the Green Revolution: Third World Agriculture, Ecology, and Politics*. London: Zed, 1991.
Singer, Peter. *Animal Liberation*. New York: Random House, 1995.
Spinoza, Benedictus. *Complete Works*. Indianapolis: Hackett, 2002.
Theobald, Paul. *Teaching the Commons: Place, Pride, and the Renewal of Community*. Boulder: Westview, 1997.
Thiel, Udo. *The Early Modern Subject: Self-Consciousness and Personal Identity from Descartes to Hume*. Oxford: Oxford University Press, 2011.
Traherne, Thomas. *Centuries, Poems, and Thanksgivings*. Edited by Herschel Maurice Margoliouth. 2 vols. Oxford: Clarendon, 1958.

———. *Christian Ethicks*. Ithaca: Cornell University Press, 1968.

———. *Church's Year-Book, Meditations and Devotions from the Resurrection to All Saints' Day*. In *Church's Year-Book, A Serious and Athetical Contemplation of the Mercies of GOD, (Meditations on the Six Days of the Creation)*, edited by Jan Ross, 1–312. Vol. 4 of *The Works of Thomas Traherne*. Suffolk: DS Brewer, 2009.

———. *Commentaries of Heaven, part 2: Al-Sufficient to Bastard*. Vol. 3 of *The Works of Thomas Traherne*. Edited by Jan Ross. Suffolk: DS Brewer, 2007.

———. *Inducements to Retirednes*. In *Inducements to Retirednes, A Sober View of Dr. Twisses his Considerations, Seeds of Eternity or the Nature of the Soul, The Kingdom of God*, edited by Jan Ross, 3–44. Vol. 1 of *The Works of Thomas Traherne*. Suffolk: DS Brewer, 2005.

———. *The Kingdom of God*. In *Inducements to Retirednes, A Sober View of Dr. Twisses his Considerations, Seeds of Eternity or the Nature of the Soul, The Kingdom of God*, edited by Jan Ross, 253–554. Vol. 1 of *The Works of Thomas Traherne*. Suffolk: DS Brewer, 2005.

———. *Roman Forgeries, Or, a True Account of False Records Discovering the Impostures and Counterfeit Antiquities of the Church of Rome / By a Faithful Son of the Church of England*. London: S. and B. Griffin, 1673.

———. *Seeds of Eternity, or, The Nature of the Soul*. In *Inducements to Retirednes, A Sober View of Dr. Twisses his Considerations, Seeds of Eternity or the Nature of the Soul, The Kingdom of God*, edited by Jan Ross, 231–52. Vol. 1 of *The Works of Thomas Traherne*. Suffolk: DS Brewer, 2005.

———. *A Sober View of Dr. Twisses his Considerations*. In *Inducements to Retirednes, A Sober View of Dr. Twisses his Considerations, Seeds of Eternity or the Nature of the Soul, The Kingdom of God*, edited by Jan Ross, 45–230. Vol. 1 of *The Works of Thomas Traherne*. Suffolk: DS Brewer, 2005.

Traherne, Thomas, and Denise Inge. *Happiness and Holiness: Thomas Traherne and His Writings*. Norwhich: Canterbury, 2008.

Traina, Cristina L. H. *Feminist Ethics and Natural Law: The End of the Anathemas*. Washington, DC: Georgetown University Press, 1999.

Trevarthen, Colwyn. "Innate Moral Feelings, Moral Laws, and Cooperative Cultural Practice." In *Free Will, Emotions, and Moral Actions*, edited by Ariberto Acerbi, et al., 385–420. Rome: Pontificia Università della Santa Croce, 2009.

———. "Proof of Sympathy: Scientific Evidence on the Personality of the Infant and Macmurray's 'Mother and Child.'" In *John Macmurray: Critical Prespectives*, edited by D. A. S. Fergusson and N. Dower, 77–118. New York: Peter Lang, 2002.

———. "The Self Born in Intersubjectivity: The Psychology of an Infant Communicating." In *The Perceived Self: Ecological and Interpersonal Sources of Self-Knowledge*, edited by Ulrich Neisser, 121–73. Cambridge: Cambridge University Press, 1993.

Vickers, Brian. *Occult Scientific Mentalities*. Cambridge: Cambridge University Press, 1986.

Wade, Gladys Irene, and Robert Allerton Parker. *Thomas Traherne*. Princeton: Princeton University Press, 1944.

Wall, J. "Fallen Angels: A Contemporary Christian Ethical Ontology of Childhood." *International Journal of Practical Theology* 8 (2004) 160–84.

Ward, Keith. *More Than Matter?: Is There More to Life Than Molecules?* Grand Rapids: Eerdmans, 2011.

Watson, Robert N. *Back to Nature: The Green and the Real in the Late Renaissance*. Philadelphia: University of Pennsylvania Press, 2007.
Whitman, Walt. *Poetry and Prose*. New York: Library of America, 1996.
Willey, Basil. *The English Moralists*. New York: Doubleday, 1976.
———. *The Seventeenth-Century Background: Studies in the Thought of the Age in Relation to Poetry and Religion*. Abingdon: Taylor & Francis, 1979.
Wirzba, Norman. *The Paradise of God: Renewing Religion in an Ecological Age*. Oxford: Oxford University Press, 2007.
Wöhrer, Franz K. *Thomas Traherne, the Growth of a Mystic's Mind: A Study of the Evolution and the Phenomenology of Traherne's Mystical Consciousness*. Salzburg: Institut für Anglistik und Amerikanistik, Universität Salzburg, 1982.
Yates, Frances Amelia. *The Rosicrucian Enlightenment*. Abingdon: Routledge, 2001.
Zagorin, Perez. *Hobbes and the Law of Nature*. Princeton: Princeton University Press, 2010.
Zhang, Jane Hongjuan. "Of Mothers and Teachers: Roles in a Pedagogy of Caring." *Journal of Moral Education* 36 (2007) 515.

www.ingramcontent.com/pod-product-compliance
Lightning Source LLC
Chambersburg PA
CBHW071247230426
43668CB00011B/1621